D1327601

Governing the UK in the 1990s

Governing the UK
in the 1990s

Edited by

Robert Pyper

and

Lynton Robins

St. Martin's Press

Selection, editorial matter, Introduction and Conclusion © Robert Pyper
and Lynton Robins 1995
Individual chapters (in order) © Martin Burch, Kevin Theakston, Tony Butcher,
Philip Norton, Michael Rush, Stephen Ingle, Kenneth Newton, Trevor Salman,
Roger Levy, David Wilson, Clive Gray 1995

First published in Great Britain 1995 by
MACMILLAN PRESS LTD
Houndmills, Basingstoke, Hampshire RG21 2XS
and London
Companies and representatives
throughout the world

A catalogue record for this book is available
from the British Library.

ISBN 0–333–58431–7 hardcover
ISBN 0–333–58432–5 paperback

10   9   8   7   6   5   4   3   2   1
04 03 02 01 00 99 98 97 96 95

Printed in Malaysia

First published in the United States of America 1995 by
Scholarly and Reference Division,
ST. MARTIN'S PRESS, INC.,
175 Fifth Avenue,
New York, N.Y. 10010

ISBN 0–312–12552–6

Library of Congress Cataloging-in-Publication Data applied for

11599995

For Anna Pyper, Robert Pyper (Senior), and
Barbara Joan Robins

Contents

PART II   PARLIAMENT AND PARTIES

List of Tables and Figures

Tables

Figures

Abbreviations

AEU	Amalgamated Engineering Union
C&AG	Comptroller and Auditor General
CAP	Common Agricultural Policy
CCLGF	Consultative Council on Local Government Finance
CCP	Common Commercial Policy
CCT	Compulsory Competitive Tendering
CFSP	Common Foreign and Security Policy
CIPFA	Chartered Institute of Public Finance and Accountancy
COHSE	Confederation of Health Service Employees
COSLA	Convention of Scottish Local Authorities
CPRS	Central Policy Review Staff
CSA	Campaign for a Scottish Assembly
DoE	Department of the Environment
DUP	Democratic Unionist Party
EC	European Community
EEC	European Economic Community
EETPU	Electrical, Electronic, Telecommunication and Plumbing Union
EMU	European Monetary Union
EPU	European Political Cooperation
ERM	European Exchange Rate Mechanism
EU	European Union
FCO	Foreign and Commonwealth Office
FDA	First Division Association
FMI	Financial Management Initiative
GCHQ	Government Communications Headquarters
GDP	Gross Domestic Product
GLC	Greater London Council
GMB	General, Municipal and Boilermakers Union
GNP	Gross National Product
IEA	Institute of Economic Affairs
IGC	Intergovernmental Conference
ILEA	Inner London Education Authority

INLOGOV	Institute of Local Government Studies
IPPR	Institute for Public Policy Research
MAFF	Ministry of Agriculture, Fisheries and Food
MEP	Member of the European Parliament
MINIS	Management Information System for Ministers
NALGO	National Association of Local Government Officers
NAO	National Audit Office
NEC	National Executive Committee of the Labour Party
NFU	National Farmers Union
NHS	National Health Service
NICS	Northern Ireland Civil Service
NIDs	Northern Ireland Departments
NIHE	Northern Ireland Housing Executive
NIO	Northern Ireland Office
NUPE	National Union of Public Employees
OFGAS	Office of Gas Supply
OFTEL	Office of Telecommunications
OFWAT	Office of Water Services
OMCS	Office of the Minister for the Civil Service
OMOV	One Member, One Vote
OPSS	Office of Public Service and Science
OUP	Official Unionist Party
PAC	Public Accounts Committee
PLP	Parliamentary Labour Party
SDA	Scottish Development Agency
SDLP	Social Democratic and Labour Party
SDP	Social Democratic Party
SEA	Single European Act
SNG	Sub-National Government
SNP	Scottish National Party
SO	Scottish Office
SSA	Standard Spending Assessment
STUC	Scottish Trade Union Congress
TECs	Training and Enterprise Councils
TUC	Trade Union Congress
UDCs	Urban Development Corporations
UKREP	United Kingdom Permanent Representative in Brussels
WDA	Welsh Development Agency
WO	Welsh Office

Notes on the Contributors

Martin Burch is Senior Lecturer in Government at the University of Manchester. He is joint author of *Public Policy in Britain* and has also published books and articles on British, Welsh and Australian politics. He is currently completing a book on British Cabinet politics.

Tony Butcher is Lecturer in Government in the Department of Social Policy and Politics at Goldsmiths' College, University of London. He is co-author of *The Civil Service Today* author of *Delivering Welfare*, and has written various articles on public administration and policy studies.

Clive Gray is Senior Lecturer in the Department of Public Policy and Managerial Studies at De Montfort University, Leicester. He has published widely on local and regional government and is author of *Government Beyond the Centre*. He is currently re-searching changing patterns in the fields of inner cities and cultural policy in Britain.

Stephen Ingle is Professor and Head of Department of Politics at the University of Stirling. He has worked in the area of British party politics for a number of years and is the author of *The British Party System*. He is also interested in politics and literature, and his book, *George Orwell: A Political Life*, was published in 1994.

Roger Levy is Professor and Head of School in the School of Public Administration and Law at the Robert Gordon University, Aberdeen. He is author of *Scottish Nationalism at the Crossroads*, as well as numerous articles on Scottish government and politics. His current research interests also include the control and management of the EU budget.

Kenneth Newton is a Professor in the Department of Government at the University of Essex and Executive Director of the

European Consortium for Political Research. He has written widely on urban and comparative politics, public opinion and the mass media

Philip Norton is Professor of Government, and Director of the Centre for Legislative Studies, at the University of Hull. He is the author of numerous books, including *The Commons in Perspective, The Constitution in Flux, The British Polity* and *Does Parliament Matter?*. He is co-author of *Back From Westminster*, joint author of *Politics UK*, and joint editor of *Parliamentary Questions*. He is President of the Politics Association.

Robert Pyper is Senior Lecturer in Public Administration at Glasgow Caledonian University . He is author of *The Evolving Civil Service* and *The British Civil Service*, joint editor of *Britain's Changing Party System*, and he has written numerous articles on aspects of UK Government.

Lynton Robins is Coordinator of Public Administration at De Montfort University. He is co-author of *Contemporary British Politics* and joint editor of *Public Policy under the Conservatives*, *Britain's Changing Party System* and *Two Decades in British Politics*.

Michael Rush is Professor of Politics at the University of Exeter. He is the author of *The Selection of Parliamentary Candidates, Parliament and the Public, Parliamentary Government in Britain* and the *Cabinet and Policy Formation*, and co-author of *The MP and His Information*. He is co-editor of *The House of Commons: Services and Facilities*, and editor of *Parliament and Pressure Politics*. He is also the author of two textbooks on political sociology, and his research interests span British and Canadian politics.

Trevor Salmon is Jean Monnet Professor of European Integration Studies in the Department of International Relations at the University of St Andrews. He is the author of *Unneutral Ireland*, co-author of *Understanding the European Communities* and *Understanding the New European Community*, and co-editor of

International Security in the Modern World. He is also the author of numerous articles on the European Union and European security matters.

Kevin Theakston is Lecturer in Politics at the University of Leeds. He is the author of *Junior Ministers in British Government, The Labour Party and Whitehall* and *The Civil Service since 1945.*

David Wilson is Professor of Public Administration and Head of the Department of Public Policy and Managerial Studies at De Montfort University, Leicester. He has written widely in a range of journals. He is co-author of *Public Administration in Britain Today* and *Local Government in the United Kingdom.*

Preface

The original idea for a book surveying the governing institutions of the United Kingdom in the 1990s stemmed from our work on *Talking Politics*, the journal of the Politics Association. Many of the contributors to this volume had authored short articles for the journal, examining aspects of UK government, and we believed there was scope for these to be expanded, updated and moulded into a self-contained text.

We were encouraged when our publisher, Steven Kennedy took a serious interest in this project and helped us to steer it towards publication. We are grateful to him for his patience and perseverance throughout. Additional thanks are due to Ian Holliday, from the University of Manchester, who read the initial typescript and made a number of useful suggestions for improvement. Naturally, we add the conventional rider that the final responsibility for the text rests with us, and we hereby absolve others from blame for any weaknesses or errors!

Finally, we would like to thank all of our contributing authors for cooperating with our schedules, deadlines and general thematic requirements.

ROBERT PYPER
LYNTON ROBINS

Acknowledgements

The publishers and editors would like to thank the Study of Parliament Group and the Joseph Rowntree Foundation for permission to use data contained in Table 5.4 and Table 10.1, respectively.

Introduction: The Nature and Challenge of Governing in the 1990s

ROBERT PYPER and LYNTON ROBINS

The practice of governing the United Kingdom in the 1990s involves confronting a unique combination of perennial problems and fresh challenges.

Most British governments in the post war period have been forced to face the difficulties associated with an erratic economic performance and industrial dislocation, as well as grappling with the implications of changing economic and political relationships with the United States of America, the Empire/Commonwealth and the countries of Western Europe. More recently, over the past twenty-five years or so, the scales of difficulty have been tipped even further by consistently high levels of unemployment, the apparently intractable nature of the Northern Ireland conflict, the demands placed upon and the stress encountered by the various components of the welfare state, and a sharpening of public scepticism regarding key elements of the UK polity (up to, and including, the monarchy).

All governments have faced real difficulties in effecting change. The challenge of translating major campaign promises and manifesto commitments into substantive achievements has been insurmountable in many cases. Here we need only consider the fate of such grand designs as the 'technological revolution' heralded by Harold Wilson, the Heath government's new regime of industrial relations, and the Thatcher government's 'control' of public expenditure. The gaping chasm which opened up between the original Thatcherite commitment to reform the rates and the disastrous, unworkable, reality of the poll tax further illustrates the sheer intractability of certain problems.

Added to the perennial problems and the continuing difficulty of effecting real change have been the issues and challenges which have emerged with particular force in the 1990s: the need to re-assess the UK's defence requirements in the light of the end of the Cold War and the collapse of state communism in Eastern Europe, the consequences of moves towards European economic and political unity, and clear evidence that Britain's economic performance in the previous decade had fallen well short of the expectations (and boasts) of the Thatcherites (Wilks, 1993, pp. 225–9). Having all but exhausted the potential financial benefits to be derived from the sale of state assets, and with the proceeds of the North Sea oil boom rapidly dwindling, the Conservative government's fourth term began with an air of foreboding.

To make matters worse for the government, the very fact that it was in its fourth term brought a price of its own. It became increasingly difficult to divert attention from the government's problems by referring to the poisoned chalice passed on by a previous, Labour, administration. The reduced majority (21 seats) with which the Conservatives were returned in 1992, and the further reduction of this due to by-election defeats, simply added the problems of party management to the government's agenda. This particular combination of an extended period in power and a relatively low parliamentary majority presented the Major government with a unique challenge, faced by no other UK government in modern times. Furthermore, within six months of its election victory, during the financial crisis which culminated in 'Black Wednesday', the government found itself completely at the mercy of events, wholly incapable of enforcing its chosen policy.

Hanging over all of this, there has been a continuing attempt, dating back at least as far as the first Thatcher administration, to reconsider the very nature of government and the proper role of the state.

The main purpose of this book is to examine the system of government in the United Kingdom as it faces up to these and the other challenges of the 1990s. Our approach will be largely institutional, although this will not detract from the analysis of policy issues.

How to Govern? The Dilemma of the 1990s

It can be argued that part of the legacy of the 1980s was a confusion about the proper role of government in the United Kingdom. The premiership of Margaret Thatcher was characterised by a fundamental tension between two competing impulses.

> Thatcherism was centred on a contradiction, a liberating impulse flooding into authoritarian channels. In part this paradox sprang from the personality of Mrs Thatcher herself, impatient, dogmatic and assertive, urging freedom for others but deeply contemptuous of what they might choose. In part it was the result of ideological cross-currents, economic liberalism eddying against social conservatism, with a government at one and the same time fearlessly radical and stolidly respectful of history and hierarchy. (Holme, 1992, p. 405)

The apparent contrast between the proclaimed aim of the recent Conservative governments to put an end to 'big', interventionist, government, to curtail dirigisme in the UK, while simultaneously exercising continuing control over the nature of our society, confronts and challenges the Major government in the 1990s.

Arguably the most graphic illustration of this is to be found in the context of local government, where the sheer scale and detailed nature of central intervention under the Conservatives (which, it might be added, shows no signs of abating in the 1990s) knows no parallels in the modern history of the United Kingdom.

Evidence of the tension between the government's apparent desire to achieve at least a partial disengagement of the state and encouragement of individual initiative, and a powerful residual hankering for control, can be found in many policy spheres. The field of education provides an example.

It is difficult to avoid concluding that the balance of schools education policy during the early 1990s has been tilted towards increased central government intervention. The detailed implementation of the 1988 Education Reform Act and associated pieces of legislation, as much as the principles contained therein, has been responsible for this (Ranson, 1992). It is true that the local management of schools schemes facilitated a delegation of some powers from local authorities to boards of governors, and can be viewed as a dilution of government (albeit local government !) control. However, the establishment of a National Curriculum in England and Wales, coupled with the active encouragement of schools to opt out of local authority control into central government grant-maintained status, together represent a potentially significant accretion of power to the centre.

Even where the process of disengagement or withdrawal has actually been accomplished, as with the privatisation of the former nationalised industries and public utilities, the government has been obliged to recognise the need for a continuing role for the state as a regulator; hence the proliferation of regulatory agencies, such as OFTEL, OFWAT, and OFGAS, in the wake of privatisations.

If we stand back from the details, we can see that a rough pattern emerges. The interventionist state is by no means at an end, and the role of government as a provider remains valid in some spheres at least. Furthermore, as we shall see in the course of this book, the tradition of 'big' government remains strong in some parts of the United Kingdom. However, put simply, the choice facing the UK government in the 1990s is really between different modes of governing. Increasingly, the government eschews the option of continuing as a large-scale direct provider, except where this remains unavoidable, and moves instead into a new governing mode as an enabler, a contractor, and a regulator.

The enabling government sees its primary role in terms of facilitating service provision by non-state bodies or partly autonomous state bodies, for example, the creation of incentives for individuals to make their own health insurance and retirement pension arrangements through private companies, and the delivery of social security benefits through an executive agency.

The government as contractor can be illustrated with reference to the contracting-out of certain functions to in-house teams or private companies, such as awarding the Group 4 organisation the contract for transferring prisoners between prisons and from prison to court. These contracts are drawn up, monitored, enforced and renewed (or not, as the case may be!) by government.

finally, the regulatory government establishes bodies to monitor the level and quality of service provided by a range of public and private sector organisations, and provide mechanisms for redress of customers' grievances, hence, the aforementioned regulatory agencies operating in the fields of former nationalised industries and public utilities, as well as the plethora of regulatory bodies covering finance and the City, broadcasting and the press, employment, and the environment.

Whilst 'reinventing' government as a fundamentally entrepreneurial rather than a bureaucratic activity may solve the most pressing difficulties in the United States (Osborne and Gaebler, 1993), both the differing tradition and more diverse nature of the UK's problems mean that market-related reforms alone cannot deliver a universal solution here. Indeed, there is increasing concern that a smaller state may precipitate a crisis in political legitimacy. In deprived areas of the United Kingdom the cumulative effects of neglect are resulting in the enabling state becoming the invisible state, and the electorate finding a new interest in politics at the extreme.

The precise balance to be struck between the government's roles as provider, enabler, contractor and regulator is, of course, a matter of policy. Policy, in this strategic sense, as well as in its more detailed manifestations, is the prevailing concern of government in this as in any other decade. However, we should be aware that the UK government is far from being the only significant actor in the processes of policy-making and implementation.

The Policy Process: Putting Government in Context

There can be a temptation, in a book of this kind, to ignore or minimise the fact that government is only one of the participants in the policy process. Political and governmental institutions must be placed in perspective, and we have to be aware of the broad context within which government operates, if we are to properly understand the nature and challenge of governing the UK in the 1990s.

It is impossible to do justice here to the complex academic debates about the strengths and weaknesses of various models of the policy process. Some of these are quite sophisticated. For example, Hogwood and Gunn (1984) have described the policy cycle in terms of nine interlinked stages, from 'deciding to decide', to 'policy maintenance, succession or termination'. Philip Norton (1993), on the other hand, has utilised a more concise model, describing four principal stages ('initiation', 'formulation', 'deliberation and approval' and 'implementation'). While recognising the value of extended, more sophisticated theoretical models, let us use Norton's four stages as the basis for our avowedly introductory comments. Our task is simply to offer some general observations in order to locate the analysis of institutions which follows within a broader framework.

A very simplistic view of the process would see policy initiated by the majority party, formulated and refined by ministers and their official advisers, deliberated upon and approved by Parliament, and implemented by the civil service or another appropriate arm of the state. It is extremely doubtful whether the policy cycle ever operated in such a mechanistic fashion, and it would be totally misleading to describe it in these terms today. As Norton notes, policy proposals 'may emanate from different sources, such as individuals, pressure groups and companies' (Norton, 1993, p. 52). Jordan and Richardson have gone further, to cite five policy-making 'arenas' over and above that occupied by the political parties: public, parliamentary, Cabinet, bureaucratic, and pressure-group (Jordan and Richardson, 1987). They might have added an international arena, encompassing bodies such as the European Union, the United Nations and NATO.

At each stage of the policy process, vital parts may be played by a variety of governmental and non-governmental bodies. Civil servants are not simply the passive administrators of policy: they invariably play an important part in setting the policy agenda with ministers and the most significant organised interests. In almost any given sphere of policy, there will be insider groups and policy elites who can exercise some influence over the policy process. In agricultural policy, for example, the role of government ministers must be considered alongside the parts played by senior civil servants at the Ministry of Agriculture, Fisheries and Food, the political and bureaucratic systems of the European Union, and the organisers of the National Farmers' Union. The latter participates in each stage of the policy process, and is used as an agent of policy implementation by the government in relation to the administration of certain types of grant. However, it should be emphasised that, over the period since 1973, MAFF and the NFU have ceded considerable power and influence to the EU, within the terms of the Common Agricultural Policy.

The precise role of organised interests and pressure groups can vary significantly over time, of course, as is illustrated by the sharp contrast between the virtual incorporation of the trade unions within the formal economic and industrial policy-making process in Britain during the 1970s, and their almost total exclusion in the 1980s and 1990s.

A developing trend in the early 1990s was for increased reliance on voluntary organisations of various kinds to implement elements of the government's social policy. For example, the rehabilitation of drug addicts is only partly tackled through the formal systems of the National Health Service: local and national charities and voluntary bodies play an important part.

The limitations of government are perhaps seen most vividly at this implementation stage of the policy cycle. The problem of translating policy into action can be so severe in some cases, partly because of the strain imposed upon the bodies charged with implementation, that the policy simply fails to achieve its objectives. A graphic illustration of this came when the Major government abandoned the Community Charge in 1991. Public opposition to the policy combined with the stress it imposed on the already creaking structure of local government to damage the process of implementation. Less spectacularly, in 1992 and 1993 the Department for Education was obliged to scale down and postpone its plans for the testing of school pupils in England and Wales when it became clear that the teachers who would have to implement the policy were being swamped by its implications.

In those spheres of policy where the government has more or less direct control over implementation, such as the delivery of social security benefits, the creation of executive agencies within the civil service has been designed to facilitate more efficient and effective translation of policy into action. Even here, however, severe problems can arise, as shown by the difficulties encountered by the Child Support Agency when attempting to enforce the government's policy on securing maintenance payments by fathers.

Further emphasis can be given to our general point about the need to place government in context when we turn to the international scene. A policy agenda may be initiated and formulated within the international arena, as was the case with the decisions by the United Nations to intervene (in different ways) in the Gulf and in Bosnia. While the UK government plays a part in initiating, formulating, approving and implementing such policies, it is one participant among many.

In other cases, the UK government's room for manoeuvre can be sharply circumscribed by the policies pursued by other governments and their institutions. A clear and specific illustration of this came on 'Black Wednesday' in September 1992, when the policy of the German government, and the Bundesbank in particular, played a vital part in forcing a series of desperate measures upon the Major government, ending with the UK's withdrawal from the European Exchange Rate Mechanism (ERM). In this case, even the commanding heights of the UK polity found themselves wholly incapable of directing policy as they would have wished. More generally, international economic conditions impinge upon the UK government's trade and employment policies, and overall industrial strategy. In this context, we begin to see the concept of national sovereignty in a broader perspective. The complex interdependence of international political, military and economic factors makes the exercise of anything resembling full sovereignty by a medium-sized European power like the United Kingdom increasingly problematic.

As our survey of UK government in the 1990s progresses, we must bear in mind these complexities of the policy process, and the limitations they can impose upon successful, unilateral, action by government.

The Book

At the very heart of the United Kingdom's system of government lie the personnel, institutions and agencies of the central executive. Central government policy-making and implementation can only be understood with reference to the complex interaction between the key components of the Whitehall machine. In Part I, the functioning of the central executive is examined in depth.

Martin Burch sets out the scope and structure (formal and informal) of the central executive's very core, the premiership and the Cabinet system, in Chapter 1. The operation of the Prime Minister's Office, the Cabinet, its committees and Secretariat, are analysed prior to an examination of the links between the PM, the

Cabinet and departments of state. Burch offers a clear picture of the core executive in transition, following a period which has witnessed the downgrading of the formal Cabinet and an enhanced role for the Prime Minister's Office and the Cabinet Office. The chapter ends with a summary of options for the development of effective policy leadership at the centre.

The relationship between ministers and civil servants, which has been the subject of intense scrutiny over recent years, is placed under the microscope by Kevin Theakston in Chapter 2. He examines the strengths and weaknesses of four models of the relationship before proposing a broadening of the analytical context in order to accommodate consideration of parliamentary factors, managerialism, ethics and secrecy. Theakston notes the potentially significant impact of the Next Steps initiative upon the minister–civil servant relationship, and this theme is picked up in Chapter 3 by Tony Butcher.

Butcher's concern is with the emergence of a new type of civil service. He charts the origins and evolution of the most ambitious structural and managerial change in the history of the UK bureaucracy. The organisational, constitutional and political implications of Next Steps are clearly laid before us in a chapter which illustrates the pace and scale of change in this area of the central executive.

The theme of change also runs through Part II, where the focus is on Parliament and the political parties. In Chapter 4, Philip Norton traces the significant behavioural, structural and procedural changes which have marked the recent history of the Commons and the Lords. He explains and analyses these with reference to specific developments within Parliament as an institution and to broader trends in UK society, politics and the system of government.

Michael Rush examines Parliament's role as a scrutineer of the executive. Having established the link between ministerial responsibility and parliamentary scrutiny, he surveys four major means of scrutiny, differentiates between 'power' and 'influence', and offers a detailed analysis of the system of select committees. The impact of this developing system on government policy and action is illustrated with reference to a range of examples. While parliamentary scrutiny of the executive has improved remarkably over recent years, gaps and weaknesses remain, and these are indicated.

In Chapter 6, Stephen Ingle turns the focus on to the political parties. The apparent shortcomings of the UK party system are set out: it fails to offer choice on many key policy issues, it has ceased to provide for an alternation in power, it fails to deliver effective scrutiny and control of the executive, and it exhibits a propensity to deliver unrepresentative governments. Ideological and organisational developments within the main parties are reviewed, and a summary is offered of the pressures for change within the parties, and the party system itself.

Although the United Kingdom remains, to a considerable extent, a centralised, unitary state, it stands as a rather anomalous and quirky strain of this political organism. In consequence, no interpretation of the UK system of government can be complete without paying significant attention to the roles of institutions and actors beyond the enclosed confines of Whitehall and Westminster. This is the purpose of Part III.

Carlyle's 'Fourth Estate of the Realm', the Victorian press, which had the capacity to act as a watchdog over the body politic, has evolved into the multi-faceted mass media of the 1990s. In Chapter 7, Kenneth Newton analyses the claim that the fourth estate has become a fifth column, undermining aspects of the UK system of government. He examines, in turn, the concentration of ownership and control, systematic political bias and political influence, while drawing appropriate distinctions between the electronic and print media. He concludes that the balance of evidence does seem to indicate the existence of a media fifth column.

The growing importance of the European Union to the UK system of government is set out by Trevor Salmon in Chapter 8. As a point of style, it should be noted that 'European Union' or 'EU' is used by Salmon and other contributors when referring to the period after November 1993, while 'European Community' or 'EC' refers to the period until that date (which marked the signing of the Maastricht Treaty). He describes the rocky route taken by the 'reluctant European' to membership of the EC in 1973. As the issue of membership *per se* gradually lost its political salience, new themes came to the fore: the attempt to remodel the Community on Britain's terms, long-running disputes about budgetary contributions, an emphasis on 'negative' as opposed to 'positive' integration, and deep domestic political divisions about the future scope and role of the EU. Salmon examines these against the background of a changing approach to European issues signalled by the advent of the Major government, and exemplified by the style and content of negotiations over the Maastricht Treaty. The impact of European Union membership on departments of state, and the roles and responsibilities of UKREP, the Foreign Office, the Cabinet and Parliament are analysed in detail.

In Chapter 9, Roger Levy provides a wide-ranging account of the special challenges associated with governing Scotland, Wales and Northern Ireland. Eschewing a purely descriptive nation-by-nation account, he adopts an analytical approach which identifies common themes and particular styles. Levy examines in turn the factors shaping the political background of these 'national regions', central government's territorial management arrangements (with specific reference to the Scottish, Welsh and Northern Ireland Offices and parliamentary committee systems), and the recurrent issue of legislative devolution.

The opportunities and consequences of the move towards the creation of 'enabling' local authorities, together with the implications of a new wave of structural change, fresh approaches to internal management and the seemingly endless reform of local government finance, are considered by David Wilson in his account of central–local government relationships. The complex interaction between two levels of government is examined with reference to the main analytical models and the working framework of the relationship. Wilson notes that genuine control has eluded the centre, despite the huge scale of intervention in the affairs of local authorities.

The process of governing beyond Whitehall and Westminster, in what Clive Gray describes in Chapter 11 as the 'other' governments, in the sphere of sub-national government, merits special attention. A typology of government beyond the centre in the UK would include local government, the National Health Service, outposts of the centre, quangos and associated organisations. As Gray notes, the fate of these bodies is intrinsic to the future of the entire system of government in the United Kingdom. In terms of employment alone, these 'other' governments are highly significant. Gray analyses the piecemeal but accelerating process of change and reform (focused on privatisation of the management function, curbing expenditure and fragmenting organisational structures) which has come to characterise this sphere, while noting (with Wilson) the relative failure of the centre to achieve many of its key objectives.

The concluding chapter addresses the issue of reform. Throughout the book, comments will be offered on the various remedies for change being put forward in virtually every sphere of the UK system of government. We end by pulling these thematic stands together, while offering a summary of the main prescriptions for specific and wide-ranging reform.

References

Hogwood, B. W. and Gunn, L. A. (1984) *Policy Analysis for the Real World* (Oxford: Oxford University Press).

Holme, R. (1992) 'After Paternalism', *The Political Quarterly*, 63(4) (October–December) pp. 404–12.

Jordan, A. G. and Richardson, J. J. (1987) *British Politics and the Policy Process* (London: Allen & Unwin).

Norton, P. (1993) *Does Parliament Matter?* (Hemel Hempstead: Harvester Wheatsheaf).

Osborne, D. and Gaebler, T. (1993) *Reinventing Government: How the Entrepreneurial Spirit is Transforming the Public Sector* (New York: Plume).

Ranson, S. (1992) 'Education 1991', in Terry, F. and Jackson, P. (eds), *Public Domain 1992* (London: Chapman & Hall).

Wilks, S. (1993) 'Economic Policy', in Dunleavy, P., Gamble, A., Holliday, I. and Peele, G. (eds), *Development in British Politics 4* (London: Macmillan).

Part I

The Central Executive

1

Prime Minister and Cabinet: An Executive in Transition?

MARTIN BURCH

In theory Britain has Cabinet government. According to this view, the executive is centred on the Cabinet and leadership is collective, being located in the group rather than a particular individual. A contrast can be made with presidential systems where leadership is more singular, being centred on one person. The traditional view of Cabinet-led government emphasises certain features: that the Cabinet is the main steering organ of British central government and has general oversight over policy; that all major decisions are reached with the active involvement or at least full awareness of all its members; and that the Prime Minister, who chairs the Cabinet, is 'first among equals': dominant, but not predominant. In fact, this traditional notion of Cabinet as being at the very centre of government (Jennings, 1959) has for a number of years been unsustainable.

A popular image is that the erosion of Cabinet government took place only recently, under the premiership of Thatcher (1979–90), and that the phenomenon was peculiar to her term in office and reflected her domineering style. Certainly, more than any other Prime Minister since the war, Mrs Thatcher personified strong leadership from the top. But, in fact, the decline of Cabinet reflects long-term trends which have their origins well before the

1979 period. The tactics and style of the Thatcher governments simply brought the consequence of these changes into greater prominence.

Many of the features of the Cabinet system today can be traced back to the First World War (Wilson, 1975; Mackintosh, 1977), though so far as the decline of Cabinet is concerned there have been two significant periods of change; first, 1945–51, which saw the introduction and establishment of a comprehensive system of Cabinet committees under the Attlee administration (1945–51) (Hennessy and Ahrends, 1983), the consequence of which was to ensure that as a matter of established practice the bulk of decision-shaping took place below the Cabinet level; and second, the period from around 1974–6 onwards which has seen a number of changes, one of the most significant of which has been a reduction in the frequency of regular Cabinet meetings from two a week to one during the parliamentary session. The consequence of these changes has been to greatly extend the already developed tendency to predetermine and decide issues outside Cabinet.

As the trends are long-term, so they reflect deep underlying causes, two of the most important of which are purely administrative: the problems of the capacity and the competence of Cabinet as an effective policy-making forum in the modern age. The capacity problem reflects the fact that the volume of business is nowadays so large that it cannot possibly be handled or even effectively overseen through Cabinet. The question of competence concerns the difficulties that lay and non-specialist Cabinet ministers are bound to have when it comes to making a full contribution to the resolution of the many complex issues which arise, especially if they have not been involved in the matter before it is placed before them in Cabinet. The consequence is that Cabinet ministers meeting together as a group are unable to contribute to many areas of discussion: they have neither the opportunity nor the know-how.

Partly in order to solve these problems of capacity and competence, the modern Cabinet system has emerged in which many of the key activities take place at sub-Cabinet level. This has a number of results for both the nature and momentum of policy-making. In the first place, it greatly weakens, and in many cases undermines, the collective ideal of decision-making. Moreover, in the absence of collective leadership, a particular problem is raised about who or what fulfils the essential tasks of providing direction, coherence and coordination to overall policy-making. For in the absence of Cabinet, control has either shifted elsewhere or is in abeyance. Moreover if control is obscured, what about responsibility? And beyond that, who might be held accountable for this or that action?

A popular answer to these questions is that we now have prime ministerial government. In other words, we have moved from the collective to the singular executive. This is a simplistic view and it would be more realistic to say that the real problem is that we may nowadays have neither (Burch, 1990a). The danger is that the essential tasks of achieving policy direction, coherence and coordination are in peril of not being adequately fulfilled, in that, with the decline of Cabinet, the exact locations of control and responsibility within the central executive have become uncertain. To some extent, as will be shown, power has shifted to the Cabinet and Prime Minister's Offices, but it has not yet been fully and formally placed there. There is, as Lord Hunt, a one-time Secretary to the Cabinet, has argued, 'a hole in the centre' of government (Plowden, 1987, p. 67).

This lack of provision for an effective central capability is partly the result of the unresolved tension which remains between, on the one hand, the principle and ideal of collective government and, on the other, the reality of a more singular executive which, despite lacking the wherewithal, is increasingly expected to lead from the top. Ideally, this tension needs to be resolved one way or the other, for at the moment the situation is unsatisfactory. Policy leadership depends not upon the strength and resources of either the Cabinet on the one hand, or the Prime Minister's and Cabinet Offices upon the other, but upon the variable ability of the particular individuals involved to effectively exploit the limited staff and information resources available to them. The resolution of this problem of policy leadership seems likely to be one of the major issues concerning the operation of Cabinet government in the 1990s.

Of course there are barriers to any kind of substantial reform. One is the departmentalism built into the structure of central government. Departments and their ministerial heads have traditionally enjoyed a high measure of autonomy. This is enshrined in one of the central conventions of Cabinet government, that ministers are individually responsible to Parliament for the work of their departments. Departmentalism has served to limit collective government, in that ministers are inclined to push the interests of their departments, as well as to impede the full development of direction and leadership at the centre of the system.

These tensions between collective and central leadership are touched on in this chapter. The bulk of the outline contains a straightforward account of the nature of the Cabinet system and the manner in which it operates, emphasising the extent to which the system has become less collective and more centred upon the core institutions especially in the period since 1974. The point is to document the centralising of the structure of the Cabinet system and to indicate the extent to which this centralising has only been partially achieved. In the conclusion we return to the issue of how the central executive might develop in the 1990s. We begin, however, with a brief examination of the formal and informal aspects of the Cabinet system.

The Scope and Structure of the Cabinet System

In institutional terms the Cabinet system consists of Cabinet and its committees, the Cabinet Secretariat which administers and services them, and the Prime Minister's Office. This constitutes the inner core of the central state and it connects into a wider set of institutions including the governing party in Parliament, the Treasury and, especially through ministers' and permanent secretaries' private offices, the departments. Beyond and through these links the Cabinet system relates to a wider set of organisations such as political parties and pressure groups (see Figure 1.1).

In order to understand the workings of the Cabinet system it is essential to distinguish between its formal, institutionalised, and informal aspects. The formal structure consists of the established offices and the powers entailed to them, the organisations involved and the functions they are expected to fulfil, and the rules of procedure and accepted ways of working within them. These create a framework within which more informal aspects of behaviour are played out. In effect what is involved here are the personal contacts which take place within the formal structure. Such contacts range from the casual 'chat' in the corridor, to encounters

Figure 1.1 The Cabinet System

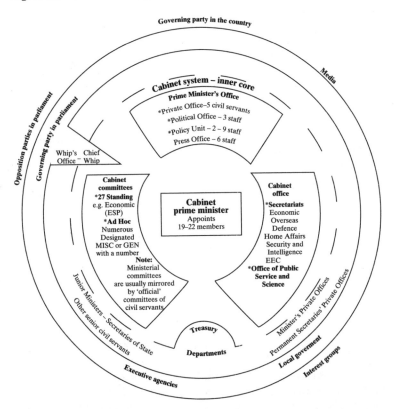

in more organised meetings – the key point is that they all take place within the Cabinet system, but outside the formal structure (Burch, 1990b). It is important to note that the informal working of the system is subject to great variety as it is very much affected by the characters, opinions and prejudices of the individuals holding this or that position.

These formal and informal structures closely interlink in terms of their development. Recurrent patterns of behaviour in the informal structure tend in time to feed through into the formal level. Initially this is reflected in changes in accepted ways of working which may eventually be refined in rules and guidelines and, later, in changes in institutions and offices and the powers attached to them. In this gradualist way the informal structure feeds into its formal counterpart. It is a central theme of this chapter that while changes in accepted practices have taken place and to some extent have been reflected in the rules, the institutions have not yet been fully developed to reflect this. Effectively, the British executive is in a transitional state. This can be illustrated by considering the main features of the various elements making up the Cabinet system and how these have altered, especially in the period since 1974.

The Cabinet and its Committees – the Decline of the Forum of Collective Government

The Cabinet consists of the senior ministers or secretaries of state who head the main departments or are in charge of the government's business, such as the leaders of both Houses of Parliament. Since 1974 it has had a membership of between 21 and 23 and it is chaired by the Prime Minister. Compared with the pattern in the early postwar period the meetings of Cabinet have been more than halved from a high of 108 meetings per year under Churchill in 1952 (Hennessy, 1986, p. 100) to lows of 41 under Callaghan in 1977 and 37 under Thatcher in 1985 and 1987. These latter figures reflect the change which began after 1974 to a once weekly, regular Cabinet meeting lasting about two hours. This practice has been continued under John Major, though he holds more extra Cabinets than was the case under his predecessor.

Because it meets relatively infrequently and for such a short period of time, there is no way that the modern Cabinet can handle or even effectively oversee the amount of business that goes through the Cabinet system. In effect Cabinet has been reduced to four major functions. First, providing information about aspects of government business: for example, each Cabinet begins with a parliamentary report and a report on foreign affairs. These usually take up about 30 to 45 minutes of the meeting, leaving even less time for the discussion of other matters. Second, dealing with issues which have not been settled at a lower level. This might be termed the residual function of the Cabinet, and it reflects the general working principle on which the modern Cabinet system is based: that in order to avoid overwhelming the machinery, issues should be settled at the lowest possible level (Burch, 1988, p. 46). Third, some major policy issues, but by no means all, are generally brought before the Cabinet for final decision, such as the annual public expenditure proposals which are considered in July and October each year (Thain and Wright, 1992, p. 12). These matters are usually largely predetermined elsewhere so the Cabinet's decision-making role is very often reduced simply to that of ratification (although the reformed public expenditure cycle introduced in 1993 could increase the Cabinet's role). Finally, some matters that are likely to prove politically awkward or embarrassing may be discussed in the Cabinet on the grounds that they might rebound on the whole government. Hot political issues are the kind that may actually go farthest in the Cabinet system. Astute ministers are prone to bring such matters before their colleagues so that if the political flak becomes heavy the group, as well as the individual minister, can share the blame. The political costs can be heavy if a minister fails to do this, as was witnessed by Mr Heseltine's difficulties following the announcement of 31 pit closures in October 1992. The timing, and to some extent the content, of the announcement was not discussed in either Cabinet or a standing Cabinet committee (Employment Committee, 1993, para. 20). So, the last category is not inclusive; many issues that do turn out to be politically explosive never reach Cabinet, at least not until they have exploded!

Formally speaking the bulk of business is handled in Cabinet committees. A Cabinet committee is a committee served by the Cabinet Secretariat and one that is recorded in the Secretary to the Cabinet's Committee Book. This distinguishes Cabinet committees from the numerous interdepartmental committees which do not come within the scope of the Cabinet system. There are two basic forms of committee: standing or permanent committees and *ad hoc* or temporary ones. The standing committees are usually designated by letters such as EDP which is John Major's coordinating committee on Economic and Domestic policy, one of the 28 standing ministerial committees established under his premiership (see Figure 1.2), whereas *ad hoc* committees are given a number and a prefix of either MISC or GEN which changes with the changeover from one Prime Minister to another: these committees are numbered consecutively during the period in office of a premier. Committees are either staffed by ministers or officials, though there are one or two mixed committees in which both ministers and civil servants take part, such as the civil

Figure 1.2 Ministerial Standing Committees of Cabinet

CHAIR   DESIGNATION AND POLICY AREAS

CHAIR					
Prime Minister *John Major* Security(4)	EDP: Economic and Domestic (13)	OPD: Defence and Overseas (6)	OPDG: the Gulf States (4)	OPDN: Nuclear Defence (4)	OPDSE: European
	OPDK: Hong Kong (8)	NI: Northern Ireland (7)	EDS: Science and Technology (12)	IS: Intelligence services (5)	
Lord Privy Seal *Lord Wakeham*	EDI: Industry, Consumers (13)	EDE: Environment (13)	EDH: Home and Social Affairs (18)*	EDL: Local Government (16)	EDI: Public Sector Pay (12)
	EDR: Urban Regeneration (12)				
Lord President *Antony Newton*	FLG: Future Legislation (9)*	LG: Legislation (12)*	EDC: Civil Service Pay (12)	EDH(H): Health (13)	EDH(D): Drug Misuse (10)
Other Ministers *As indicated*	OPD(E): European Questions (15)* *Foreign Sec.*	OPD(AE):Eastern Europe (9) *Foreign Sec.*	OPD(T): Terrorism (8) *Home Sec.*	EDL(L): London (13) *Environment Sec.*	
	EDH(U): Urban Policy (15) *Environment Sec.*	EDH(A): Alcohol Misuse (12) *Ch. of the Duchy of Lancaster*	EDH(W): Women's Issues (11) *Employment Sec.*	EDX: Public Expenditure (7) *Chancellor of the Exchequer*	

Note: As at end 1993. The number is brackets refer to the designated membership of the committee (including the chair), though other ministers can be invited to attend if matters come up which are relevant to their areas of responsibility. Subcommittees are distinguished by a bracketed initial after the main initials, e.g. EDH(H), but they may have a stand-alone status and do not necessarily report to their 'main' committee. Some junior ministers are members of some of the subcommittees as well as the LG and EDL committee. Apart from EDP, EDH and OPD these committees do not meet on a strictly regular basis, but only as business requires.

*The Chief Whip is a full member of these committes, though he may attend others as required.

Source: Cabinet Office, 1993.

contingencies unit which meets on a regular basis during national strikes or states of emergency (Hennessy, 1986, p. 31).

Ministerial Cabinet committees have the function of either preparing business for decision at a higher level, possibly in Cabinet, or reaching decisions on matters of policy on their own account on behalf of the Cabinet. It is the role of official committees to prepare papers and to isolate and clarify options for the consideration of Ministers, usually at committee level. The power of ministerial Cabinet committees to take final decisions without reference to Cabinet is made absolutely clear in one of the main rule books of the Cabinet, *Questions of Procedure for Ministers* (Cabinet Office, 1992, para. 4). Thus, formally speaking, it is the Cabinet *and* its committees which must be considered the main forums for decision-making.

The number of Cabinet committees and Cabinet committee meetings has tended to fall in recent years, especially under Mrs Thatcher. In terms of the numbers of meetings of Cabinet committees, the reduction began under the premierships of Wilson and Callaghan, though both used the committee system extensively as a means of handling and determining business; Callaghan in particular had a penchant for using *ad hoc* committees at both the ministerial and official level. So while less time was spent in Cabinet the committee system remained extensively in use, though not to the same extent as under Heath's premiership (1970–4). Under Thatcher the trend away from Cabinet was sustained and, significantly, less activity took place at the committee level. On average over her period in office, the total number of meetings of all forms of Cabinet committee (standing and *ad hoc*/ministerial and official) per year was well less than half that sustained by her Conservative predecessor, Edward Heath. Moreover, under Mrs Thatcher the most precipitate fall took place in the number of meetings of ministerial committees. This tendency to spend less time in committee has been continued under John Major, though not to the same extent as under Mrs Thatcher. For instance, by the beginning of 1993, after more than two years in office, Major had created only 24 *ad hoc* committees.

What is clear from the evidence is that while the use of Cabinet has declined, more business has been settled at the sub-Cabinet level. This raises the question as to where, if not in Cabinet, or even Cabinet committee, business has been handled? One answer is that there has been an increase in 'ministerial correspondence': matters involving perhaps two or three departments which are settled through memos and letters following informal liaison. The correspondence might then be circulated to members of a relevant Cabinet committee for their information. This has tended to keep some business out of the Cabinet system altogether. Also Cabinet committees have been used more efficiently to produce decisions rather than pass them on to other committees or to readdress them at subsequent meetings. The most important answer, however, is that more business has been handled and extensively predetermined at the informal level before being brought into the formal structure of Cabinet and committee for final determination. This is a development which began before Mrs Thatcher, though the technique was greatly developed under her premiership.

The greater reliance on *ad hoc* committees under the Callaghan administration is indicative of this trend. Admittedly these committees are part of the formal structure, but they are less institutionalised than the standing committees and allow the Prime Minister, and those advising him or her, greater flexibility when it comes to determining the membership and remit of the committee. It is the personnel at the centre of the Cabinet system whose opportunities for managing and steering business are enhanced by the development of *ad hoc* committees. Of an even more informal nature has been the tendency, most evident during Mrs Thatcher's period, to initiate or substantially shape issues in a wide range of types of informal groupings: these usually centre on the Prime Minister (Prior, 1986, pp. 135–6; Seldon, 1990, p. 115). Under Thatcher these varied from the most structured form of informal gatherings such as committees chaired by the Prime Minister which were not listed as Cabinet committees and which were not necessarily serviced by the Cabinet Secretariat, to less structured meetings such as those which took place between the Prime Minister and her staff and one other minister and his staff (Burch, 1990b, p. 7).

This development of informal contacts partly reflected Mrs Thatcher's personal style of government, but it was not unusual during the Callaghan premiership. For example, questions to do with interest rates and the value of the currency were discussed and shaped in what was referred to as the Prime Minister's 'economic seminar' (Donoughue, 1987, p. 101). The practice has been continued under John Major, even though his approach to Cabinet government is different from that of his predecessor. Major's system is more collegiate and also more oligarchical in that the informal aspects are centred on a group of key Cabinet ministers, notably, along with the Prime Minister, Douglas Hurd, Michael Heseltine, Lord Wakeham, Kenneth Clarke, and at times the Chief Whip, Richard Ryder.

Overall the pattern that emerges, especially in the period since 1974, is a further downgrading of the Cabinet as the central point of decision in the system, and a further shift of business to the sub-Cabinet level and more extensively into the informal structure. This tendency to use informal mechanisms to predigest issues before bringing them to a formal point of decision reflects deeper and more long-term factors than the style of this or that Prime Minister. Clearly it can help the speed and efficiency of decision-making if matters are already developed and explored before being taken into wider and more formal forums. The upshot is that the principle and practice of collective government has continued to be undermined, while the opportunities to exert influence by those usually at the centre of the system has been extended. These changes have further reduced the Cabinet's ability to act as the primary steering mechanism of executive government through providing policy direction, control, cohesion and coordination. As a consequence some responsibility for these tasks has tended to fall upon those in the Cabinet Secretariat and the Prime Minister's Office. Yet the position and resources of these central institutions have not been enhanced to the extent required to enable them to handle these steering and leadership tasks adequately. Moreover their right to act in these areas, as against the interests of the collective executive and the prerogatives of individual departments, remains strongly contested.

The Central Institutions Enhanced

The Cabinet Secretariat

The primary responsibility for the day-to-day administration and management of the Cabinet system is located in the Cabinet Secretariat which forms a part of the wider Cabinet Office headed by the Secretary to the Cabinet. The Secretariat is in effect made up of five sections each with a particular area of responsibility covering economic policy, home affairs and legislation, overseas and defence policy, European affairs, and national security and intelligence information. An important change took place in the organisation of the Cabinet Office in May 1992 with the creation of the Office of Public Service and Science, which brought together responsibilities for the general administration of the civil service (including the creation of executive agencies, efficiency, market testing and the Citizen's Charter), and science policy by incorporating what was formerly a sixth secretariat dealing with science and technology. This new unit within the Cabinet Office is headed by a Cabinet minister, the Chancellor of the Duchy of Lancaster (William Waldegrave until July 1994, David Hunt thereafter) (Treasury and Civil Service Select Committee, 1993, pp. 1–5).

The most important of the Secretariats from the point of view of the management and handling of business within the Cabinet system are those dealing with economic, home affairs and legislation and overseas and defence matters. These primarily fulfil the tasks of scheduling and setting the agendas of Cabinet and committee meetings, ensuring that the papers are available and circulated to those involved, and taking and circulating the minutes and conclusions of meetings. They also provide 'handling briefs' for the chairmen of committees, outlining the nature of the issue at hand and the points that need to be settled. These tasks involve only about 35 to 40 members of the office's senior staff. With the exception of the Secretary to the Cabinet all the senior officials involved are on secondment from the departments for short periods, usually of between one to three years.

The administration of the flow and handling of business is governed by a series of accepted practices which to some extent are laid down in codes or rules of guidance for officials and ministers. One set of formal rules is contained in the document already referred to, *Questions of Procedure for Ministers*. There are also written guidelines laid down for the benefit of officials such as committee clerks, members of the Secretariat and those in the departments primarily involved in liaising with the Cabinet system. A list of precedents is also kept in the Secretariat. These guidelines cover such matters as the requirements for preliminary consultation before a matter can be brought before Cabinet or a Cabinet committee, how and to whom documents are to be circulated and the format for committee minutes and Cabinet conclusions. The bulk of present practices have been long established. They reflect an accumulation of administrative experience and help to ensure that the system works smoothly. They are not rigid precepts and are capable of accommodating special cases, but they form the basis on which the system normally works.

The task of creating and developing these guidelines is not the responsibility of Cabinet ministers either individually or collectively. These rules are usually changed at the margin as difficulties or new requirements arise. The precepts governing the handling of business in the Cabinet and its committees are essentially matters for the Prime Minister advised by, and often on the instigation of, the Secretary to the Cabinet and other members of the Secretariat. The important matter of determining the exact composition, terms of reference and flow of business to Cabinet committees is also a matter for the Prime Minister again closely advised by Secretariat officials. Given that the accepted procedures and the structure and flow of business to Cabinet and Cabinet committees can greatly affect the outcome of a proposal, this power to establish and alter the framework of rules and institutions is a very important one: it is firmly located at the centre of the system.

Over the period since 1974 the operation of the Cabinet Secretariats has undergone five important changes which have served to enhance their position at the centre of the Cabinet system. First, the organisation of the flow of business has become much more regularised and planned over the short term. This involves close and regular liaison between the Secretary to the Cabinet and officials from the Secretariats and the Prime Minister's Office. A key meeting takes place between these officials towards the end of each week (under John Major's premiership on a Thursday) and produces proposals for the flow of business to Cabinet and its committees over the next two to four weeks, subject to the approval of the Prime Minister (Seldon, 1990, p. 110; Donoughue 1987, pp. 27–8). Since 1974, this procedure has been periodically supplemented by a 'forward look' covering up to three to six months ahead in terms of what is likely to come up and where in the Cabinet system it should be handled. This procedure has enhanced the position of the Secretariat in relation to the shaping and pace of business being developed in the departments.

Second, the Secretariat has been more effective in ensuring that business is clarified and focused by the time it reaches Cabinet or one of its committees. This partly reflects the more organised process of forward planning mentioned above, but also the more stringent requirements for consultation before an item can be settled. In addition to the need to consult the Treasury on matters of spending and the Foreign Office if the item has any implications for overseas policy, these now include consultations with the Treasury if extra staffing is likely to result from a proposal, or if the item has implications for accommodation or general financial policy. Any consequences for Britain's membership of the European Union must be laid out. A requirement since 1983 has been some assessment of what a new policy will cost, what it is meant to achieve and how its achievement will be measured. More recently, there has been the need for any aspects of potential legal liability to be clarified. The effect of these changes has been to strengthen the issue-vetting role of the Secretariats and to ensure that, if and when, business reaches a formal point of decision, in Cabinet or committee, it is more extensively refined and predetermined.

Third, the policy responsibilities of certain sections of the Cabinet Office and the Secretariat have been extended from time to time to take on matters relating to the development of issues of a cross-departmental nature. Some of this accretion of functions has been temporary as in the case of the Constitutional Unit dealing with devolution from 1975–9. Other functions have been acquired on a more permanent basis such as the oversight by the European Secretariat of European Union matters, and a more substantive role for the Economic Secretariat in the annual public expenditure exercise. The effect has been that in these areas of special responsibility members of the Cabinet Office have been able to take on a more active role in policy-making rather than generally leaving that to the departments. To this must be added the placing of certain central functions in the Cabinet Office which affect all government departments. These include the responsibility for the government's overall efficiency programme and the carrying out of the 'Next Steps' programme of civil service reform which involves transferring service delivery functions and personnel from the direct control of central departments to executive agencies (see Chapter 3 below).

Fourth, the appointment of the Secretary to the Cabinet as Head of the Civil Service in 1981 led to the reorganisation of the workload within the Secretariats and the granting of greater autonomy to the deputy secretaries (Seldon, 1990, p. 105). Arguably this change strengthened the position of the Prime Minister *vis-à-vis* the Secretary to the Cabinet in that advice to the Prime Minister is now channelled directly from the deputy secretary level rather than through the intermediary of the Cabinet Secretary.

The final change has been the growth in the importance of European Union (EU) business and the important role in coordinating these matters which is fulfilled by the European Secretariat. It is the job of the Secretariat to pull together policy formulation on EU matters. This is done through a range of official committees which process through into a ministerial committee on European questions (OPD (E)). The Secretariat also establishes detailed negotiating positions for those officials who are engaged in carrying out British government business in Brussels. As James argues, in this area the Secretariat is 'not just co-ordinating policy but managing and formulating it' (1992, p. 201).

Taken together these five changes have fortified the position of the Secretariats when it comes to coordinating and giving some coherence to policy. They have also marginally enhanced the Secretariats' responsibility for the control and direction of policy in certain areas, though only at either the behest of the Prime Minister or as a secondary consequence of the job of organising business. In the main it is not the task of the Secretariat to lead policy, but to organise, and occasionally galvanise, initiatives engendered by others. Notably also, the links and level of liaison between the Prime Minister's Office and the Cabinet Office have been fortified. An active Prime Minister can draw on these links if he or she chooses.

The Prime Minister's Office

So far as the Cabinet system is concerned the main powers which are vested in the Prime Minister are those of appointing ministers and some of the very top civil servants; managing the machinery of the Cabinet system and especially the establishment of committees; and supervising the flow of business. These powers provide the Prime Minister with opportunities to give a measure of policy leadership if he or she chooses to exploit them. The Prime Minister is also in a position to coordinate and give coherence to government business by virtue of the fact that he or she is the only party politician in government who has full access to the material flowing through the system.

Of course all these powers are exercised under constraint and are in no sense absolute. For instance the power to hire and fire ministers depends on the pool of talent available in Parliament, the right opportunity arising in which changes in personnel can be made and the need to balance various factions and personnel within the party (Thatcher, 1993, p. 25). Equally the power to re-construct the pattern of Cabinet committees and the way business is handled is constrained by, as we have seen, the myriad of ac-cepted procedures and ways of operating. Also the amount of ma-terial going through the system is substantial so that prime ministerial oversight tends to be intermittent and selective.

The problem is that in attempting to fulfil these tasks the Prime Minister is assisted by a relatively small staff, at least in compari-son with those available to chief executives in other countries. For example, the US President has 400 staff and the German Chancellor 450 (Blondel, 1993, pp. 134–5). Although under Major the size of the Downing Street staff has increased, with a comple-ment of 107 it still remains small in international terms. As a con-sequence the Prime Minister's ability to give policy leadership is both circumscribed and erratic. The key staff (excluding typists, messengers and so forth) are organised into four distinct sections: the private and political offices, the policy unit and the press section. The format of the organisation of the office has been kept relatively constant in the post-1974 period, though the details of its operation have varied somewhat according to the personal dis-positions of this or that Prime Minister.

The private office serves as the main access point to the Prime Minister from the departments and the other parts of the Cabinet system. It is staffed by career civil servants who usually serve for a term of between two to three years before moving on to senior posts in the departments. There are currently five private secre-taries under John Major and these are headed by the Prime Minister's principal private secretary. The number of private sec-retaries has hardly changed since 1945 when there were four. The main difference is that the organisation of the office has become more structured so that, with the exception of the principal secretary, each covers a particular area of prime ministerial business: overseas, economic, parliamentary and home affairs. A further secretary keeps the Prime Minister's diary. The principal private secretary oversees the Number Ten office and he draws together the papers which go to the Prime Minister. In addition to organising the flow of business to the Prime Minister and the appointments of visitors to see him, the private secretaries provide briefings for the Premier on issues and developments and keep notes on his meetings and conversations (Jones, 1987, p. 51).

There is also a political secretary and a small political office in Number Ten. This handles the Prime Minister's relations with the party in the country and his party political correspondence. It is partly funded by Conservative Central Office. The third element making up the Number Ten office is the press section which deals with media relations and has a staff of five press officers, plus five support staff (Seymour-Ure, 1989). It works through daily briefings of the parliamentary lobby correspondents (Negrine, 1989, p. 158). Finally, there is the Policy Unit which under John Major is currently headed by Sarah Hogg and has a total staff of eight, plus five support staff. The role of the unit in the broadest sense is to provide the Premier with policy ideas and policy advice on papers received in the Prime Minister's Office. In addition to the unit, the Prime Minister's Office contains one or two advisers on specific areas of policy.

The main changes since 1974 have been in the operation and functions of the Prime Minister's Office. In the first place, there has been an enhancement in the status of the Office as an established part of British central government. In 1977 it was for the first time given its own designation, separate from the Cabinet Office, in the *Civil Service Yearbook*, which is the major publication listing all the main departments. Within the Office the most important change has been the creation of the Policy Unit. This was established by Harold Wilson in 1974 and it has turned out to be a significant innovation at the very core of central government. The unit has always remained small with eight or nine full- and part-time members under Wilson and Callaghan (1974–9). Initially, under Thatcher, it was kept to a small size numbering about four, including one or two civil servants. Following the abolition of the Central Policy Review Staff (CPRS) in 1983

(Blackstone and Plowden, 1988, ch. 9), the unit was expanded to a complement of eight or nine, a level which has only been slightly expanded since Thatcher's departure.

Under Wilson and Callaghan the unit concentrated on forward policy analysis over the medium to long term (Donoughue, 1987, pp. 20ff.) especially in the economic policy field (Willetts, 1987, p. 44). Under Thatcher it developed a far more departmentally-related role. In addition to the general provision of policy advice it attempted to monitor the government's main economic strategy. It also served to originate new policy ideas in the fields of economic and domestic policy and, if these were approved by the Prime Minister, to liaise with departments to see if these ideas could be further developed. Thatcher also appointed a number of special advisers in the areas of efficiency, overseas and defence, and economic policy. These had a free-standing status within the Office and could be drawn into the work of the Policy Unit on some issues or report to the Prime Minister direct. John Major has continued this practice by employing advisers on foreign affairs and efficiency and competition.

The press office has also taken on a more substantial role in the coordination of government information. This was particularly developed under the premiership of Margaret Thatcher who made periodic attempts to centralise the coordination of government information services, latterly under the control of her press secretary, Bernard Ingham (Harris, 1990, p. 170). These attempts at coordination were never wholly successful. They did, however, mark a shift from established operating principles and they involved the use of the information service in a more cross-departmental way. The departure of Mrs Thatcher led to a reversion to the practice whereby the head of the government information service is not a member of the Prime Minister's Office (Devereau, 1992), though the centralising of the service which took place under Mrs Thatcher has remained.

Overall there has been a change in the functions of the Prime Minister's Office since 1974, though this has entailed only a marginal increase in key staff and resources. The important point is that there has been a change in the purposes and position of the Office *vis-à-vis* other institutions. The Prime Minister's ability to know what is going on in the rest of the government machine has been enhanced, and his or her potential to initiate policy ideas from the centre has been expanded, though only on a limited range of issues. These changes, taken together with those affecting the Cabinet Secretariat, have tended to bias the operation of the Cabinet system more substantially towards the central elements within it. They mark a further weakening of the collective executive, but they are not sufficient to ensure the establishment of a singular executive legitimately regarded as, and capable of, providing policy leadership and coherence. Despite this shift in emphasis the centre still remains largely dependent on the departments for advice, many policy initiatives and nearly all detailed proposals. Departmentalism and the autonomy associated with it still remains a central part of the British system.

The Departments: Independence and Coordination

The Formal Links into the Departments

The last set of relationships making up the Cabinet system are the contact points into the departments. These operate through a limited range of formal channels at both the ministerial/political level and the civil service/official level. The two sets of contacts overlap. The most high-profile of these is provided by the senior minister or secretary of state who links the two entities as both Cabinet member and head of the department. Contact is maintained either through him directly or via the intermediary of his private office. Other channels are junior ministers and their private offices; the permanent secretary and his private office; and other senior officials who may be involved in providing information for Cabinet papers or participating in official Cabinet committees.

Most private offices of ministers and junior ministers are not unlike that of the Prime Minister with a principal private secretary and a number of assistant secretaries (Kaufman, 1980, p. 33). It is through these offices that all communications to and from the minister will pass, including Cabinet and committee papers (Bruce-Gardyne, 1986, p. 33). Moreover it is usually members of the private office or the permanent secretary that school the minister in the practices and accepted ways of proceeding within the Cabinet system (Theakston, 1987, p. 103).

Like ministers, the permanent secretary is also served by a private office. He or she will be involved in various official Cabinet committees as well as the weekly meeting between all permanent secretaries, which is nowadays held under the chairmanship of the Secretary to the Cabinet. This assists the coordination of the overall flow of business across departments. Junior ministers are particularly confined by the existing machine and practices. This is very much reflected in the opportunities to influence the flow of materials provided by access to Cabinet and committee papers. The private offices of the secretary of state and the permanent secretary will see much the same range of Cabinet and committee materials, but the private offices of junior ministers, and the junior ministers themselves, will only have access to selected items from Cabinet conclusions and relevant committee minutes (Bruce-Gardyne, 1986, p. 42). Those senior officials who are involved in the work of official Cabinet committees will see those sections of Cabinet and ministerial committee papers and minutes which are relevant to them or require action from their section of the department. Others who may have access to Cabinet and committee papers are the special advisers to ministers.

So far as the relationship with the Cabinet system is concerned there have been two main changes over the period since 1974: the more effective use of junior ministers and the more extensive development of the system of special advisers. Much has depended, however, on the use made of these personnel by each ministerial department head.

Nearly all departments have four junior ministers (ministers of state and parliamentary secretaries); some of the larger ones have six or seven (Drewry and Butcher, 1988, p. 162). Since the amalgamation of ministries into larger units in the late 1960s and early 1970s (Pollit, 1984) it has become the accepted practice that junior ministers take on the responsibility for specific areas of the department's work (Theakston, 1987), though the final responsibility still remains with the secretary of state. Nowadays, junior ministers are drawn directly into the Cabinet system through their participation in Cabinet committees either in their own right or as a deputy for their departmental head. For instance, five of the ministerial standing committees set up under John Major's premiership are almost wholly constituted from junior ministers. The effect of these changes, in those cases where they have worked effectively, has been to lighten the burden of work upon the secretary of state.

Special (or political) advisers provide an extra source of information and advice for ministers. The first of these were appointed by some Labour ministers in the 1960s and the practice was continued during Edward Heath's premiership: they were few in number and wholly concerned with advising on departmental business (Klein and Lewis, 1977). The big change came in 1974 when Harold Wilson regularised and extended the exercise to involve 28 special advisers, including nine part-timers. Initially, under Mrs Thatcher, the system was cut back, so that in 1979 the number had dropped to fourteen (Treasury and Civil Service Committee, 1986, pp. li–liii), but after 1983 the numbers grew once more to around twenty. The practice has been maintained under John Major and in 1992 there were 24 special advisers located in nearly all the main departments. Advisers are used for different purposes according to how the minister wishes to deploy them. Some are concerned with advising on specific areas of the department's activities. Others provide the minister with advice over the whole range of departmental activities and very often on matters coming before Cabinet and its committees for which the minister is not responsible but may wish to make an informed contribution. This latter practice has served to increase the competence of the minister when it comes to dealing with Cabinet and committee business falling outside his departmental brief.

These formal and established linkages provide a limited number of access points into departments. This ensures a regular means whereby business and messages from the Cabinet system are drawn in, but the linkages also serve to filter and control what departments will send out into the Cabinet system, and this has helped to maintain a degree of departmental control and autonomy. These formal links are supplemented by a number of informal networks which cross departments and are often centred around personnel within the Cabinet system.

Informal Networks Across the Cabinet System

The main networks are centred on the Prime Minister's Office and the Secretariat. As Heclo and Wildavsky have noted, Whitehall is like a village; it is relatively compact and operates on the basis of personal contacts and the exchange of gossip and information (Heclo and Wildavsky, 1974). The private secretaries in the Prime Minister's Office are closely connected into the private offices of ministers and permanent secretaries. This private office grapevine is, as Kaufman points out, 'one of the most powerful networks in Whitehall' (1980, p. 48). Members of the Secretariat have close contacts with the relevant departments and these are facilitated by the practice of recruiting senior members from the departments on a two- or three-year secondment. These two are the most established networks linking the Cabinet institutions into the wider government machine. They are supplemented by the personal contacts between ministers who are drawn together before formal meetings in Cabinet and committee and in the House of Commons, either when called on to vote or in the course of handling legislative business. Additionally there is close interconnection between permanent secretaries and other senior officials across departments.

The nature of these networks has hardly changed in the period since 1974. If there is a trend, it is towards strengthening the position of the Cabinet system institutions at the hub of the network, so that the flow of information has become more focused on the centre. Also, amongst the constellation of departments a more significant position has been taken on by the Treasury. This partly reflects the continuing concern of governments since the mid-1970s with the control and constraint of public spending. This is reflected in the fact that the Chief Secretary to the Treasury, the minister in charge of public spending, has since 1977 been a full member of the Cabinet, that only the Treasury has been granted an automatic right of appeal from committee to Cabinet and that the requirements for Treasury vetting before business is discussed in committee or Cabinet have been extended and tightened (Lawson, 1992, pp. 273 and 383; Thain and Wright, 1993).

In addition, two new networks have begun to emerge. One involves special advisers and the Policy Unit at Number 10 which has periodically attempted, with only limited success, to draw together advisers in departments (Donoughue, 1987). Under the Conservative governments since 1979, coordination of special advisers has also been attempted from Conservative Central Office. The other network involves the information officers in the departments who have increasingly been coordinated from Number 10, again not wholly successfully.

It is in relation to its departmental component that the Cabinet system has changed least substantially in the period since 1974. The advisory resources available to ministers have been marginally augmented through the system of special advisers, while the more effective use of junior ministers and their greater involvement in the Cabinet system has meant a decrease in the burden of departmental business falling on the secretary of state. In theory, this allows him or her a greater opportunity to master those aspects of business within the Cabinet system which do not directly concern the department. This change, however, is limited and has not taken place uniformly across all departments. Nor can it be assumed that each secretary of state has made the best use of the opportunities available. What is clear is that departmentalism remains embedded in the working of the system: this imposes clear limits on any attempt to strengthen the central institutions in the Cabinet system. At the informal level, there is some evidence that linkages and contacts are more located towards the centre, reflecting in part the strengthening of the central institutions (including the Treasury) which have been documented in this chapter. Whether these changes at the informal level will in turn lead to changes in formal organisations and institutions remains to be seen.

Conclusion: Possibilities for the 1990s

In sum there have been two major changes in the central executive in the period since 1974. First, there has been a further downgrading of Cabinet as the key point in the system. Consequently much business is now handled at the sub-Cabinet level and much of it is preshaped within the informal structure. Second, the position of the Cabinet and Prime Minister's Office has been enhanced so that the system is more centralised in its operation. The effect of these two changes has been to move even further away from a truly collective executive to one that is more singular. Yet the shift of emphasis is only partial and in essence the tension between a collective and a singular executive remains unresolved. Responsibility for the tasks of policy leadership, coordination and coherence remains uncertain and contested. Arguments about the effective allocation of these tasks seem likely to feature in debates about the central executive in the 1990s. Along what avenues might these debates develop?

There are three possibilities for developing effective policy leadership in the central executive: one builds on the principle of a collective executive; one builds on the principle of a singular executive made fully responsible and accountable; and one builds on both, but emphasises the need to enhance the ability of the Cabinet system in general to effectively coordinate and develop policy. All imply a further weakening of the strong departmentalism which underlies the British system.

Strengthening the collective dimension must involve augmenting the position of Cabinet and the information available to Cabinet ministers. There are three areas worth exploring. First, providing the Cabinet collectively with more policy advice and comment across the range of government business. One way to do this would be to reintroduce a body like the Central Policy Review Staff (Wass, 1984, p. 39). The original idea behind the CPRS was that it should serve the Cabinet and provide advice and analysis on the development of the government's overall strategy and on key and emerging policy issues. The problem with the CPRS was that it was too apolitical and became increasingly marginalised. A revised CPRS would need to have far more substantial party political input and be brought more effectively into Cabinet system processes than was previously the case. Second, more could be done to enhance the advisory resources available to ministers so far as the coverage of issues outside the remit of their departments is concerned. An initial step might be to enhance the system of personal advisers and to insist that their primary function would be to consider and advise on those aspects of Cabinet and committee papers which fall outside ministers' departmental briefs. More radically, a system of ministerial *Cabinets* might be introduced, modelled on the practice in France. The danger in either of these reforms is that they might enhance rather than ameliorate departmentalism. Third, the Cabinet could meet more often, and all matters going through the system and concluded in committee could be brought before it. The problem for ministers would be finding the time, and the danger, from the point of view of the efficiency of decision-making, is that matters might be reopened at a relatively late stage in their development. Far better, perhaps, to ensure that ministers are fully informed about decisions reached elsewhere, and to hold special, general strategy and monitoring sessions of Cabinet. The problem of time might be overcome by once again experimenting with a smaller Cabinet.

This was originally tried by Churchill in 1951 when he created a number of 'overlord' ministers. It was not a success as the problem of separate departments was not tackled at the same time. However, recent changes in the core size of the central ministries under the 'Next Steps' programme through the hiving-off of the delivery of services to executive agencies has created an opportunity for innovation and experiment. The implications of this 're-structuring of the central state' for the Cabinet system have not yet been fully thought through (Burch, 1993). The dimensions of the reform are dramatic: by June 1993, 90 executive agencies had been created and a further 20 were in the pipeline involving the removal of more than 67 per cent of the civil service from the day-to-day administrative control of the central departments (Treasury and Civil Service Committee, 1993, pp. 206ff.). In theory this would leave ministers and their advisers with more time to consider longer-term policy questions. It also opens up the opportunity to amalgamate some of the 'slimmed down' ministries and set up a formally constituted, small inner Cabinet charged with the overall coordination and steerage of government business.

An alternative would be to develop further the directive powers and resources of the central institutions: the Secretariats, and the Cabinet and Prime Minister's Offices. This would enhance the singular as opposed to the collective executive and might be resisted as contrary to the British tradition. However, as has been shown, recent developments have been in this direction. Better, perhaps, to recognise this trend and to formalise it so that the lines of responsibility are clear and issues of accountability and parliamentary scrutiny can be more adequately dealt with. This would mean enhancing the staff and advisory sources available to the Prime Minister either through extending the function of the Cabinet Secretariat or the Prime Minister's Office or by amalgamating them into a fully fledged Prime Minister's Department (Jones, 1983; Weller, 1983). Indeed this proposal was discussed within government in 1983, though no action was taken partly as a result of opposition from ministers.

Strengthening the centre might also involve placing more cross-departmental responsibilities in the central institutions. Again there has been a clear trend in this direction especially in relation to the administration and organisation of the civil service, the government's programme for more efficient management in government and the development of 'Citizen's Charters' covering many aspects of the public service. As we have seen, under John Major these functions have been drawn together within the Cabinet Office in the Office of Public Service and Science. Moreover the tendency of modern campaigning, media attention and popular awareness to focus on the single leader may have served to enhance the leadership potential of modern Prime Ministers *via-à-vis* their Cabinet colleagues (Foley, 1993, ch. 5). Consequently there may be an argument for openly acknowledging that in an age of mass politics, the position of Prime Ministers is unavoidably enhanced, and that this requires to be recognised in the prescribed distribution of powers and resources, if for no other reason than to ensure that their activities are more effectively subject to oversight and control.

The third reform alternative is to attempt to combine elements of both the collective and singular executive by standardising existing arrangements and enhancing the advisory staff available to Cabinet ministers and the Prime Minister alike: perhaps by taking up some of the proposals mentioned above. This might enhance the capability of the system but it would not solve the problem. For, while Cabinet collectively and the Prime Minister would be better resourced, the tension between collective and singular executives would remain and responsibility for policy leadership would still be highly contested.

References

Blackstone, T. and Plowden, W. (1988) *Inside the Think Tank* (London: Heinemann).

Blondel, J. (ed.) (1993) *Governing Together* (London: Macmillan)

Bruce-Gardyne, J. (1986) *Ministers and Mandarins* (London: Sidgwick & Jackson).

Burch, M. (1988) 'The British Cabinet: A Residual Executive', *Parliamentary Affairs*, 41, pp. 34–48.

Burch, M. (1990a) 'Power in the Cabinet System', *Talking Politics*, 4, pp. 102–8.

Burch, M. (1990b) 'Cabinet Government', *Contemporary Record*, 4, pp. 5–8.

Burch, M. (1993) 'The Next Steps for Britain's Civil Service', *Talking Politics*, 5 (3) pp. 166–171.

Cabinet Office (1992) *Questions of Procedure for Ministers* (London: Cabinet Office) mimeo.

Cabinet Office (1993) *Ministerial Committees of the Cabinet* (London: Cabinet Office) mimeo.

Devereau, M. (1992) 'Do We Need Government Information Services', *RIPA Report*, 13.

Donoughue, B. (1987) *Prime Minister* (London: Jonathan Cape).

Drewry, G. and Butcher, T. (1988) *The Civil Service Today* (Oxford: Basil Blackwell).

Employment Committee (1993) *Employment Consequences of British Coal's Pit Closures*, HC Paper 1992–93/263-I (London: HMSO).

Foley, M. (1993) *The Rise of the British Presidency* (Manchester: Manchester University Press).

Harris, R. (1990) *Good and Faithful Servant* (London: Faber).

Heclo, H. and Wildavsky, A. (1974) *The Private Government of Public Money* (London: Macmillan).

Hennessy, P. (1986) *Cabinet* (Oxford: Basil Blackwell).

Hennessy, P. and Ahrends, A. (1983) 'Mr. Attlee's Engine Room: Cabinet Committee Structure and the Labour Government 1945–51', *Strathclyde Papers on Politics*, 26 (Glasgow, University of Strathclyde).

James, S. (1992) *British Cabinet Government* (London: Routledge),

Jennings, I. (1959) *Cabinet Government*, 3rd edn (Cambridge: Cambridge University Press).

Jones, G. (1983) 'Prime Minister's Departments Really Create Problems', *Public Administration*, 61, pp. 79–84.

Jones, G. (1987) 'The United Kingdom', in Plowden, W. (ed.), *Advising the Rulers* (Oxford: Basil Blackwell).

Kaufman, G. (1980) *How to Be a Minister* (London: Sidgwick & Jackson).

Klein, R. and Lewis, J. (1977) 'Advice and Dissent in British Government: The Case of the Special Advisers', *Policy and Politics*, 6, pp. 1–25.

Lawson, N. (1992) *The View From No. 11* (London: Bantam).

Mackintosh, J. (1977) *The British Cabinet*, 3rd edn. (London: Stevens).

Negrine, R. (1989) *Politics and the Mass Media in Britain* (London: Routledge).

Plowden, W. (ed.) (1987) *Advising the Rulers* (Oxford: Basil Blackwell).

Pollitt, C. (1984) *Manipulating the Machine* (London: Allen & Unwin).

Prior, J. (1986) *A Balance of Power* (London: Hamish Hamilton).

Seldon, A. (1990) 'The Cabinet Office and Co-ordination', *Public Administration*, 68, pp. 103–22.

Seymour-Ure, C. (1989) 'The Prime Minister's Press Secretary', *Contemporary Record*, 3, pp. 33–5.

Thain, C. and Wright, M. (1992) 'Plannning and Controlling Public Expenditure in the UK, Part 1: the Public Expenditure Survey', *Public Administration*, 70, pp. 3–25.

Thain, C. and Wright, M. (1993) *The Treasury and Whitehall*, forthcoming.

Thatcher, M. (1993) *The Downing Street Years* (London: HarperCollins).

Theakston, K. (1987) *Junior Ministers in British Government* (Oxford: Basil Blackwell).

Treasury and Civil Service Committee (1986) *Civil Servants and Ministers: Duties and Responsibilities*, Vol. II, HC Paper 1985–86/92-II (London: HMSO).

Treasury and Civil Service Committee (1993) *The Role of the Civil Service: Interim Report*, Vol. II, HC Paper 1992–93/390-II (London: HMSO).

Wass, D. (1984) *Government and the Governed* (London: Routledge & Kegan Paul).

Weller, P. (1983) 'Do Prime Minister's Departments Really Create Problems?' *Public Administration*, 61, pp. 59–78.

Willetts, D. (1987) 'The Role of the Prime Minister's Policy Unit', *Public Administration*, 65, pp. 443–54.

Wilson, S. (1975) *The Cabinet Office to 1945* (London: HMSO).

2

Ministers and Civil Servants

KEVIN THEAKSTON

I have read Mr Giffen's very able and interesting memorandum. I do not clearly apprehend whether he approves or disapproves the proposal which he discusses; but in any case I agree with him. (Ministerial comment on a file)

I turned to my Private Secretary and said, 'Now you must teach me how to handle all this correspondence.'…'Well, you put all your in-tray into your out-tray', he said, 'and if you put it in without a mark on it then we deal with it and you need never see it again.' (Ministerial diary entry)

[The Under Secretary] brought me a very difficult letter of complaint from one of the opposition front bench on a constituency matter … I had no idea what it all meant or what I was supposed to do about it. It turned out that I didn't have to do *anything* about it. She explained that some of the facts were wrong, and other points were covered by statutory requirements so that I didn't have any alternatives anyway. This is the kind of Civil Service advice that makes a Minister's life easy. No decision needed, not even an apology required. Nothing to do at all, in fact. Great. I asked her to draft a reply, and she'd already done it. She handed it across my desk for me to sign. It was impeccable. (Ministerial diary entry)

I wish they'd tell me what to do instead of giving me both sides of the argument! (Comment of newly appointed minister to an MP)

Four scenes from ministerial life in Whitehall, or to be precise three incidents from the real world of government and one from the television comedy series *Yes, Minister* (see if you can tell which one – the answer is at the end of the chapter!).

The relationship between elected politicians in ministerial office and the unelected permanent civil servants who advise them and implement their policies has long fascinated observers of the British system of government, and has long been a subject of controversy and argument, too. Governments today face problems so complex, it is said, that inexpert and transient ministers are reduced to selecting between the options served up by their officials rather than relying on their own judgement. There is something in this argument – but to portray ministers as mere puppets in the hands of civil servants is an exaggeration – though it should be pointed out that it is *not* a new one. The first quote cited at the start of this chapter, for instance, relates not to a baffled minister in a recent government but to a Victorian Cabinet minister!

There is nothing new under the sun. Here is Tony Benn speaking in 1981: 'The deal that the civil service offers a minister is this: if you do what we want you to do, we will help you publicly to pretend that you're implementing the manifesto on which you were elected ... I've seen many ministers, of both parties ... fall for that one' (Young and Sloman, 1982, p. 19). And here is Walter Bagehot, writing in a less conspiratorial vein in 1867 about something maybe not too different:

Ministers have to make good their promises [made in opposition], and they find a difficulty in doing so ... When they come to handle the official documents, to converse with the permanent under-secretary – familiar with disagreeable facts, and though in manner most respectful, yet most imperturbable in opinion – very soon doubts intervene ... The late Opposition cannot, in office, forget those sentences which ... admirers in the country still quote ... so the new Minister says to the permanent under-secretary, 'Could you not suggest a middle course? I am not of course bound by mere sentences used in debate ... but' ... And the end always is that a middle course is devised which *looks* as much as possible like what was suggested in opposition, but which *is* as much as possible what patent facts ... prove ought to be done. (Bagehot, 1963, p. 160)

What one observer sees as civil service manipulation in pursuit of its own political ends, another interprets as the inevitable process of bringing politicians face to face with what one top mandarin once called 'ongoing reality'.

'Britain's Ruling Class' was how Peter Kellner and his co-author Lord Crowther-Hunt (a former Labour minister) described the higher civil service in the subtitle of their book *The Civil Servants*, published in 1980. The claim was rather overblown even then, but reading their account of a mandarinate confident in its power and secure in its role in the government of the country, one could see what they meant – here was a force to be reckoned with, a body whose acquiescence in their plans the politicians could not take for granted. A decade later things looked very different. There appeared to be no doubt about the ability of the Conservative government elected in 1979 to impose its will upon Whitehall. Ministers, not mandarins, were in the driving seat.

There was certainly a lively argument about the power and role of the civil service in the 1970s and 1980s. Richard Crossman and Tony Benn provided plenty of ammunition for Labour critics but the hostility and suspicions of many Thatcherites meant that attacking the mandarins became a bipartisan pastime. We had been here before, however, as was just pointed out. In the 1930s, for instance, one finds left-wing politicians denouncing the Treasury for sabotaging the MacDonald Labour government, a Conservative Party leader complaining about the bureaucracy's 'bias towards stagnation and the paralysing fear of error', and writers such as Harold Laski (on the left) and Ramsay Muir (in the centre) detailing Whitehall's powers of obstruction and its 'management' of ministers. But plenty of ministers in, and observers of, different governments have, over the years, also reported positive experiences and evaluations – that civil servants were invaluable aides, the neutral and efficient instruments of whichever party was in office. So, just what *is* going on in Whitehall?

The combination of obsessive secrecy and self-serving leaks makes it difficult to fathom ministers' and officials' relationships and relative power, as does the cryptic nature of the official files when they are finally opened after 30 years. The available evidence can be patchy and anecdotal. There is a fair amount of folklore masquerading as analysis: if you get in first you create the

myth, as a critic of the Crossman Diaries observed. To say that
the experience of each minister is to some extent unique and that
minister – mandarin relations are highly variable and can change
over time is true enough but does not take us very far. And there
is a very real sense in which the long-running controversy about
power – 'ministers versus civil servants: who has more influence
over policy?' – is perhaps an over-simplified way in which to
frame that particular question as well as being an issue that can
too easily divert attention away from other complex and important problems concerning the organisation and workings of the
British administrative machine.

Four Models

My aim in this chapter is to set out the main ways in which the interactions of ministers and top-level bureaucrats in Whitehall
have been understood by political scientists (and sometimes by
participants too!); to review some of the evidence relating to these
models; and then to try to broaden the discussion by bringing up
some of the wider questions alluded to above.

The Formal – Constitutional Model

In British constitutional theory and orthodox textbook accounts
the position is quite straightforward: the civil service has no constitutional personality or responsibility distinct or separate from
that of the government of the day; it is a non-political and neutral
bureaucracy loyally committed to the aims and the interests of
that government; the duty of officials is to ensure that ministers
are fully apprised of the problems, constraints and options they
face, but then it is also their duty to make the best of the policy
ministers lay down and to put into effect their decisions, for which
ministers are responsible. This is the normative theory of the
British constitution: that ministers, not civil servants, should have
the final power because they carry the final accountability to
Parliament and the public.

Participants in government (politicians and officials) frequently
say that this is what life in Whitehall is really like; conversely,
critics' reform schemes are often intended to close what they

claim to be the gap between reality and this model. For both sets of people, the model is important – as a description or as a normative standard. Officials referring to their 'political masters', ministers announcing 'their' decisions – both are speaking the language of this model of political control and bureaucratic subservience. The continued existence of a permanent, anonymous and 'neutral' career bureaucracy is underwritten by this model – which is why the civil service top brass were so anxious to re-affirm its continued validity in the 1980s in the face of controversies over Whitehall 'politicisation' and 'whistle-blowing'. It also became an issue when the Major government's economic policy fell apart in the autumn of 1992 and there were calls for the sacking of Sir Terence Burns, appointed chief economic adviser in 1979 and now permanent secretary to the Treasury, as one of the chief architects of the failed policies. Roy Hattersley pointed out that this would be constitutionally dubious and would let unsuccessful ministers off the hook – for him, this model described the conduct of government as it was and as it should be (*Independent Magazine*, 29 August 1992; *The Times*, 13 October 1992).

The Adversarial Model

That ministers find it difficult to translate formal authority into real power over the Whitehall bureaucracy is a familiar argument. The reasons are various. The sheer size of the civil service is an obvious problem: in 1900, we had 50 000 civil servants controlled by about 60 ministers, today we have over half a million civil servants and around one hundred ministers. Ministers' tenure in office is limited: on average Cabinet ministers head their departments for only two and a half years (there have been eight different ministers in charge of the Department of Trade and Industry since 1983!). They are just starting to get on top of the jobs when they are reshuffled to a different post (or sacked). There are many pressing demands on ministers' time: only about a third of their working week is spent running their departments, as opposed to *representing* them in Parliament, Whitehall committee rooms, television studios and on other public occasions. There are strongly held 'departmental views' which shape the advice ministers receive and which affect the implementation of policy – many ministers are swiftly 'domesticated' and adopt their department's priorities as their own. Add to all this the imbalance in information and expertise between politicians and bureaucrats and the existence of Whitehall networks closed to ministers (the informal civil service grapevine and a labyrinthine structure of committees, working parties and so on), and the problems in exerting effective political control over the civil service machine are apparent.

Some of the civil service's critics go beyond these points to allege that minister – mandarin relations are conflictual, that there is a constant struggle for power and control over policy between elected politicians and permanent bureaucrats, and that Whitehall actively obstructs or sabotages ministerial initiatives. In other words, life in Whitehall is like *Yes, Minister* without the jokes.

Crossman and Benn have popularised the left-wing version of this model in which a devious and conspiratorial civil service (a conservative if not actually Conservative force) represents a formidable obstacle to the achievement of a Labour government's socialist programme. Benn (1980, p. 62) argues that 'the problem arises from the fact the civil service sees itself as being above the party battle, with a political position of its own to defend against all-comers, including governments armed with their own philosophy and programme'. Whitehall prefers consensus politics, he maintains: 'they are always trying to steer incoming governments back to the policy of the outgoing government, minus the mistakes that the civil service thought the outgoing government made'(Young and Sloman, 1982, p. 20). The mandarinate has been seen in strikingly similar terms – as a set of adversaries rather than allies – by some supporters of the Thatcherite project. 'Whitehall is the ultimate monster to stop governments changing things', complained Sir John Nott from the economic liberal wing of the Conservative Party (Hennessy, 1989, p. xiii). And a former adviser to Mrs Thatcher, Sir John Hoskyns, grabbed the headlines in the mid-1980s with a stream of vitriolic attacks on the civil service – sack all officials aged over 50 and import several hundred politically committed outside businessmen to run departments, he recommended (Hoskyns, 1983, 1984). Whitehall, it is argued, aims to maximise continuity and is committed to defending the status quo – whether in the form of narrow departmental interests or, more broadly, the postwar social democratic/Keynesian consensus – against any radical challenges.

Village Life in the Whitehall Community

On this view, life in Whitehall is *not* lived in a state of permanent conflict and struggle between ministers and civil servants. The adversarial model over simplifies and distorts. Relations are in fact, complex and fluid, and the lines of division are usually to be found not *between* the political and bureaucratic elements in government, but *within* them, as alliances of ministers *and* officials compete with each other to advance particular goals or defend common interests. Ministers and officials may well sometimes fight, but they also cooperate and bargain, as Hugh Heclo and Aaron Wildavsky showed in their classic study of *The Private Government of Public Money* (1981).

Politicians and top-level civil servants interact so closely that they constitute a single 'government community', a community marked by a consensus on norms of behaviour (the 'rules of the game') and by the exclusion of 'awkward' outsiders (including MPs). Public spending decisions, for instance, are effectively determined inside a small, exclusive network of around 200 officials and ministers. Ties of mutual dependence bind ministers and mandarins together – they must trust each other and fight each other's battles. Civil servants, according to Heclo and Wildavsky, prefer a strong minister to a cipher because they rely on him to fight for his department in Cabinet, to have clear ideas about future policy, to win a proper share of resources for the department's programmes, and to represent it effectively in Parliament and to the public. 'Civil servants hate a weak minister', they were told by one of their interviewees. 'He reflects badly on the department. If he waffles in debate or is getting kicked about by his colleagues it affects the department. His permanent secretary, when he goes to the Reform Club, will be embarrassed and pitied by other permanent secretaries' (Heclo and Wildavsky, 1981, p. 133). For their part, ministers need officials for advice on the detailed formulation and implementation of policy, to manage their departments efficiently (ministers lack the time and interest to be concerned with the details of organisation, administrative procedures and all but the most senior appointments and promotions), and to maintain effective control over government expenditure (looking both to its efficiency and to its regularity, as monitored by the Public

Accounts Committee). Ministers and officials thus have a close, interdependent, working relationship.〕

Other comparative research into governments in a number of Western democracies, which fits in with this model, suggests that both politicians and senior officials are involved in making policy but, while operating closely together, they make distinctive contributions based upon different perspectives on the problems of governing. Officials provide expertise, a 'safety first' orientation and established links to organised group interests; politicians contribute political sensitivity and ideological energy; policy-making is the story of their interaction (Aberbach, Putnam and Rockman, 1981). This view goes beyond the formal – constitutional model, but denies that the battle-lines are as starkly drawn as they are in the adversarial model.

The Public Choice Model: Bureaucratic Expansionism

〔This fourth model is part of the wider New Right/public choice critique of the workings of modern democracies and governments. It originated in the work of certain American theorists but gained a practical relevance on this side of the Atlantic by informing Thatcherite attacks on waste and inefficiency in government. The focus here is less on civil service power as such than on the consequences of that power. Assuming bureaucrats to be self-interested budget-maximisers, this is a model of bureaucratic growth (Niskanen, 1973). Sir Humphrey will scheme to expand the budget and size of his department (and so his own power and status). A witless Jim Hacker will let him get away with it or, worse, connive and present the resulting increase in public spending as showing the success of his policies. The result is a bloated, inefficient and wasteful bureaucracy – 'overproviding' services, exploiting the taxpayer and serving its own rather than the public's interests.〕 · *Match with Gov of today!*

The *Yes, Minister* television series actually drew much of its inspiration from this model, according to one study (Borins, 1988). A content analysis of the scripts showed that Sir Humphrey's behaviour and motives were in line with the theory of bureaucratic empire-building! More importantly, these ideas found a receptive audience in Mrs Thatcher's Conservative Party. In the 1970s and 1980s some Conservative politicians argued that Whitehall was really a natural ally of the Labour Party because of its belief in the merits of action by the state and reported difficulties with civil servants over proposed cut backs in government functions and spending (the resistance frustrating the Heath government but not the more determined Thatcher administration). For instance, when Sir Keith Joseph argued, at the Department of Industry and then at Education in the early 1980s, that his ministry's spending was too high, officials apparently regarded him as a freak and fought for more resources all the same, as the model would predict (Bruce-Gardyne, 1986, p. 205). *Support this argument.*

Like the formal – constitutional model, this approach has strong normative overtones as well as purporting to describe real-world bureaucratic behaviour. That is to say that its proponents typically canvass a number of reforms designed to curb the bureaucracy's budget-expanding proclivities (contracting-out or privatising services, more openness about and stronger controls over departments' costs and spending, and so on).

What's Going on in Whitehall?

How far can these different models help us make sense of what has been happening inside government over the past couple of decades?

Taking the public choice model first, we should note that this has come in for withering theoretical and empirical assault. The regularly uncovered horror stories of waste, mismanagement and incompetence in Whitehall and the spiralling public spending of the postwar decades would certainly seem to support this model. But it has been justly criticised for its narrow assumptions about officials' motivations and for its overly monolithic view of bureaucracy. Even when state spending was increasing rapidly, the form of government growth was not that expected by the theory: the major expansion actually came outside Whitehall. Furthermore, retrenchment and cutbacks since the mid-1970s have arguably changed the nature of the game (though some departments continued to prosper – e.g. Defence until the late 1980s). Power and prestige in Whitehall belong to the Treasury and the Cabinet Office – which are relatively small departments concerned with expenditure control and policy coordination, respectively, and not

the big-staff, big budget leviathans of public choice theory.
Overall, there are too many weaknesses with public choice theory
to make it a convincing analysis of bureaucratic behaviour and de-
cision-taking in Whitehall.

Heclo and Wildavsky's 'village life' model has been tremen-
dously influential as apparently the most plausible and 'realistic'
interpretation of the inner life of British central government. So
much of what we know about how government decisions get
made, pieced together from leaks and insiders' accounts, seems to
bear out this model. However, we should note two important
weaknesses with Heclo and Wildavsky's version of the workings
of British 'political administration'. One is that, by focusing on the
internal operations of the Whitehall community, it neglects the
important ways in which the bureaucracy's extensive links with
outside interest groups ('policy communities') can constrain political leadership and influence the direction of policy (civil servants
too can be constrained by these links – there are frequent allegations that some departments are 'captured' by their 'client'
groups, for instance the Ministry of Agriculture and the NFU). A
second drawback with this approach is that ministers are more
than players in the Whitehall game, they are also party politicians
with wider concerns and ideological goals. In office they may
often succumb to 'departmentalitis', but there are also instances of
united political teams imposing their will on the 'natives' rather
than themselves 'going native'. The 'village life' model probably
underestimates the importance of party and ideological factors in
the relations of ministers and mandarins – factors which were
perhaps more important in the 1980s than before. 'There is probably no domestic department left that retains a "departmental
view" that would be at odds with Thatcherism', concluded a study
of Mrs Thatcher's impact on the civil service, testimony to the
success with which her government was able to dominate the
'Whitehall village' (Wilson, 1991, p. 333).

A proper assessment of the formal – constitutional and the adversarial models is best made in the context of a discussion of the
experience in office of recent Labour and Conservative governments. Some preliminary points about the formal – constitutional
model should be made, however. To the extent that this approach
is taken to involve a distinction between policy-making and administration, as two separate spheres and activities, it is, of course,

a caricature of the actual division of labour between ministers and top-level officials. It is impossible to maintain any such distinction in the practical conduct of government. Perhaps less than 1 per cent of the work of a department goes before ministers; ministerial 'control' in this situation is therefore less a matter of issuing orders and more the result of indirect influence – 'climate-setting', officials' anticipations of how ministers will react, and so on. Senior mandarins inevitably play important political (but not partisan) and policy-making roles. In the Department of Health, for instance, only capital projects (hospital building) costing over £50 million go to ministers for approval; projects up to that limit are approved at civil service level. Sir Robin Butler, the country's most senior mandarin, has described the civil service's role as 'to inform government policies, to refine them, to make them practicable' – terms which suggest a positive and creative input into policy-making (*Contemporary Record*, April 1990, p. 20). The subtle interconnections of the spheres of 'policy' and 'administration' pose difficult problems for British constitutional doctrine, in which *ministers* carry sole responsibility. However, the development of the Parliamentary ombudsman and of House of Commons select committees to probe the workings of the bureaucracy, together with pressures for 'open government' reform, represent attempts to get behind the façade of government and are based on a recognition that officials are more than mechanical implementers of ministerial decisions.

Turning to Labour's experience in office (this sections draws on Theakston, 1992), it certainly seems to be the case that opinion on the question of civil service power and obstruction reflects evaluations of the success or otherwise of Labour governments. This was less of an issue in the party after the 1945–51 government than after (and during) the 1964–70 and 1974–9 terms of office. Writing their memoirs in the 1950s, Attlee and his ministers had nothing but praise for the civil service, its efficiency and its loyalty. In fact, Whitehall had worked in a textbook fashion to put Labour's 1945 programme into practice. Searching for 'what went wrong' after the 'failures' of the Wilson and Callaghan governments, however, many on the Labour left seized on the higher bureaucracy as a scapegoat. Marcia Williams, for instance, a close Wilson confidante, wrote of Labour's 'defeats' in the 'battle' against the civil service; ' Whitehall: The Other Opposition' was the revealing title of a critical *New Statesman* article in 1974 – the adversarial model with a vengeance! Left-wing critics argued that without major reform – to broaden the class base of recruitment, to reinforce ministers by appointing teams of political advisers and giving politicians more control over top-level appointments – the mandarins could not be relied upon to assist in Labour's socialist project, rather they would systematically sabotage it.

Leading Labour ministers in the governments of the 1960s and 1970s, however, such as Wilson, Callaghan and Denis Healey, firmly reject allegations of bureaucratic sabotage or political prejudice on the part of civil servants. Ministers who complain about civil service power are weak or incompetent, Healey robustly argues. Blaming the bureaucrats is just an unconvincing alibi. Benn's well-known difficulties with his officials came about because he was out of step with his political colleagues – the story would have been different if he had had prime ministerial and Cabinet backing. The general point here is that governments are not necessarily united entities, so that what might at first appear to be civil service obstruction of a minister is in fact something rather different, with officials rightly concerned to keep in line with the collective policy laid down by Number 10 and the Cabinet.

Overall, the historical record seems to suggest that Labour's problems, frustrations and 'failures' in office are political in origin rather than due to Whitehall sabotage or obstruction, with key factors being the party's poor preparations in opposition and its lack of a clear policy strategy. Too often, Labour governments enter office not having done their homework before achieving power and armed with sketchy or ill-thought-out plans; they quickly become the prisoners of events. Civil servants showing that their schemes have unforeseen drawbacks or are unworkable, and then conveying the bad news of real-world constraints and dilemmas (acting as 'stewards of the inevitable' in Rose's (1987, p. 421) vivid phrase), might seem to some politicians to be obstructive but are actually performing their proper and legitimate role in the system.

The experience of the Conservative government after 1979 was to make nonsense of the claim made by Marcia Williams (Lady Falkender) in 1983 that 'the battle to establish the precedence of the elected Government over a non-elected Civil Service has still to be resolved'. Despite initial scepticism in some parts of

Whitehall (including inside the Treasury) towards its radical programme, with numerous press leaks naturally fuelling suspicions
of disloyalty, all the signs were that any civil service resistance or
foot-dragging that there may have been after 1979 failed to stymie
the Thatcher government. A long-serving Conservative minister,
Norman Fowler, symbolically entitled his memoirs *Ministers
Decide*. 'The only situation in which the civil service itself is likely
to initiate change', he argued, 'is when there is a policy vacuum
because ministers are not clear about what they want to do.
Whatever else, that was not a frequent complaint about the
Thatcher Governments' (Fowler, 1991, p. 112). An elected government with radical intentions and clear priorities *was* able to
impose its will upon Whitehall.

'The constitutional textbooks are truer now than they have
been some for time', the political columnist Hugo Young observed in 1990 (*FDA News*, May 1990). This is not to say that the
apparent political and ministerial control of policy-making was
uncontroversial. Constitutionally, Whitehall is not neutral
between the government and the opposition, but it is supposed to
be neutral in a party-political sense. However, with one party in
power for so long, and pursuing such controversial policies, could
this vital distinction be maintained? The Thatcher government's
critics argued that the civil service was being transformed into an
instrument of ministers in ways that went beyond or subverted the
traditional practices. Mrs Thatcher's unprecedented deep personal involvement in top-level appointments triggered off a fierce
debate about the 'politicisation' of the civil service. The Whitehall
information machine – and particularly the Number 10 press
office – seemed to be blurring the distinction between explaining
government policies and party-political image-building. There
were fears voiced that officials were now encouraged to implement decisions without asking questions rather than giving objective advice. Officials with views out of line with those of ministers
were 'sidelined' and ignored in the preparation of welfare
reforms, it was alleged. More starkly, Lord Bancroft, a former
head of the civil service (summarily dismissed by Mrs Thatcher in
1981), commented that the 'grovel count' was higher than it had
been under other governments. The classic civil service 'snag-
hunting' function of presenting to ministers critical judgements or
unpalatable facts which may frustrate their plans seemed to have

partially atrophied. Hugo Young talked of the loss of 'institutionalised scepticism' in British public administration. Perhaps ministers were having it too much their own way and the mandarins were too subservient?

If these allegations that the neutrality of the civil service had been subverted were true, it would suggest that relations between Whitehall and a future non-Conservative government would be extremely adversarial unless and until a massive purge of a Thatcherised mandarinate was executed. It would appear, though, that rather than applying a partisan litmus test, Mrs Thatcher looked for a dynamic, 'can do' style when appointing permanent secretaries. The head of the civil service pledged before the 1992 election that whoever occupied Number 10 could count on Whitehall's loyalty. Although some Labour politicians had their doubts, Neil Kinnock seemed prepared to accept such assurances, as did his successor, John Smith. For his part, John Major appears to have a more stable relationship with the civil service than Mrs Thatcher – where she was suspicious of the Whitehall machine and looked to outside think-tanks and personal advisers and gurus for ideas on policy, he relies more on top civil servants, it is said (*The Economist*, 1 December 1990, p. 39). However, such was the disarray in the conduct and in the policies of his government by mid-1993 that civil servants were reported to be frustrated by ministerial indecision, the lack of a firm lead, and by governmental losses of nerve in relation to backbench protests and external buffeting (*Financial Times*, 11 June 1993). In addition, the drive to extend 'market testing' and contracting-out within the civil service soured the government's relationship with its officials.

If the next election comes in 1996 – 97, Whitehall will have known only Conservative masters for 17 – 18 years. But all the signs are that both politicians and bureaucrats believe it could then switch to working on the conventional basis for a government of a different political complexion, and they are probably right – there is life in the formal – constitutional model yet!

Conclusion : The Need to Widen the Focus

The 'Jim Hacker versus Sir Humphrey' way in which this subject is commonly addressed is unsatisfactory and incomplete not only because there are alternative models of minister – mandarin relations, as we have seen, but also because it neglects the wider context, the *system* in which politicians and bureaucrats are located. In British government, issues of power, organisation, functioning and accountability are all interconnected. Limited space means that all that can be done here is to highlight some of the broader issues and briefly suggest their relevance to the topic under discussion.

One important issue which shows why we need to be aware of that wider system is the question of how well-prepared the real-world Jim Hackers are for their ministerial roles. It has been said that being a professional politician in Britain means being an amateur minister. Ministerial careers follow an essentially Victorian pattern: Cabinet ministers spend an average of twelve years in Parliament and three to four years as a junior minister before becoming secretaries of state. Their political and parliamentary apprenticeships do not equip ministers with specialist policy knowledge or managerial and executive skills and experience, and arguably this compromises their capacity to exercise effective political leadership. Other European governments have less frequent reshuffles and also tend to appoint minister with relevant expertise. However, the problem is that far-reaching changes in British political life, including the workings of the party system, the organisation of Parliament and the outlook of politicians themselves, would be necessary before a new breed of ministers could emerge on this side of the Channel (Theakston, 1987; Rose, 1991).

The parliamentary context is important in another way. The unremitting pressures of parliamentary criticism and of party competition mean that the presentation of policy and dealing with essentially tactical questions – next week's debate or some awkward parliamentary questions, the line to be taken in press briefings, the latest interdepartmental squabble – can squeeze out strategic planning, proper policy analysis and the effective management of programmes. The issue then becomes not the distribution of power between ministers and mandarins but rather the *style* (and outcome) of policy-making, resulting from the nature of the system and the responses of both ministerial and civil service residents of the 'Whitehall village'. The executive capacity of British central government is what is at stake here – how well can the machine develop and implement coherent and effective policies for the long term, as opposed to keeping the ship of state afloat and focusing on the short term in a reactive fashion? The record of successive governments suggests that the brutal answer is: not very well at all.

Related to this is the issue of the dominance inside the civil service of the generalist administrator, who has long been a target of Whitehall's critics and would-be reformers. But the latter have, however, usually neglected the influence of the overall system in producing and sustaining the need for that type of bureaucrat – not least the need of ministers for the sort of support and services that generalists give them. The limited resources of political parties (and their associated 'think-tanks') mean that partisan sources cannot be looked to to supply policy-planning and analysis on the necessary scale or of the required quality. And the 'closed' nature of the policy debate in Whitehall – encompassing ministers, officials, and 'insider' interest groups – is also a problem in this respect. Reducing analysis of British government to a zero-sum game between ministers and civil servants misses these wider dimensions and problems.

In the early years of the Thatcher government there was much talk of the 'minister as manager'. Michael Heseltine at the Department of the Environment provided the new model with his concern for 'value for money', information systems and the nuts and bolts of departmental organisation, though his sceptical colleagues remained unconvinced. The emphasis changed with the launch of the Next Steps initiative in 1988 and the start of a process of establishing a range of agencies to manage the executive operations of government and absorb the bulk of civil servants (see Chapter 3). This scheme puts ministers – supported by a small core of civil service policy advisers – at arm's length from the detailed management of services.

Important issues raised – but not so far resolved – by this development concern the arrangements for ensuring the proper accountability of the new agencies and whether it will in fact prove to be possible for ministers (and top officials) to hold back from their day-to-day running, given the concerns of MPs for constituency cases and the way in which political storms can arise out of low-level administrative decisions. Will ministers and senior mandarins really now start to focus properly on long-term strategy and the development and analysis of coherent policies? The Next Steps changes may well create a civil service more amenable to ministerial control, it has been suggested, but at the risk of increasing the scope for political influence over appointments (will officials on short-term contracts trim their advice and be more anxious to please ministers?) (Greer, 1992, pp. 226–7).

Finally, the issues of secrecy and civil service ethics, put on the agenda by the Ponting and Westland cases in the mid-1980s, are also relevant to this discussion of ministers and mandarins. Constitutionally, ministers and Parliament define what is in the public interest, not civil servants. If civil servants are permitted to 'whistle-blow' in the public interest (as they define it), what will that do for their relations with their political masters? And how would moves towards more 'open government' affect the relations of confidence and trust necessary between ministers and their civil service advisers? Would wary politicians be tempted to apply tests of personal or political loyalty to the bureaucracy's topmost ranks, 'politicising' the civil service in the search for reliable support, or could these innovations be easily accommodated by Whitehall without disturbing the established relations between ministers and mandarins? At the moment, there are more questions than answers here but this is bound to remain an issue in the 1990s.

Note

The quotes opening the chapter are from, respectively: Sir Austen Chamberlain (1935) *Down the Years* (London: Cassell) p. 308; Richard Crossman (1975) *The Diaries of a Cabinet Minister, Vol. 1: Minister of Housing 1964–66* (London: Hamish Hamilton and Jonathan Cape) p. 22; Jonathan Lynn and Antony Jay (1983) *Yes Minister*, vol. 3 (London: BBC) p. 14; Gerald Kaufman (1980) *How To Be A Minister* (London: Sidgwick & Jackson) p. 140.

References

Aberbach, J., Putnam, R. and Rockman, B. (1981) *Bureaucrats and Politicians in Western Democracies* (Cambridge, Mass.: Harvard University Press).

Bagehot, W. (1963) *The English Constitution* (London: Fontana).

Benn, T. (1980) 'Manifestos and Mandarins', in *Policy and Practice: The Experience of Government* (London: Royal Institute of Public Administration) pp. 57–78.

Borins, S. (1988) 'Public Choice: "Yes Minister" made it popular, but does winning the Nobel Prize make it true?, *Canadian Public Administration*, 31, pp. 12–26.

Bruce-Gardyne, J. (1986) *Ministers and Mandarins* (London: Sidgwick & Jackson).

Fowler, N. (1991) *Ministers Decide* (London: Chapman).

Greer, P. (1992) 'The Next Steps Initiative: The Transformation of Britain's Civil Service', *Political Quarterly*, 63, pp. 222–7.

Heclo, H. and Wildavsky, A. (1981) *The Private Government of Public Money*, 2nd edn (London: Macmillan).

Hennessy, P. (1989) *Whitehall* (London: Secker & Warburg).

Hoskyns, Sir J. (1983) 'Whitehall and Westminster: An Outsider's View', *Parliamentary Affairs*, 36, pp. 137–47.

Hoskyns, Sir J. (1984) 'Conservatism is Not Enough', *Political Quarterly*, 55, pp. 3–16.

Kellner, P. and Crowther-Hunt, Lord (1980) *The Civil Servants* (London: Macdonald).

Niskanen, W. (1973) *Bureaucracy: Servant or Master?* (London: Institute of Economic Affairs).

Rose, R. (1987) 'Steering the Ship of State: One Tiller but Two Pairs of Hands', *British Journal of Political Science*, 17, pp. 409–33.

Rose, R. (1991) *Too Much Reshuffling of the Cabinet Pack?* (London: Institute of Economic Affairs).

Theakston, K. (1987) *Junior Ministers in British Government* (Oxford: Basil Blackwell).

Theakston, K. (1992) *The Labour Party and Whitehall* (London: Routledge).

Wilson, G. (1991) 'Prospects for the Public Service in Britain: Major to the Rescue?', *International Review of Administrative Sciences*, 57, pp. 327–44.

Young, H. and Sloman, A. (1982) *No, Minister: An Inquiry into the Civil Service* (London: BBC).

3

A New Civil Service? The Next Steps Agencies

TONY BUTCHER

The late 1980s saw the launching of an initiative that has been described by the government as a 'quiet revolution' in the management of the civil service, and which is considered by others to be 'the most ambitious attempt at civil service reform in the twentieth century' (Treasury and Civil Service Committee, 1990, para. 1). Known as the 'Next Steps' programme, the initiative involves the separation of the small core of civil servants involved in the policy-making and ministerial support functions of government departments from the vast majority of civil servants, who are involved in the service delivery or executive functions of central government. The intention is that by the end of the century most of the latter group will have been transferred to semi-autonomous executive agencies, headed by chief executives who are set performance targets and given certain financial and managerial freedoms. The hope is that the reforms will lead to greater efficiency and effectiveness in the civil service and to a better quality of service to the public. By the middle of 1993, just over 60 per cent of the British civil service were working in Next Steps agencies or organisations operating on Next Steps lines.

The Next Steps programme is of profound significance for the British civil service. As well as transforming the structure and culture of the civil service, it raises important questions about parliamentary and other forms of accountability. Some observers maintain that the programme will mean the end of the unified civil service which has been such an important feature of British government since the Fisher reforms of the early interwar period. But before we discuss the Next Steps programme, its origins, and its implications, we need to look back at some earlier developments. This is only the latest in a series of attempts since the 1960s to improve management in the civil service. It is with these earlier 'first steps' that we begin.

The First Steps: From Fulton to Thatcher

Concern about efficiency and effectiveness in the civil service has been on the political agenda since the early 1960s. In 1961, the Plowden Report, best known as the blueprint for central government's public expenditure survey system, was highly critical of the failure of senior civil servants to devote enough time to management as compared with policy advice. But the real starting point for discussions of efficiency and effectiveness in the civil service was the Fulton Report of 1968. A key theme of the Fulton findings was the promotion of efficiency in the service and, like Plowden, the report was very critical of the fact that too few civil servants were skilled managers.

Central to Fulton's discussion of efficiency was the argument that in order to function effectively, large organisations needed a structure in which units and individual staff have clearly defined authority and responsibilities for which they can be held accountable. It concluded that there was scope for organising executive activities in such a way that the principle of 'accountable management' could be applied within government departments. Some of the evidence to the Fulton Committee went even further, arguing that accountable management could be most effectively introduced where activities were 'hived off' to semi-autonomous boards outside government departments. Such bodies would be outside the day-to-day control of ministers and the scrutiny of Parliament. Whilst recognising that the separation of policy-making from its execution would raise parliamentary and constitutional issues, the report recommended a thorough review of the whole subject. In making this suggestion, Fulton was influenced by the Swedish system of government, where there is a policy-making core of only a few thousand civil servants, and autonomous agencies and boards are responsible for the delivery of services (Fulton Committee, 1968, ch. 5).

The Fulton proposals were endorsed by the then Labour government and the idea of accountable management was taken up by Mr. Heath's Conservative government in the early 1970s as part of its 'new style of government'. The concept was reflected in the development of such departmental agencies as the Defence Procurement Executive and the Property Services Agency. But progress in this area was slow, as it also was in the related area of 'hiving off', where few activities met the Conservative government's criteria [one of which was that the activity did not require regular ministerial involvement (see Pollitt, 1984, p. 102)]. The Heath government, and the Labour government which followed it, found only a few activities to be suitable for hiving off, notably those which formed the now defunct Manpower Services Commission. As the House of Commons Expenditure Committee observed in its 1977 report on the progress of the Fulton recommendations, the Civil Service Department was 'unenthusiastic' about the prospects for an extension of hiving off, arguing that the process might create more problems than it solved in areas with a high policy content (Expenditure Committee, 1977, para. 91).

The First Steps: The Thatcher Years

The election of Mrs Thatcher's Conservative government in 1979, with its promise to reduce waste and bureaucracy in the public sector, and its enthusiasm for managerialism and value for money, marked a turning point in the debate about efficiency and effectiveness in the civil service. In addition to large cuts in civil service staffing – the size of the civil service fell by nearly a quarter between 1979 and 1990 – the Thatcher governments introduced a series of measures designed to improve the management of government departments. The Prime Minister appointed Sir Derek (now Lord) Rayner, the then managing director of Marks & Spencer, as head of her Efficiency Unit to advise on ways of improving efficiency and eliminating waste in government departments. Under Rayner's direction, the Efficiency Unit initiated a series of small-scale efficiency scrutinies which looked in detail at particular areas of civil service work and made recommendations aimed at identifying economies and improving efficiency.

It was a Rayner scrutiny which led in 1980 to the introduction of MINIS (Management Information System for Ministers) in the Department of the Environment, designed to enable ministers to understand how the work of the department was organised and to identify who was responsible for the different areas of activity. MINIS was strongly endorsed by the House of Commons Treasury and Civil Service Committee, which called for the introduction of the system, or its equivalent, in all government departments, a call which was taken up by the government in 1982, when it launched the FMI (Financial Management Initiative) designed to promote devolved budgetary authority and accountable management in government departments. Parallel changes took place in policies for civil service training and career management, all intended to further encourage cost-consciousness and better management.

Thus a series of important developments took place in the early 1980s in an attempt to create a more efficient and effective civil service. By the late 1980s, the devolution of managerial and budgetary responsibility was a major feature of the Whitehall system. But, despite these developments, many supporters of the 'new managerialism' remained disappointed. There were criticisms that the FMI had only scratched the surface of the civil service's management problems, and suggestions were made that middle and lower managers were sceptical about the benefits of the changes (see, for example, National Audit Office, 1986, para. 20). There was a view that more radical changes were required.

The Ibbs Report

Disappointment with what was seen as the slow progress of the FMI and other reforms led the Efficiency Unit (apparently prompted by the Prime Minister) to undertake an efficiency scrutiny of the progress achieved in improving management in the civil service. The scrutiny was carried out under the supervision of Sir Robin Ibbs, the ICI executive brought in to carry on the work of Rayner.

The original version of the Ibbs Report was presented to the Prime Minister just before the 1987 general election. It was said to envisage turning most government departments into small policy units and devolving their service delivery functions to self-governing boards, in charge of their own budgets and free to set their own pay scales, on the lines of the Swedish system of government admired by the Fulton Committee. According to press reports, the scale of the proposals generated fierce opposition from the Treasury and some Cabinet ministers. The Treasury was apparently deeply concerned that the proposals would weaken its capacity to control public spending and civil service pay, while some ministers were said to be alarmed at the loss of 'political clout' in Cabinet if their departments were transformed into policy units.

A version of the Ibbs Report was eventually published in February 1988 (Efficiency Unit, 1988). Although recognising that some progress had been made in civil service management since 1979 – civil servants were now more cost-conscious and management systems were in place – the report concluded that there were still substantial obstacles in the way of further progress (Efficiency Unit, 1988, Annex B, I: paras 2–12):

1. There was insufficient focus on the delivery of government services, as opposed to policy-making and ministerial support, even though 95 per cent of civil servants worked in service delivery or executive functions.
2. There was a shortage of management skills, and of experience of working in service delivery functions, among senior civil servants. As one senior civil servant told the scrutiny team: 'the golden route to the top' was through policy and not through management.
3. Long-term planning was squeezed out by short-term political pressures.
4. There was too much emphasis on spending money and not enough on getting results.
5. The civil service was too big and diverse to run as a single entity. An organisation with nearly 600 000 employees, with responsibilities as varied as driver licensing, catching drug smugglers, and the processing of parliamentary questions, was bound to develop in a way which fitted no single operation effectively.

Thus Ibbs argued that despite the various initiatives taken since the election of the first Thatcher government in 1979, there was still a long way to go. In particular, the report identified what it described as an 'insufficient sense of urgency' in the search for better value for money and improved services (Efficiency Unit, 1988, para. 1).

A key characteristic of the British civil service has long been its unified nature, as reflected in service-wide terms and conditions, uniform grading and the concept of a service in which officials can transfer to posts in other departments. Ibbs, however, argued that the advantages which a unified civil service was intended to bring were outweighed by the practical disadvantages. Thus it said that uniform grading frequently inhibited effective management, whilst the concept of a career in a unified civil service was seen as having 'little relevance for most civil servants', whose horizons were bounded by their local office or department (Efficiency Unit, 1988, para. 12). As Fry (1988, p. 431) observed, unlike Fulton, which had endorsed a unified civil service, Ibbs was prepared to envisage it breaking up.

Ibbs recommended that the aim should be to establish what it described as 'a quite different way' of conducting the business of government. This different approach involved a move away from the concept of a unified civil service responsible for both policy formulation and the delivery of services. What Ibbs called 'the central civil service' should consist of a relatively small 'core' responsible for servicing ministers and managing departments, who should be the 'sponsors' of particular government policies and services. The actual delivery of particular services should be carried out by a range of agencies employing their own staff, who might or might not be Crown servants (Efficiency Unit, 1988, para. 44). Agencies would operate within a policy and resources framework set by the parent department. This framework would set out the policy, budget, specific targets and the results to be achieved. Once the policy objectives and budget had been set, the managers of the agency should have as much independence as possible in deciding how these objectives were met. There should be freedom in such matters as recruitment of staff, pay, grading and structure (Efficiency Unit, 1988, paras 19–21). It was envisaged that such changes would result in 'the release of managerial energy' within the civil service (Efficiency Unit, 1988, para. 50).

Thus, like the Fulton Report twenty years earlier, the Ibbs Report emphasised the importance of delegating authority to managers as a means of improving efficiency and effectiveness in the civil service. As we shall see later, like Fulton, the Ibbs proposals also raised important constitutional implications.

The Next Steps Programme

On the same day as the publication of the Ibbs Report, the Prime Minister announced that the government had accepted the report's main recommendations and that, 'to the greatest extent practicable', the executive functions of central government were to be carried out by agencies, which would be headed by chief executives, and whose staff would continue to be civil servants. The government committed itself to a continuing programme for establishing such agencies, and Peter Kemp, a deputy secretary in the Treasury, was appointed as project manager, with the rank of second permanent secretary in the Office of the Minister for the Civil Service (OMCS), to oversee the implementation of the Next Steps programme. (Following the 1992 general election, the OMCS was absorbed by the newly created Office of Public Service and Science and Kemp was replaced.) The staff of agencies were to remain as civil servants and were to be subject to the traditional rules relating to individual ministerial responsibility.

The reforms announced by the Prime Minister were hailed by the press as a 'revolution' and described as 'the biggest shake-up of the civil service in a century'. But after the earlier press speculation, the government's decision on the Ibbs Report was viewed by more sceptical observers as an anti-climax. The preliminary list of candidates for agency status, which included Her Majesty's Stationery Office (HMSO), the Meteorological Office and the Royal Parks, was a modest one, and, with the exception of the Employment Service side of the Department of Employment, did not involve large numbers of civil servants. The staff of the new agencies were to remain within the bounds of ministerial responsibility, and it later emerged that the policy and resources framework for each agency was to be set up by the responsible minister in consultation with the Treasury.

Progress with the Next Steps

Amid press reports of Treasury opposition to large departments becoming agencies, the Next Steps programme got off to a slow start. The first agency, the Vehicle Inspectorate, was not established until August 1988, and by the end of March 1990, just over two years after the publication of the Ibbs Report, only twelve agencies, employing a modest total of just over 10 000 staff, had actually been set up. This slow progress was the subject of criticism from the House of Commons Treasury and Civil Service Committee, which has monitored the development of the initiative since its early days. The programme's project manager, however, argued that the programme was making good progress, and that it was not the intention to go in for cosmetic change, but to ensure that the initiative brought about real and lasting reforms (Treasury and Civil Service Committee, 1989, Evidence, p. 3).

Despite these assurances, there continued to be widespread scepticism about the success of the Next Steps programme. It was viewed by many as just the latest chapter in the saga of unsuccessful attempts at reforming central government since the early 1960s. Thus one observer, in evidence submitted to the Treasury and Civil Service Committee in 1990 (Treasury and Civil Service Committee, 1990, Evidence, p. 60), referred to the belief that the Next Steps programme would eventually stagger into 'the Museum of Public Administration', to take its place alongside such initiatives as the Fulton Report in 'the gallery of failed reforms'.

In the event, the programme was considerably expanded in April 1990, when a further eighteen agencies were added (including one in Northern Ireland), making a total of 30, employing a total of some 66 000 civil servants. This new batch of agencies included the Employment Service, which, with some 35 000 staff, was the first really sizeable agency.

By June 1993, 60 more agencies had been established (including seven in Northern Ireland). These included the transformation of the social security benefits operation of the Department of Social Security into the Benefits Agency, which, with over 64 000 staff, is the flagship of the whole Next Steps programme. The Department of Social Security is the clear leader in the move towards setting up agencies to deliver services, with some 97 per cent of its staff working in five separate Next Steps agencies. Even departments

TABLE 3.1   *The Top Ten Next Steps Agencies, 1993*

	Staff
Benefits Agency	64 055
Employment Service	44 490
Her Majesty's Prison Service	39 060
Defence Research Agency	10 110
Social Security Contributions Agency	9 370
Land Registry	9 190
RAF Maintenance	6 180
Northern Ireland Social Security Agency	5 830
Valuation Office	4 965
Scottish Prison Service	4 625

Source: Treasury and Civil Service Committee, 1993, Evidence, pp. 208–9.

which have not formally introduced Next Steps agencies have taken the philosophy of the programme on board. Thus, although Her Majesty's Customs and Excise has not established any executive agencies, and the Board of Inland Revenue has set up only one executive agency (the Valuation Office), both departments are operating fully on Next Steps lines. Thus Customs and Excise has set up 30 Executive Units and the Inland Revenue has set up 33 Executive Offices, the managers of which are individually responsible for budgets and performance.

A total of nearly 348 000 civil servants (including nearly 9000 in Northern Ireland) were working in agencies and other organisations operating on Next Steps lines in June 1993. Over 40 per cent of these civil servants worked in just three agencies (see Table 3.1). A further 20 areas of departmental activity, including the Court Service, and employing a total of over 28 000 civil servants, had been identified as candidates for future agency status.

Setting Up Agencies

As the official history of the launching of the Next Steps programme explains, setting up an agency involves several stages (Goldsworthy, 1991, pp. 22–5). First of all, it is necessary to decide whether the activity concerned needs to be carried out at all. If the department decides that the activity is to continue, it must then consider full-scale privatisation and contracting out. The issue of privatisation has been a controversial one, with fears being expressed by Labour MPs that the Next Steps programme is the stepping stone to the full-scale privatisation of the civil service. In the event, the government only announced firm plans for privatising one agency – Driver Vehicle Operators Information Technology (formerly the information technology arm of the Driver and Vehicle Licensing Agency) – which was sold in December 1994, although other agencies, including the Vehicle Inspectorate, the National Engineering Laboratory and Companies House, have been identified as possible candidates for privatisation. (We shall discuss the government's plans for the possible longer-term privatisation of civil service functions, together with the related issue of market testing, later in the chapter.)

Agency status is only considered if ministers conclude that neither privatisation nor contracting out are suitable for the activity concerned. Departments then have to consider such questions as whether ministers need to be involved in the activity on a day-to-day basis, and whether it is capable of becoming a separate administrative unit (National Audit Office, 1989, para. 12).

Before agencies are established, parent departments are also expected to subject each potential agency activity to a rigorous 'review analysis' of its readiness for agency status, the functions it will be carrying out, and the benefits being sought from the agency approach. This analysis must satisfy both the responsible minister and the Treasury that the proposed agency will have 'a robust management structure', in order that it can operate from the very start without being a drain on the public purse and be able to provide services to its customers (National Audit Office, 1989, para. 18).

Once it has identified a candidate activity, the department consults with the Next Steps project team and the Treasury about the operational details of setting up the agency. A framework agreement is then drawn up for the new agency, setting out the contract between it and the parent department.

Types of Agencies

Agencies vary widely in size, structure and relationships with parent departments. They range from the Wilton Park Conference Centre with a staff of only 25 to the Benefits Agency with just over 64 000 staff. However, it is possible, using the typology employed by the Fraser Report of 1991 (Efficiency Unit, 1991, Annex A), to identify four broad groups of agency:

(a) Mainstream agencies – agencies which are fundamental to the mainstream policy and operations of their parent departments. Such agencies tend to be large in relation to their parent department and have a major impact on expenditure. Examples of mainstream agencies include the Benefits Agency and the Employment Service.

(b) Regulatory and other statutory agencies – agencies which execute, in a highly delegated way, statutory (usually regulatory) functions. Such agencies carry out tasks which are derived from the objectives of their parent department, but which are not closely connected to its main activities. Many are self-financing. The Vehicle Inspectorate is an example of this type of agency.

(c) Specialist service agencies – agencies which provide services to departments or other executive agencies, using particular specialist skills. The Social Security Information Technology Services Agency is a specialist service agency.

(d) Peripheral agencies – agencies which, although they report to a minister, are not linked to the main aims of a department and operate very much at arm's length. An example is Historic Royal Palaces.

Framework Agreements

Given the range of activities which have been given agency status, it is hardly surprising that some commentators have remarked on 'how little they have in common' (Davies and Willman, 1991, p. 16). The former project manager of the Next Steps programme, Peter Kemp (Treasury and Civil Service Committee, 1988, Evidence, Q. 14), maintained that there was 'no hard and fast pattern' for agencies – the concept of an agency was 'more a frame of mind' and an approach to the way government works. But what agencies do have in common is that they all work within the terms of a framework document agreed by the parent department, with the chief executive being judged on the success of the agency in meeting the performance targets set by the department.

Framework agreements have been described as being perhaps 'the key element' in the Next Steps programme, and are seen as implying a 'quasi-contractual' relationship between the minister and the chief executive (Treasury and Civil Service Committee, 1990, paras 14–15). Although they vary from agency to agency, being custom-built to meet the needs of specific agencies, they typically include information on the aims and objectives of the agency; the relationship between the agency and its parent department, including parliamentary accountability; planning and finance; pay and personnel matters; and the arrangements for reviewing the framework agreement (Treasury and Civil Service Committee, 1989, paras 20–1).

Next Steps Agencies at Work

The central theme of the Next Steps programme is that civil servants should become, in the words of one commentator, 'more innovative and pro-active rather than reactive'. This involves transforming the culture of the civil service by the adoption of the values and practices of the private sector (Greer, 1992, p. 224).

Thus, as befits organisations which have been created by a government which emphasises the introduction of more businesslike practices into the civil service, agencies produce annual business plans with detailed performance targets for the year ahead, as well as medium-term corporate plans. Performance targets are designed to bring about improvements in the quality of service, financial performance and efficiency. Thus the targets for the giant Benefits Agency in 1992–93 included clearing 60 per cent of Family Credit claims in thirteen days, and achieving £460 million worth of benefit savings from the detection and prevention of fraud. One of the targets for the Employment Service in the same year was to place 1.425 million unemployed people into jobs.

Responsibility for the day-to-day management of agencies lies with the chief executives, who are all appointed on fixed-term contracts and paid bonuses if they meet their targets – the chief executives of the three largest agencies in the Department of Social Security may be paid up to 12.5 per cent of their basic salary as an annual bonus. In the early years of the Next Steps programme, most chief executives came from within the civil service, but outsiders now make up just over one-third of the total number. Open competition has become the normal way of recruiting to these top positions, with successful candidates coming not only from within the civil service, but also from the private sector and other public sector organisations such as local authorities and the National Health Service. The first chief executive of the giant Benefits Agency is a former chief executive of Gloucestershire County Council.

Agency Freedoms

As we saw earlier, a major theme of the Ibbs Report, and an important requirement for cultural change, was the argument that those running agencies should be given as much independence as possible in their operations and should be given freedoms in recruitment and pay. Under the terms of their framework agreements, chief executives have delegated responsibilities in the field of pay and personnel management. A number of agencies have introduced group incentive schemes, whereby staff are rewarded if the agency meets its targets. Other agencies have introduced their own pay and grading structures, and all agencies with more than 2000 staff are responsible for their own pay bargaining from April 1994. Greater flexibility has also been introduced into recruitment arrangements, with agencies having the freedom to recruit directly most of the staff that they need.

There have also been developments in the area of financial delegation. A number of agencies, including the Vehicle Inspectorate and Companies House, have been designated as trading funds, allowing them to run their financial affairs more like private companies, with profit and loss accounts.

Agency–Department Relations

Despite the various pay, personnel and financial freedoms given to Next Steps agencies, there has been criticism that the Treasury and individual departments have been unwilling to grant agencies sufficient autonomy. One researcher has argued that the delegations of authority given to agencies have been minor, and that all of them could have been gained without agency status (Treasury and Civil Service Committee, 1991, Evidence, p. 108). Commenting on the relationship between departments and agencies, a former

Cabinet Secretary (Hunt, 1991, p. 97) has warned of the danger of 'departmental neo-colonialism' – the over-zealous monitoring or second guessing of agencies by their parent departments. An independent review of the progress of Next Steps agencies reported that the volume of contacts between agencies and their parent departments has been very high, with almost all those questioned reporting weekly contacts with departmental officials, and 25 per cent having weekly contact with ministers (Price Waterhouse, 1991, p. 9).

The danger of excessive interference by departments in the affairs of agencies has also been highlighted by the Treasury and Civil Service Committee (1990, paras 58–62), which has argued that parent departments must learn to develop a 'hands-off' management role and allow agencies to carry out the work delegated to them. This view was reinforced in 1991 by the head of the Efficiency Unit, who stated that there was a need to change the environment in which agencies operate 'from being restrictive to becoming enabling' (Treasury and Civil Service Committee, 1991, Evidence , Q. 342), and recommended greater freedoms for chief executives (Efficiency Unit, 1991, para. 2.7).

This kind of 'hands-off' approach was, of course, central to the philosophy of the Ibbs Report, which argued that once agencies had been established, ministers and senior civil servants should have enough confidence in the system 'to be able to concentrate on their proper strategic role of setting the framework and looking ahead to plan policy development' (Efficiency Unit 1988, para. 47). As one commentator has observed, assuming that senior civil servants develop such strategic skills, they are more likely to be in a position to provide greater support for their 'political masters' on strategic issues. It has also been suggested that because chief executives on fixed-term contracts will be 'anxious to make an impression', they are likely to have closer and more productive relations with ministers (Greer, 1992, pp. 226–7). Thus the Next Steps programme could transform the relationship between ministers and their senior officials discussed in Chapter 2.

Agencies and Accountability

One issue which has been the subject of much debate is that of accountability. According to the government, the creation of Next

Steps agencies involves no change in the traditional arrangements for accountability: ministers will continue to account to Parliament for all the work of their departments, including the work of agencies. Some observers, however, are sceptical and point to the problem of reconciling these traditional arrangements with the Next Steps philosophy of delegating greater managerial freedom to civil servants.

As Drewry and Butcher (1991, p. 228) note, the basic problem of accountability is quite simply stated, although it cannot be easily resolved. 'How can ministers credibly cling to their virtual monopoly of accountability to Parliament, via traditional modes of ministerial responsibility ... in respect of agencies whose chief executives are expected to take managerial initiatives at arm's length from ministerial control?'

There are various ways in which ministers and the chief executives of agencies can be held to account by Parliament (Treasury and Civil Service Committee, 1991, paras 70–89). MPs may ask parliamentary questions about the work of an agency. In addition, the chief executives of agencies can be called to appear before select committees, and, as agency accounting officers, can also appear before the Public Accounts Committee.

Problems have arisen in all these areas (see Treasury and Civil Service Committee, 1991, paras 73–89), but especially with the arrangements for dealing with questions from MPs to ministers concerning the work of agencies. The general principle on which the system works is that while ministers answer questions which relate to strategic matters, in the case of parliamentary questions concerning day-to-day operational matters delegated to an agency, the minister will normally arrange for the chief executive to write to the MP. The replies from chief executives are placed in the House of Commons Library and its Public Information Office. Following criticisms that such information was not readily accessible to the public, the replies from chief executives are now published in Hansard.

Despite the various arrangements for parliamentary accountability, they have been the subject of much criticism. One observer has described them as 'a muddle', which sets up 'a new variety of quasi-responsibility for which we have no agreed constitutional label' (Marshall, 1991, p. 469). Others argue that there is a need to supplement the system of parliamentary accountability by strengthening the machinery for the redress of consumer grievances through the development of such procedures as ombudsmen and user councils (see, for example, Davies and Willman, 1991, p. 36 and pp. 70–5; Treasury and Civil Service Committee, 1993, Evidence, Q. 528).

A New Civil Service?

The Next Steps programme, with its creation of executive agencies operating at arm's length from parent departments and its emphasis upon the values and practices of the private sector, is transforming the structure and culture of the civil service. Although it clearly builds upon earlier initiatives like the FMI, we are seeing the development of a new form of civil service.

Some observers suggest that the development of Next Steps agencies, along with the variations being introduced in pay, personnel and financial arrangements, is the beginning of the end of the unified civil service. Thus the civil service unions have referred to the danger of the civil service slipping away into either 'a confederation of loosely-related bodies' or 'a vague historical concept' (Treasury and Civil Service Committee, 1990, Evidence, p. 41).

In reply to such fears, the Head of the Home Civil Service, Sir Robin Butler, has referred to the future shape of the civil service as being 'unified but not uniform' (Treasury and Civil Service Committee, 1989, para. 55). But, as Chapman (1992, p. 3) points out, the sense of unity that Sir Robin believes still exists in the civil service is undermined by the fact that agencies, which now make up well over half of the service, are 'being positively encouraged to develop their own team spirit and loyalties'. The Next Steps programme has deliberately set out to engender feelings of enterprise and initiative in agencies: in Chapman's view, 'there can be no doubt that these have resulted in a fundamental change from an ethos … which contributed to the identity of the civil service' (Chapman, 1992, p. 3).

Thus for some observers, the result of the Next Steps programme is the emergence of a civil service very different to the one inherited by the Conservative government in 1979. Other observers are less certain, arguing that the programme has not gone

far enough in its attempts to improve the efficiency and effectiveness of the civil service. Thus one assessment, responding to the
government's description of the initiative as a 'quiet revolution',
has argued that 'Quiet it is. A revolution it isn't' (*The Economist*,
21 December 1991, pp. 28–9). According to this view, despite the
rhetoric, chief executives have only been given a little extra
freedom, and are not always inclined to make use of that.

There are those who argue that the major drawback of the Next
Steps programme is that central government is not exposed to
competition from outside providers. Thus the Confederation of
British Industry has argued that while the introduction of Next
Steps agencies may lead to some improvement, it will not
'yield the full benefit' of opening services up to competition
(Confederation of British Industry, 1988, p. 101, quoted in Mather,
1991, p. 78). For them, the best option is competitive tendering
for the opportunity to carry out central government functions. In
a similar vein, the former general director of the right-wing
Institute of Economic Affairs, Graham Mather, has argued that
though a framework for change, the Next Steps programme has
been cautious. Mather argues that the imprecision in the framework agreements between departments and agencies 'lets departments who are unsure of their real priorities and objectives off the
hook'. In his view, the 'umbilical cords' between parent departments and agencies should be severed. He proposes that Next
Steps agencies should only be set up after a review of various
options. First of all, there should be a consideration, involving independent consultants, of the full privatisation of the function involved. A second stage should be to draw up a specification for
competitive tender for the provision of the function. If this failed,
it might be possible for there to be a management buy-out
(Mather, 1992, p. 3; see also Mather, 1991, p. 79).

Beyond the Next Steps: Market Testing

The value of competition in the search for quality and value for
money in the public services was a key theme of the government's
Citizen's Charter, published in 1991 and designed to improve the
standard of services provided by government departments and
other public sector organisations. Competition was seen as one of

the main ways of making public services respond to the wishes of their users, or 'customers', and the Charter stated that the government was going to subject much more work in central government to 'market testing' – i.e., testing the cost of providing a service in-house against that of purchasing it from the private sector (Prime Minister, 1991, p. 33). Although contracting out in central government departments had been a feature of the civil service since at least the mid-1980s, it had been confined to traditional support services such as office cleaning and catering.

The government's plans for market testing were set out in the White Paper, *Competing for Quality*, published in November 1991 (HM Treasury, 1991). The White Paper made proposals for extending competition in the provision of public services and it was suggested that the services provided by central government and other public bodies should increasingly move to relationships which are contractual rather than bureaucratic. It further suggested that contracting out in central government departments, which had hitherto been confined to support services, should move to areas 'closer to the heart of government', such as the delivery of clerical and executive operations, and specialist and professional skills (HM Treasury, 1991, p. 12).

The government later announced that central government activities worth nearly £1.5 billion and involving more than 44 000 staff were to be market-tested in the period from April 1992 to October 1993 (Prime Minister, 1992, pp. 60–4). The activities involved in this first round of the programme ranged from audit and legal services in the Department of Social Security to vehicle excise duty refunds in the Department of Transport. A second round of market testing, involving work worth an additional £800 million, started in October 1993.

The market-testing initiative, like the Next Steps programme, has aroused much debate, heightened by conflicting statements on the real agenda of the exercise. Thus the Chancellor of the Exchequer, in his foreword to the White Paper on competition, stated that the government had 'no dogmatic preference' for either the private or the public sector, and that the best public sector managers can match anything achieved in the private sector (HM Treasury, 1991, p. ii). On the other hand, an internal paper said to have been circulated at very senior levels in government departments two months before the publication of the

White Paper stated that government policy was to restrict the size of the public sector, and that in general the presumption was that 'services should, wherever possible, be provided by the private sector rather than the public sector' (*FDA News*, July 1992, pp. 1–2).

In arguments reminiscent of those that have revolved around the Next Steps programme, critics of these new developments argue that the government has failed to think through the constitutional implications of market testing. One issue which has been raised is the tension between the traditional ethos of the civil service and the business culture associated with the new initiative. Thus Bogdanor (1992) has argued that 'it is not clear what weight has been given to public interest considerations such as impartiality and incorruptibility against the commercial considerations of the market', while the Council of Civil Service Unions has warned that there are areas of work in the civil service being subject to market testing and contracting out which 'give rise to the potential for severe conflicts of interest and corruption to arise' (Treasury and Civil Service Committee, 1993, Evidence, p. 106).

In the event, the early implementation of this particular phase of the civil service's managerial revolution was not quite as straightforward as the government had hoped. Legal obstacles to market testing emerged, and the first round of the programme was accompanied by confusion over the implications of a European Community directive protecting workers transferred from one employer to another. The savings made as a result of the first round of market testing – some £100 million – were much smaller than expected when the initiative was launched, and testing was completed on less than half the £1.5 billion target (*Guardian*, 5 November 1993).

In the meantime, concern about the future structure of the civil service had been fuelled even further by the announcement in late 1992 that the government was initiating a review of central government activities in order to 'develop the successful privatisation programme of the last decade'. Describing this new initiative as 'a long march through Whitehall', the Financial Secretary to the Treasury emphasised that in every government department the 'back to basics' test would be applied to every activity of government. The government was no longer simply looking for candidates for privatisation: it should ask itself what it must keep – 'what is the inescapable core of government?' (quoted in Treasury and Civil Service Committee, 1993, para. 11). The future is unclear. It will be some years before we can fully evaluate the impact on the civil service of the market-testing initiative or the outcome of the government's review of the possible privatisation of some civil service functions. In the words of the general secretary of the First Division Association, the trade union for senior civil servants, speaking about market testing: 'It may amount to very little or we may see the wholesale privatisation of functions generally acknowledged to be appropriate for a politically neutral, non-commercialised civil service' (Symons, 1992, p. 2). What is certain is that the civil service will continue to be at the heart of political debate in the 1990s.

References

Bogdanor, V. (1992) 'Going Private Is the Next Step to Oblivion', *Guardian*, 29 August.
Chapman, R. A. (1992) 'The End of the Civil Service?', *Teaching Public Administration*, XII (2), pp. 1–6.
Confederation of British Industry (1988) *The Competitive Advantage* (London: CBI).
Davies, A. and Willman, J. (1991) *What Next? Agencies, Departments and the Civil Service* (London: Institute for Public Policy Research).
Drewry, G. and Butcher, T. (1991) *The Civil Service Today*, 2nd edn (Oxford: Basil Blackwell).
Efficiency Unit (1988) *Improving Management in Government: The Next Steps* (London: HMSO).
Efficiency Unit (1991) *Making the Most of the Next Steps: The Management of Ministers' Departments and their Executive Agencies* (London: HMSO).
Expenditure Committee (1977) Eleventh Report, 1976–77, *The Civil Service*, Vol I, HC 535-I (London: HMSO).
Fry, G. (1988) 'Outlining "the Next Steps"', *Public Administration*, 66, pp. 429–39.
Fulton Committee (1968) *The Civil Service*, Vol. I, Report, Cmnd 3638 (London: HMSO).
Goldsworthy, D. (1991) *Setting Up Next Steps* (London: HMSO).
Greer, P. (1992) 'The Next Steps Initiative: The Transformation of Britain's Civil Service', *Political Quarterly*, 63, pp. 222–7.

HM Treasury (1991) *Competing for Quality*, Cm 1730 (London: HMSO).

Hunt, Sir J. (1991) 'The Cabinet and "Next Steps"', in Vibert, F. (ed.), *Britain's Constitutional Future* (London: Institute of Economic Affairs).

Marshall, G. (1991) 'The Evolving Practice of Parliamentary Accountability: Writing Down the Rules', *Parliamentary Affairs*, 44, pp. 460–9.

Mather, G. (1991) 'Government by Contract', in Vibert, F. (ed.), *Britain's Constitutional Future* (London: Institute of Economic Affairs).

Mather, G. (1992) 'Markets in the Machinery', *FDA News*, 12 (January) pp. 3–4.

National Audit Office (1986) *The Financial Management Initiative*, HC 588 (London: HMSO).

National Audit Office (1989) *The Next Steps Initiative*, HC 410 (London: HMSO).

Pollitt, C. (1984) *Manipulating the Machine* (London: Allen & Unwin).

Price Waterhouse (1991) *Executive Agencies Survey Report: Facts and Trends*, Edition 3.

Prime Minister (1991) *The Citizen's Charter*, Cm 1599 (London: HMSO).

Prime Minister (1992) *The Citizen's Charter: First Report: 1992*, Cm 2101 (London: HMSO).

Symons, E. (1992) 'A Year of Surprises', *FDA News*, 12 (June) p. 2.

Treasury and Civil Service Committee (1988) Eighth Report, 1987–88, *Civil Service Management Reform: The Next Steps*, HC 494 (London: HMSO).

Treasury and Civil Service Committee (1989) Fifth Report, 1988–89, *Developments in the Next Steps Programme*, HC 348 (London: HMSO).

Treasury and Civil Service Committee (1990) Eighth Report, 1989–90, *Progress in the Next Steps Initiative*, HC 481 (London: HMSO).

Treasury and Civil Service Committee (1991) Seventh Report, 1990–91, *The Next Steps Initiative*, HC 496 (London: HMSO).

Treasury and Civil Service Committee (1993) Sixth Report, 1992–93, *The Role of the Civil Service: Interim Report*, HC 390-I and 390-II (London: HMSO).

Part II

Parliament and Parties

4

Parliament's Changing Role

PHILIP NORTON

It is impossible to reach a proper understanding of UK government in the 1990s without giving detailed consideration to the role of Parliament. Parliament in the United Kingdom has a distinguished history. Its has its origins in the thirteenth century, and it has maintained many of the procedures and much of the terminology employed centuries ago. All of this is in sharp contrast to many of the legislatures of other Western industrial nations, which, in their present form, have a history of less than fifty years. Such legislatures are conscious creations, the products of codified constitutions.

However, in terms of the roles of the legislature in the political system, the differences are not as great as the historical origins might suggest. As a result of industrialisation and mass politics, most Western legislatures are, at best, minor actors in the policy-making process. They are now more likely than not to be reactive, or policy-influencing, bodies (Mezey, 1979; Norton, 1987a). The US Congress stands as an exceptional legislature due to its policy-making capacity. The UK Parliament does not.

The UK Parliament is one of a large number of reactive legislatures. The crafting – the 'making' – of a coherent programme of public policy rests with government: party ensures that this programme is approved. In so far as Parliament's history bears on its present relationship to government, it has served to hold back its development as a more specialised, committee-oriented institution on the lines of many of its continental counterparts. Nineteenth-century perceptions of a 'good legislature' (propagated, for example, by Walter Bagehot) have lingered. Thus, great emphasis is placed on the floor of the House, where men of independent means come together to discuss the merits of the measures proposed by the Queen's ministry (Bagehot, 1867; and see Norton, 1990a). Although committees were utilised, they remained subordinate and advisory. As party grew in importance, parliamentary committees were employed less often for investigative inquiries. For most of the twentieth century, the House of Commons (and even more so the House of Lords) was to remain a chamber-oriented institution, its members mainly men of wealth whose interests were not confined to politics and who, if not offered ministerial office, were quite capable of going off to pursue other careers (see King, 1981). Government grew in responsibilities, size and organisational sophistication. Economic and other interests became more organised and demanding, those demands being channelled directly to government. Various groups were effectively coopted into the policy-making process. Parliament failed to develop the capacity to keep abreast of these developments. It remained in the family of reactive legislatures, but it was becoming one of the weaker brethren.

Parliament 1945–70

Parliament appeared to have limited consequences for the political system in the quarter-century from 1945 to 1970, limited both for government and for the citizen.

Government was little troubled by Parliament. A party majority was ready to assent to any and every measure introduced by ministers. Between 1945 and 1970, no vote was ever lost because of government supporters entering the opposition lobby. By the end of the 1960s, Samuel Beer (1969) noted that party cohesion was so close to 100 per cent that there was no longer any point in measuring it. Ministers had to appear to justify government in debates, but debates on the floor provided little opportunity for structured scrutiny and little threat to well-briefed ministers.

Links between Parliament and citizen were notable more for their absence than their strength. Peers had no direct relationship with citizens and MPs were not much troubled by constituents. The party label rather than the candidate determined the outcome in parliamentary elections and the candidate, once elected, was not always a frequent sight in the constituency. During the 1940s and 1950s, most MPs gave home addresses which were not in or near their constituencies (Norton and Wood, 1993). Some lived considerable distances from their seats and paid infrequent visits (see Mitchell, 1983, p. 183; Norton and Wood, 1990, p. 197). Constituents for their part did not make extensive demands of MPs. They did on occasion write to them, or – where the Members held surgeries – visit them, but the numbers involved were relatively modest (see for example Couzens, 1956). For some Members, it was possible to reply in longhand. For some, it was apparently too much trouble.

Constituents often had little sight of the MP in the constituency. They also had little sight of the MP at Westminster. For those living a long distance from Westminster, the opportunities to see the House in action were limited. Reports in the press were generally confined to the serious newspapers and reports on the broadcast media were rarely carried as lead items. For most citizens, Parliament thus constituted a fairly closed institution, difficult to see and, thanks to the protective embrace of party, difficult to penetrate.

In short, the dominance of party allowed government to take Parliament for granted. That same dominance allowed most MPs to take their seats for granted. Parliament consequently had a small number of significant consequences for the political system. It was an important legitimising body, giving the seal of approval to measures laid before, it, and it was the principal recruiting agency for the political elite: the road to political office ran through Parliament (Norton, 1993b, chs 3, 8). But as a body for influencing public policy and for exercising a powerful scrutiny of the administration of government, it had a limited, if not marginal, impact. Of the various consequences of Parliament, what Robert Packenham (1970) identified as the law-making or decisional consequences came close to the bottom of the list (Norton, 1993b, ch. 1).

The years since 1970 have seen a notable change in the consequences of Parliament. MPs and peers have proved relatively more independent in their parliamentary behaviour. Both Houses

– the Commons in particular – have become more specialised, and have acquired the resources to subject government to more detailed and consistent scrutiny. MPs and peers have also become more active as citizens – both individually and organised in pressure groups – have made greater demands of them. The purpose of this chapter is, first, to sketch these developments; second, to explain why they have occurred; third, to explain their effect on Parliament and its relationship to government and citizen; and, finally and briefly, to consider the implications for the future.

A Changing Institution

Since 1970, Parliament has become relatively more independent, more specialised, more professional, and – possibly most importantly of all – more accessible than at any time in the previous seven decades of the century.

Independence

The independence of MPs has increased since 1970. Government backbenchers have proved more willing to vote against their own side. There was a sudden increase in cross-voting by Conservative backbenchers in the 1970–4 Parliament: they proved more willing to vote against the whips on more occasions, in greater numbers and with much greater effect than at any time previously in the twentieth century. Two-thirds of Conservative MPs voted against the whips on at least one occasion, resulting on six occasions in government defeats (Norton, 1975, 1978). Cross-voting spread to the government backbenches following Labour's return to office in 1974. Labour MPs were frequent dissenters, with some of the dissenting lobbies being notably large (Norton, 1980). The Labour government of 1974–9 suffered 42 defeats on the floor of the House, a majority (23) as a result of some of its own backbenchers voting with the opposition. (The remaining nineteen were the result of opposition parties combining against a minority government.) Though the size of government majorities from 1979 to 1992, and especially from 1983 to 1992, were such as to absorb occasions of limited cross-voting, the incidence of cross-voting continued unabated (Norton, 1985; Saalfeld, 1988). Even the government's majority was not an absolute protection. Each Parliament from 1979 onwards has witnessed one or more occasions when the government failed to carry the day in the division lobbies.

Even the largest parliamentary majority enjoyed by the Conservative Party since 1935 was insufficient to stave off defeat on the second reading of the Shops Bill on 14 April 1986, when 72 Conservative MPs voted with the opposition (Bown, 1990). It was the only time this century that a government with a clear overall majority had lost a second reading. The return of a Conservative government with an overall majority of 21 in April 1992 heralded a Parliament in which cross-voting by a number of backbenchers has greater effect and was notably prominent. Within a matter of months, the government witnessed serious dissent on the closure of coal pits and the bill to ratify the Maastricht Treaty (Norton, 1993c). During the passage of the European Communities (Amendment) Bill – to ratify Maastricht – the government was defeated on an amendment on the proposed new EC Committee of the Regions and then, more significantly, was forced to accept an amendment – requiring the House to reach a resolution on the social chapter of the treaty before the treaty could be ratified – rather than be defeated on it. The bill was eventually passed in July 1993 – a year later than planned – but the government was then defeated in its attempt to get the House to pass a resolution on the social chapter. It only succeeded by making the vote one of confidence. This Parliament was seen as one in which backbenchers were, on some issues, pitting themselves effectively against ministers. The contrast with pre-1970 Parliaments was a sharp one.

The change should not be overstated. Cohesion remains a notable feature of the House of Commons (Rose, 1983). Even the most rebellious of MPs will vote with their own side in at least nine out of every ten votes. However, it is not so much the frequency as the scale of the dissent that makes the difference between victory and defeat. Occasional dissent by a large number of backbenchers is a greater threat to government than regular cross-voting by a handful of Members. The possibility of defeat may be occasional but, unlike in Parliaments before 1970, it is real.

Nor is a behavioural change confined to the House of Commons. The 1970s witnessed clashes between a Conservative House of

Lords and a Labour government. What has been more remarkable has been the willingness of a Conservative Upper House to defeat a Conservative government (see Baldwin, 1985; Shell and Beamish, 1993). The Thatcher government suffered more than 150 defeats at the hands of their Lordships. The willingness to defeat the government did not end with a change of premiership in 1990. The Major government suffered defeats on a number of measures at the end of the 1987–92 Parliament and at the beginning of the new 1992 Parliament. Nor has the behavioural change been confined to the division lobbies. Since 1970, peers have attended the House in greater numbers than before – average daily attendance now exceeds 300 – and engage in greater parliamentary activity. The House now sits for more hours than it ever did in the 1950s and 1960s (Norton, 1993b). Friday and late-night sittings are no longer the rarities that they once were.

Specialisation

Both Houses are now more specialised than ever before. In the Commons, this has been achieved primarily through the introduction of departmental select committees. Before 1979, select committees were used sporadically and on no systematic basis. In 1979, fourteen committees were appointed 'to examine the expenditure, administration and policy' of the principal government departments (see Drewry, 1989). In the 1992 Parliament, the number increased to sixteen. The committees have had a number of consequences, foremost among them the creation of a more specialised House. The committees have provided the means for more structured and continuous scrutiny of departments than was ever possible on the floor of the House. Concomitantly, they have provided the opportunity for MPs to specialise in a particular sector of public policy and to eke out information for the benefit of the committees and for the House as a whole (see Judge, 1990; Norton 1993b).

The House of Lords has also engaged in some degree of specialisation through the use of committees. The two principal committees have been those on the European Communities (Grantham and Moore Hodgson, 1985; Norton, 1993b) and Science and Technology (Hayter, 1991; Grantham, 1993). Both committees undertake thorough reviews in the area of their very different competences and both make use of a large number of peers. The European Communities Committee works primarily through five subcommittees and draws on between fifty and eighty peers each session. The Science and Technology Committee draws not just on a significant number of peers but on highly qualified peers, numbering among its members many leading scientists. The House also on occasion uses *ad hoc* committees to investigate particular topics, including bills. (The subject of a bill of rights, for example was considered by such a committee.) In 1992, a committee on the work of the House recommended the greater use of *ad hoc* and legislative committees.

Professionalism

Parliament, primarily the House of Commons, has also been characterised by an increase in professionalism in recent years. This has taken two forms: more career-oriented MPs and a better-resourced House. MPs are increasingly likely to be devoted to making a life-time career in politics (King, 1981). They are likely to seek election after having spent a decade or so in a profession or, increasingly likely, in a politics-related career. The 1992 Parliament was notable for the number of new entrants coming from careers as political advisers. Though some may have outside interests, the pursuit of politics constitutes their abiding passion. Once elected, they are keen to stay in Parliament and to advance. As we shall see, they are also more likely to live in their constituencies.

A change in the nature of Members has also been paralleled by a change in the resources available to Members. Pay and allowances have increased significantly – albeit from a relatively low or non-existent base – since the 1960s. A secretarial allowance (of £500) introduced in 1969 has developed into an office allowance of almost £40 000 (as of 1992, when MPs voted – against government advice – to increase it by 40 per cent to bring it to that level), thus allowing for the hire of secretarial and research staff. Travel and accommodation allowances have been introduced. Though MPs are still allocated lockers (and a pink ribbon in which to hang their swords) each one now has a desk space, though not until the second phase of a new parliamentary building programme is completed will each MP actually have an individual office. Library resources have also increased significantly. By international standards, the resources available to a British MP are, at best, modest. By comparison with the British MP of thirty or forty years ago, they are lavish. Changes in the Lords have not been so marked. As we have already noted, peers are relatively active, with a greater number than before putting in a regular attendance. An increasing number are former MPs for whom service in the Upper House constitutes the final phase of a career in politics.

Accessibility

Both Houses have become notably more accessible in their activities. This takes two forms. One is in terms of visibility. The actions of both Houses are more open to the public gaze. The other is in terms of an active relationship between members and those outside the House. MPs and peers now devote a considerable proportion of their time and energies responding the the demands made of them by citizens.

In recent years, Parliament has become more accessible to those wanting to see what it is doing. Standing committees and most select committees meet in public session (unless the members direct otherwise) and the deliberations of the House and its committees have been opened to the broadcast media. Sound broadcasting of proceedings began in both Houses in 1978. The televising of proceedings began in the House of Lords in 1985 and in the House of Commons in 1989. The programmes on the Lords between 1985 and 1989 attracted relatively high viewing figures. Coverage of the Commons and its committees was more extensive than originally anticipated and generally welcomed by MPs and broadcasters (see Hetherington, Weaver and Ryle, 1990; Select Committee on the Televising of Proceedings of the House, 1990). The entry of the cameras immediately made Parliament a more visible institution to the public. It has been estimated that coverage of some activity in Parliament in a single news programme on television is watched by as many people as could sit in the public gallery of the House of Commons over a period of one hundred years.

Those outside Parliament thus have a greater opportunity than ever before to see what is going on within Parliament. For many, though, the interest has extended beyond watching what goes on to seeking to influence what goes on. There has been a remarkable rise in the demands made of MPs and peers by individuals and by pressure groups. This has been the most significant development of the 1980 and early 1990s.

The increase in the demands made of MPs by constituents is shown most graphically in the increase in the volume of constituency correspondence. In the 1950s, a typical MP received about twelve to twenty letters a week (Richards, 1959). In the 1960s, the figure was between 25 and 74 letters a week (Barker and Rush, 1970). By the 1980s, the average MP was receiving in one day more letters than the MP of the 1950s was receiving in one week. One survey by the Letter Writing Bureau 1986 suggested that the average Member received just over thirty letters a day. Many letters are from constituents asking for particular action to be taken by the MP and it is not unusual for the constituency correspondence of a Member to include ten to twenty – sometimes more – casework letters a day.

Constituency demands have generally been matched by activity on the part of MPs. This is reflected especially in the volume of correspondence from MPs to ministers. Most such correspondence involves Members writing on behalf of constituents, usually forwarding constituents' letters for comment and, where appropriate, action. The volume of MP-to-minister correspondence was substantial by the beginning of the 1980s, about 10 000 letters a month being written to ministers by MPs. By the end of the decade, the volume had increased to 15 000 a month. One survey in 1990 found that ministers answered 250 000 letters a year, mostly from MPs (Elms and Terry, 1990).

Constituency correspondence occupies an increasing proportion of MPs' time as does constituency activity generally. MPs now spend more time in their constituencies than before – they are more likely than before to live in or near their constituencies – with one survey in the 1980s finding that more than one in five of those questioned spent thirteen days or more each month in the constituency while the House was sitting (see Norton and Wood, 1990, p. 199). For constituents, the MP thus appears a far more accessible figure.

MPs have also been found to be accessible by those citizens who form themselves into pressure groups. Representations from groups seeking some action – popularly known a lobbying – is not new but what has been remarkable since the late 1970s is the growth in the scale of the activity. Before the 1970s sectional interest groups in particular concentrated their energies not only predominantly but often exclusively on government departments. That predominance remains but the exclusivity does not.

Pressure groups of all varieties now make frequent use of contact with MPs. One survey of more than 250 organised groups in 1986 found that the overwhelming majority – almost 75 per cent – maintained 'regular or frequent' contact with one or more MPs (Rush, 1990, p. 280). Those maintaining such contact variously ask MPs to take particular action, such as tabling an amendment to a bill, arranging a meeting at the Commons or with a minister, tabling a motion, or sponsoring a Private Member's Bill. The most frequent request is to table a parliamentary question (Rush, 1990, p. 281; Franklin and Norton, 1993). Though constituency correspondence has increased in recent years, the amount of material received by MPs from pressure groups has grown at an even more remarkable rate. In the wake of the 1992 election, a number of MPs claimed to be receiving several hundred pieces of correspondence – usually printed material – each week.

Nor is such lobbying confined to MPs. Peers are regular targets of lobbyists. Of the organisations questioned in the 1986 survey cited above, more than 70 per cent said they had used the House of Lords to make representations or to influence public policy (Rush, 1990, p. 160). Peers are approached for more or less the same reasons as MPs: to help arrange meetings and to table parliamentary questions. Of peers questioned in a separate survey by Nicholas Baldwin, just over two-thirds had asked an oral question on behalf of a pressure group (Baldwin, 1990, p. 163). Peers, like MPs, are inundated with campaigning letters from groups. Such correspondence is supplemented by meetings arranged by these groups, with parliamentarians being invited to meals, receptions and different types of presentations. These activities are augmented by those of full-time lobbyists, known professionally as political consultants.

Before 1979, there were very few firms of political consultants. Since then, their number has burgeoned (see Grantham and Seymour-Ure, 1990). By the beginning of the 1990s, there were about forty such firms as well as probably a three-figure number of free-lance consultants. These consultants advise clients on how to lobby Westminster – and Whitehall – and also undertake lobbying on behalf of clients. Their use by firms and other organisations has become extensive. One survey of 180 sizeable companies in 1985 found that 40 per cent used the services of political consultants (*Financial Times*, 23 December 1985). Most leading UK companies appear now to retain consultants or to utilise in-house consultants. They not only facilitated lobbying, they also encourage it. It is in their commercial interests to do so. For organisations with an interest in influencing public policy, there is a reluctance to be left behind by others who are utilising such professional help. They therefore follow suit. Political lobbying has been one of the growth industries in Britain in recent years. Political consultants are now very visible in the corridors of Westminster.

Parliament has thus changed significantly, in some respects dramatically, over the past twenty years. It is a far more active, open and accessible institution than at any time previously in the twentieth century. The MP of the 1990s bears little resemblance to the MP of the 1950s. Just before his retirement from the House of Commons in 1992, Father of the House Sir Bernard Braine estimated that the workload of a Member had increased tenfold since he first entered the House in 1950. The change, as we have seen, has been qualitative as well as quantitative.

What explains this remarkable change in the nature of the institution? And what are the consequences for Parliament in the context of the political system?

Why?

There is no single explanation for the changes we have identified. Rather they are the consequences of a number of disparate developments. These developments can be grouped under four broad heads: those of society, politics, government, and Parliament.

Society

The principal change under this heading is the postwar growth of educational opportunities and a greater awareness, through improved mass communications, of the political process itself. This has resulted in what has been termed cognitive mobilisation (Inglehart, 1977; Dalton, 1988) and has two consequences of relevance for our analysis.

First, it helps explain the growth in the number of pressure groups since 1960. Individuals are more aware of issues and of the processes through which action may be take to affect outcomes; they are also more confident of their ability to be involved. Consequently, more people have joined groups and the number of groups has burgeoned.

Second, it helps explain in part the change in the background of those entering the House of Commons. The phenomenon of the 'grammar school boy' entering politics has been marked in the 1960s and since as those entering state grammar schools in the late 1940s and the 1960s came of political age. They have displaced some, but not all, of those for whom political life – as a result of other pressures we shall identify – become overly demanding and too great a drain on energies they wish to devote to other pursuits.

Politics

This heading is employed to encompass a development that links social change and political activity. The years since the 1960s have witnessed a decline in the class–party nexus in British politics (Franklin, 1985). Party voting on the basis of class has become less predictable. This constitutes a significant explanation for greater volatility in voting intentions. This volatility is reflected both in the opinion polls and in the number of 'safe' seats lost by parties in by-elections. The proportion of by-elections resulting in seats changing hands has increased dramatically since the 1960s (Norton, 1992a). Four consecutive election victories by the Conservative Party since 1979 have masked an underlying volatility – a volatility of which MPs are aware. At the beginning of 1990, the Conservatives were more than twenty points behind Labour in the opinion polls. The fear of losing the next election was a significant influence in the Conservative leadership contest later that year and, indeed, an explicit reason for Margaret Thatcher deciding to stand down after the first ballot (see Norton, 1992b).

This volatility can be argued to have had an impact on MPs' responsiveness to constituency demands. MPs are now more career-oriented. They want to be in Parliament and, equally importantly, they want to stay in Parliament. Greater volatility in voting intentions constitutes a threat to re-election. One potential, albeit not guaranteed, protection against such volatility is to acquire a reputation for being a good constituency Member. That may, at least, help deter supporters from defecting. There is some evidence that there is some electoral reward for constituency activity (see Norton and Wood, 1993). Greater awareness of this may encourage further attentiveness.

Local parties also appear increasingly conscious of the importance of being seen to be active in the constituency, hence a greater insistence on candidates prepared to live in the constituency and engage in constituency activities.

Government

This heading encompasses both the growth of government since 1945 and the attempts to roll back the frontiers of the state since 1979. The advent of the welfare state in particular has had important consequences for Parliament. As government has acquired greater responsibilities, not least in terms of welfare provision, the greater the contact between the individual citizen and public agencies – notably in the provision of health care and the distribution of particular benefits. The more extensive such contact, the greater the potential for individuals to have some complaint about the service on offer or the substance of what is being provided. When a grievance exists, the local Member of Parliament is seen as the first port of call (see Marsh, 1985). The greater the growth of government responsibilities, the greater the volume of requests to MPs from constituents for intervention to assist with rectifying some problem with a public agency or to seek an authoritative explanation for some action. The government agency does not have to be a central government agency: local government problems also prompt citizens to contact the MP.

The attempt by government since 1979 to achieve greater autonomy in policy-making has also had consequences in terms of Parliament's contact with citizen – this time organised in groups. As government has sought some arm's-length relationship with groups, especially peak economic groups, so the greater the need felt by such groups to seek an alternative source through which to influence public policy (see Norton, 1991a). Hence the greater attractiveness of Parliament. As government has appeared less hospitable, so Parliament has started to take on a more attractive hue. That attraction has been reinforced by developments within the institution itself.

Parliament

Parliament has become more attractive to groups because of the behavioural and structural changes that have taken place since 1970 (Norton, 1991a). A relatively more independent legislature means that parliamentarians may be able to achieve some change that previously they would not have wished to or been able to. A more specialised legislature provides groups with specific targets for their lobbying and parliamentary bodies with some degree of knowledge in their particular section. The changes within Parliament themselves are the consequence of what may be characterised as internal pressures.

The causes of the behavioural change are the subject of serious academic dispute (see, for example, Franklin, Baxter and Jordan, 1986; Norton, 1987b). This writer has advanced the 'poor leadership' thesis, identifying Edward Heath's uncompromising style of prime ministerial leadership as the trigger for backbenchers to take their dissent to the division lobbies (Norton, 1978). Once dissent had been triggered, it generated a momentum that outlived the premiership of the person responsible for setting it in train. This momentum was facilitated by a greater awareness of what could be achieved by cross-voting and also by a realisation that many of the previous constraints presumed to operate had little effect or relevance (for example, the belief that a government defeat necessitated the government's resignation or a dissolution) (see Norton, 1980, 1985). As the dissent developed in the 1970s, so many backbenchers discarded their old deferential attitude towards government in favour of what Samuel Beer (1982) termed a more participant attitude.

This attitudinal change had relevance for the structural changes we have identified. Many MPs wanted to be involved in scrutinising the activities of government. The specialised means to do so were lacking: the floor of the House was not adequate for detailed and sustained scrutiny and voting against the government in the division lobbies was a blunt weapon for influencing government. Pressure built up in the House for better means of scrutiny, resulting – in conjunction with a reform-minded Leader of the House, Norman St John Stevas – in the creation of the departmental select committees in 1979. They constituted the best-known of several structural and procedural reforms (Norton, 1986) in that Parliament, supplemented by Members insisting on increased pay and research allowances (the latter especially in 1986 and 1992) and by Members deciding to let the television cameras in to record their proceedings.

The causes of the behavioural and structural changes in the Lords have been identified in the confluence of two independent developments (Baldwin, 1985). One was the influx of life peers, providing much-needed new blood to the House. Life peers provide a disproportionate proportion of the active members of the House and attendance has risen as the number of life peers has grown. The other development was the failure of the Parliament (No. 2) Bill – to reform the House – in 1969. Peers realised that reform in the near future was unlikely and that it was therefore up to them to make the existing chamber work. A third influence may be identified in the period since 1979. The Conservative government of Margaret Thatcher adopted essentially a neo-liberal approach to politics, in contrast to the Tory approach that had characterised most previous Conservative premiers (see Norton and Aughey, 1981). Conservative peers enjoyed a preponderance of numbers in the upper House but within their ranks the Tory strand of thought was notably to the fore. Hence the potential for clashes between the House and the government. The potential, as we have seen, was variously realised.

With What Effect?

What have been the consequences for Parliament of the changes we have identified? The answer is already implicit in much of what we have written. In terms of the relationship of Parliament to government, the effects have been important but modest. It is in terms of the relationship of Parliament to citizen that the impact has been greatest.

Parliament and Government

In terms of the consequences of Parliament for the political system, those of 'law making' and administrative oversight are, as we have noted, generally among the least significant (Norton, 1993b). The changes of recent years have not necessarily resulted in these functions moving further up the ladder – other functions have increased in significance – but they have become more significant than before. Both Houses of Parliament are now more active than before and devote more energy to subjecting the conduct of government to critical scrutiny. That task, at least in the Commons, is no longer confined principally to the floor of the House. There is an important qualitative change as well. Both Houses are now better informed, especially as a result of the work of select committees. Members are relatively more willing to act independently if persuaded of the case for doing so.

The result is an improvement in the capacity of Parliament to subject government to scrutiny and to influence what government does. There has been no fundamental change. Parliament remains a reactive legislature, one among the many in the category of policy-influencing legislatures. Its scope for independent action – like that of government – has been constrained by membership of the European Community, but within the sectors in which policy-making remains within the nation state it is now a more effective policy-influencing body than it was in the decades before the 1970s.

Parliament and Citizen

The biggest and most observable change has been in the relationship of Parliament to citizen. Parliament is now a far more visible, and far more accessible, body to citizens – be it the individual as constituent or citizens collected together in an organised group. Demands made of parliamentarians have increased – and MPs and peers have responded in a manner that has generally proved acceptable to those making the demands. Constituents have generally proved satisfied with the response provided by the local MP. The greater the degree of contact, the greater the degree of satisfaction with the MP (see Norton, 1993b; Norton and Wood, 1993). As Ivor Crewe (1975; p. 322) once aptly put it, 'familiarity appears to breed content'. Likewise with group activity. The 1986 survey of organised groups found that, of those who sought to influence legislation through Parliament, an absolute majority – 55.5 per cent – claimed they had been 'very' or 'quite' successful; less than 6 per cent said they had been unsuccessful (Rush, 1990, p. 193).

This assessment of the responsiveness of MPs may also have encouraged a growing self-confidence on the part of those seeking to influence the parliamentary process. The 1987 British Social Attitudes Survey detected a 'widespread and growing self-confidence on the part of the electorate to try to bring influence to bear on Parliament' (Jowell, Witherspoon and Brook, 1987, p. 58). Contacting the MP in order to influence government or legislation is the course of individual action favoured by citizens over other means available and is the one that is increasingly used – with a result that proves acceptable to the citizen (Norton, 1990b, pp. 24–5).

Parliament may thus be seen to be fulfilling more effectively than ever before a number of related functions (see especially Norton, 1993b). It serves as a safety valve, allowing the views of individuals and groups to be expressed via a formal authoritative body. It serves as an important articulator of particular interests, ensuring that the needs and demands of constituents and of groups are made known to government. These are essentially functions flowing from representations made to parliamentarians by citizens. There is also an important educative function fulfilled by the parliamentarians' contact with citizens: the latter are better informed about both the issue in question and also about the political system. And, ultimately, if citizens are favourably impressed by the response they receive, then the greater the perception of the legitimacy of the process they are employing.

The Future?

Given these changes and their effect, what of the future? Does not the increased significance of Parliament as a safety valve, interest-articulator, scrutineer of government and policy-influencer suggest an increasingly central and important role for Parliament? Not necessarily. These changes, if allied with increased resources, offer a notable opportunity to the House. Against that must be put two challenges: one the likely outcome if resources are not improved, the other the developing outcome as a consequence of membership of the European Union. Opportunity is taken to denote a potentially positive development, a challenge to denote a potentially negative one.

Opportunity

Parliament is in danger of becoming a victim of its own success. The more demands that are made of it, the greater the difficulty it has in coping with them. Both Houses of Parliament have, so far, managed to cope with the pressures from individuals and from pressure groups. However, the increase in the resources available to meet these demands has not kept pace with the demands themselves. MPs in particular are now having difficulty finding the time to deal with all the demands made on their time. They are in danger of being overloaded with business (Norton, 1992c). Some activities, such as attending party committees, are already suffering (see Norton, 1993d). Without increased resources, giving greater opportunities for research and to release MPs from fairly mundane tasks, the demands made of MPs – and peers – are increasingly like to run ahead of the capacity of the Members to deal with them. If Parliament is to maintain its legitimacy in the eyes of electors it has to be able to meet their expectations.

Individual Members need improved working conditions and enhanced research and secretarial support. Committees of the House need greater support services and, in the case of standing committees, greater powers to take evidence. Various surveys of Members have tapped a desire for reform of working practices and a strengthening of resources (Norton, 1991b). A number of proposals for reform have flowed from committees of both Houses: a select committee of the Commons in 1992 recommended a reform of sitting hours and – following earlier recommendations of the procedure committee – the timetabling of government bills. As we have already noted, a committee of the Lords in 1992 recommended greater use of committees for the scrutiny of bills. A comprehensive scheme for reform of the legislative process was advanced by a commission of the Hansard Society in 1993.

MPs themselves have already taken some steps to increase their resources. In 1992, as we have already recorded, they increased their own office cost allowance by 40 per cent, thus allowing the recruitment of more secretarial and research support. A number of MPs on both sides of the House continue to press for the implementation of more substantial reforms, such as those advanced by the Hansard Society, including timetabling of bills and referring bills to committees that can take evidence.

If both Houses increase the resources available to members and to committees, then the remaining years of the 1990s offer a tremendous opportunity to Parliament to meet the increasing demands made of it and thus play a greater role in the British polity. The potential is there. MPs have taken some limited steps to fulfil it, as have members of the House of Lords, but it has yet to be fully realised.

Challenges

What if Parliament fails to increase resources to keep pace with the demands made of it? If demands continue to increase, then it runs the danger of being overloaded and of collapsing under the strain. Its significance would thus clearly diminish and both Houses would be more vulnerable to pressures for radical reform. Various calls have been made for a radical overhaul of the political system, including the House of Lords – and less notably – the House of Commons. A reform of the constitution may be brought about because of wider concerns than those focused on Parliament, but a failure on the part of Parliament to cope with the demands made of it by citizens would buttress the case advanced for change.

The other challenge comes from membership of the European Union. As a consequence of membership, policy-making competence in various sectors has passed to the institutions of the European Union. The effect has been to limit the policy domain within which government and Parliament can independently determine public policy. The Single European Act, which came into force in 1987, and the Maastricht Treaty, which came into force in 1993, have further strengthened the institutions of the EU in relation to the institutions of the nation states. Membership also has a significant constitutional dimension, threatening – though not yet destroying – the doctrine of parliamentary sovereignty. The doctrine stipulates that the outputs of Parliament are binding and cannot be set aside by any court. In 1990 the EC Court of Justice ruled that the courts had the power to suspend an Act of Parliament. The doctrine remains extant in that Parliament can repeal the Acts providing the legal base for membership of the EU. Even so, the practical effect is that the doctrine is being eroded and may eventually disappear.

The consequence for Parliament is that the sphere in which it can influence public policy is constrained. That is true of all national parliaments in the EU. That is a challenge. There is also an element of opportunity. If Parliament establishes closer links with the European Parliament and the other institutions of the Union it may be able to exert some influence on EU law-making. It has so far failed to develop such links. Membership thus constitutes a challenge, limiting the sphere within which Parliament can exert influence.

Parliament is thus limited by membership of the European Union but within the context of that limited sphere it has played a more significant role than before. If membership of the EU places increased strains on political systems, not least through a perceived democratic deficit, then the burden falling on the shoulders of national parliaments may be even greater. Parliament thus faces the new century with the potential to play an enhanced role in the political system. If it fails to generate the means to do so, it runs the risk of receding into insignificance and collapsing under the strain.

References

Bagehot, W. (1867) *The English Constitution* (London: Fontana, 1963 edn).

Baldwin, N. D. J. (1985) 'The House of Lords: Behavioural Changes', in Norton, P. (ed.), *Parliament in the 1980s* (Oxford: Basil Blackwell).

Baldwin, N. D. J. (1990) 'The House of Lords', in Rush, M. (ed.), *Parliament and Pressure Politics* (Oxford: Oxford University Press).

Barker, A. and Rush, M. (1970), *The Member of Parliament and His Information* (London: Allen & Unwin).

Beer, S. H. (1982) *Britain Against Itself* (London: Faber).

Bown, F. (1990) 'The Defeat of the Shops Bill, 1986' in Rush, M. (ed.) *Parliament and Pressure Politics* (Oxford: Oxford University Press).

Couzens, K. (1956) 'A Minister's Correspondence', *Public Administration*, 34, pp. 237–44.

Crewe, I. (1975) 'Electoral Reform and the Local M.P.', in Finer, S. E. (ed.), *Adversary Politics and Electoral Reform* (London: Anthony Wigram).

Dalton, R. (1988) *Citizen Politics in Western Democracies* (Chatham, NJ: Chatham House).

Drewry, G. (1989) *The New Select Committees*, revised edn (Oxford: Oxford University Press).

Elms, T. and Terry, T. (1990) *Scrutiny of Ministerial Correspondence* (London: Cabinet Office Efficiency Unit).

Franklin, M. (1985) *The Decline of Class Voting in Britain* (Oxford: Oxford University Press).

Franklin, M. and Norton, P. (1993) (eds) *Parliamentary Questions* (Oxford: Oxford University Press).

Franklin, M., Baxter, A. and Jordan, M. (1986) 'Who Were the Rebels? Dissent in the House of Common 1970–1974', *Legislative Studies Quarterly*, 11, pp. 143–59.

Grantham, C. (1993) 'Select Committees', in Shell, D. and Beamish, D. (eds), *The House of Lords at Work* (Oxford: Oxford University Press).

Grantham, C. and Moore Hodgson, C. (1985) 'The House of Lords: Structural Changes', in Norton, P. (ed.), *Parliament in the 1980s* (Oxford: Oxford University Press).

Grantham, C. and Seymour-Ure, C. (1990) 'Political Consultants', in Rush, M. (ed.), *Parliament and Pressure Politics* (Oxford University Press).

Hansard Society (1993) *Making the Law: The Report of the Hansard Society Commission on the Legislative Process* (London: Hansard Society).

Hayter, P. D. G. (1991), 'The Parliamentary Monitoring of Science and Technology', *Government and Opposition*, 26, pp. 147–66.

Hetherington, A., Weaver, K. and Ryle, M. (1990) *Cameras in the Commons* (London: Hansard Society).

Inglehart, R. (1977) *The Silent Revolution* (Princeton, NJ: Princeton University Press).

Jowell, R., Witherspoon, S. and Brook, L. (1987) *British Social Attitudes: The 1987 Survey* (Aldershot: Gower).

Judge, D. (1990) *Parliament and Industry* (Aldershot: Dartmouth).

King, A. (1981) 'The Rise of the Career Politician in Britain – and its Consequences', *British Journal of Political Science*, 11, pp. 249–85.

Marsh, J. W. (1985) 'The House of Commons: Representational Changes', in Norton, P. (ed.), *Parliament in the 1980s* (Oxford: Basil Blackwell).

Mezey, M. (1979) *Comparative Legislatures* (Durham, NC: Duke University Press).

Mitchell, A. (1983) *Westminster Man* (London: Thames Methuen).

Norton, P. (1975) *Dissension in the House of Commons 1945–74* (London: Macmillan).

Norton, P. (1978) *Conservative Dissidents* (London: Temple Smith).

Norton, P. (1980) *Dissension in the House of Commons 1974–1979* (Oxford: Oxford University Press).

Norton, P. (1985) 'The House of Commons: Behavioural Changes', in Norton, P. (ed.), *Parliament in the 1980s* (Oxford: Basil Blackwell).

Norton P. (1986) 'Independence, Scrutiny and Rationalisation: A Decade of Changes in the House of Commons', *Teaching Politics*, 15, pp. 69–98.

Norton, P. (1987a) 'Parliament and Policy in Britain: The House of Commons as a Policy Influencer', in Robins, L. (ed.), *Topics in British Politics 2* (London: Political Education Press).

Norton, P. (1987b) 'Dissent in the House of Commons: Rejoinder to Franklin, Baxter, Jordan', *Legislative Studies Quarterly*, 12, pp. 143–52.

Norton, P. (1990a) (ed.) *Legislatures* (Oxford: Oxford University Press).

Norton, P. (1990b) 'Parliament in the United Kingdom: Balancing Effectiveness and Consent?', in Norton, P. (ed.), *Parliaments in Western Europe* (London: Frank Cass).

Norton, P. (1991a) 'The Changing Face of Parliament: Lobbying and its Consequences', in Norton P. (ed.), *New Directions in British Politics?* (Aldershot: Edward Elgar).

Norton, P. (1991b) 'Reforming the House of Commons', *Talking Politics*, 4(1), pp. 16–20.

Norton, P. (1992a) 'Parliament in the UK: The Incumbency Paradox', Paper presented at the Annual Conference of the American Political Science Association, Chicago, USA, September.

Norton, P. (1992b) 'The Conservative Party from Thatcher to Major', in King, A. *et al., Britain at the Polls 1992* (Chatham, NJ: Chatham House).

Norton, P. (1992c) 'The House of Commons: From Overlooked to Overworked', in Jones, B. and Robins, L. (eds), *Two Decades in British Politics* (Manchester: Manchester University Press).

Norton, P. (1993a) 'Congress: Comparative Perspectives', in Bacon, D. C. and Davidson, R. H. and Keller, M. (eds), *The Encyclopedia of the United States Congress* (New York: Simon & Schuster).

Norton, P. (1993b) *Does Parliament Matter?* (Hemel Hempstead: Harvester Wheatsheaf).

Norton, P. (1993c) 'Parliament', in Catterall, P. (ed.), *Contemporary Britain: An Annual Review 1993* (Oxford: Basil Blackwell).

Norton, P. (1993d) 'The Party in Parliament' in Seldon, A. and Ball, S. (eds), *The Conservative Party in the Twentieth Century* (Oxford: Oxford University Press).

Norton, P. and Aughey, A. (1981) *Conservatives and Conservatism* (London: Temple Smith).

Norton, P. and Wood, D. (1990) 'Constituency Service by Members of Parliament: Does it Contribute to a Personal Vote?', *Parliamentary Affairs*, 43(2), pp. 196–208.

Norton, P. and Wood, D. (1993) *Back from Westminster* (Lexington, Ky: Kentucky University Press of Kentucky).

Packenham, R. (1970), 'Legislature and Political Development', in Kornberg, A. and Musolf, L. D. (eds), *Legislatures in Developmental Perspective* (Durham, NC: Duke University Press).

Richards, P. G. (1959) *Honourable Members* (London: Faber).

Richards, P. G. (1967) *Parliament and Foreign Affairs* (London: Allen & Unwin).

Rose, R. (1983) 'Still the Era of Party Government', *Parliamentary Affairs*, 36, pp. 282–99.

Rush, M. (1990) (ed.) *Parliament and Pressure Politics* (Oxford: Oxford University Press).

Saalfeld, T. (1988) *Das britische Unterhaus 1965 bis 1986* (Frankfurt: Peter Lang).

Select Committee on the Televising of Proceedings of the House, House of Commons (1990) *First Report: Review of the Experiment in Televising the Proceedings of the House*, Session 1989–90, HC 265-I (London: HMSO).

Shell, D. and Beamish, D. (1993) (eds) *The House of Lords at Work* (Oxford: Oxford University Press).

Wilson, H. H. (1961) *Pressure Group* (London: Secker & Warburg).

5

Parliamentary Scrutiny

MICHAEL RUSH

Ministerial Responsibility and Parliamentary Scrutiny

It is the distinguishing feature of parliamentary government that not only is the executive drawn from the legislature but, crucially, it is constitutionally responsible to it. The fact that almost without exception all ministers are members of either the House of Commons or the House of Lords clearly facilitates Parliament's ability to render them accountable to the legislature, but it is the doctrine of ministerial responsibility that is the constitutional basis of parliamentary scrutiny.

Ministerial responsibility takes two forms – collective and individual – and the ultimate sanction in both cases is the forced resignation of the government as a whole or of an individual minister respectively. In practice, however, governments rarely fall through being defeated in the House of Commons. The last to do so was the minority Labour government led by James Callaghan, which was forced into and lost the general election of 1979. The last occasion before that was in 1924 and before that in 1895, although Neville Chamberlain resigned as Prime Minister in 1940 after his normal majority fell drastically. Resignations by individual ministers are more common, either because a minister is unwilling to accept government policy on a particular matter or range of matters – collective responsibility – or because the minister regards resignation as an appropriate response when an error of policy or administration has occurred – individual responsibility.

However, the former are far more common than the latter and re-markably few resignations take place on the grounds of individual responsibility, in the main because disagreement over policy from time to time is inevitable, but admissions of error to the point of resignation are embarrassing and unpalatable to governments.

Does this mean that ministerial responsibility is largely a consti-tutional fiction? The short answer is, not necessarily: it is a matter of opinion whether the House of Commons in general and gov-ernment supporters in particular are unduly supine, but bringing down a government or forcing the resignation of a minister are only the ultimate forms of enforcing ministerial responsibility. The longer and more important answer is that in the context of day-to-day politics and policy-making ministerial responsibility is the foundation of parliamentary scrutiny. It is precisely because of ministerial responsibility that members of both Houses of Parliament can demand that the government publicly explains and defends its actions and policies. Ministers are answerable to Parliament for their conduct of public policy and administration. The doctrine therefore underpins all debates, all parliamentary questions, all committee activity – the means by which Parliament seeks to exercise its scrutiny.

The Means of Parliamentary Scrutiny

Parliamentary scrutiny is exercised by both Lords and Commons using essentially the same tools, though to different degrees and effect. The great bulk of parliamentary business – more than four-fifths – is nowadays devoted to government business, either in the form of specific legislation or the scrutiny of government policy and administration. Furthermore, the government has consider-able control over parliamentary business, not only because it nor-mally has an overall majority in the Commons, but also because, with or without a majority, it retains substantial powers of initia-tive. Governments commonly secure the passage of well over 90 per cent of their bills through Parliament, occasionally even 100 per cent as in 1987–88 and 1988–89. More often than not when government bills do not complete their passage it is because the parliamentary timetable has become too crowded. Government legislation may be modified while it is going through Parliament,

TABLE 5.1   *Division of Time on the Floor of the House of Commons;*
            1985–86

	Hours (%)
Business initiated by the government	55
Business initiated by the opposition	10
Business initiated by backbench MPs	35
Total	100

Source: J. A. Griffith and Michael Ryle *Parliament: Functions, Practice and Procedures* (London; Sweet & Maxwell, 1989) p. 12.

but in most cases the government accepts changes rather than having them forced upon it. Similarly, the government normally wins any divisions that take place during or at the end of debates on policy and administration, but it is misleading to measure parliamentary scrutiny in terms of votes won and lost. Ultimately, parliamentary scrutiny is about exposing the government and its activities to public debate and is therefore a more complex and subtle business than counting Members through the division lobbies. Moreover, the opportunities for scrutiny are more widespread than the government's ability to secure the passage of its programme would suggest, as the division of time on the floor of the House of Commons shows in Table 5.1.

Parliament has at its disposal four major means of parliamentary scrutiny: legislative procedure, debates on non-legislative business, parliamentary questions, and investigatory committees. Through these the government is subject to scrutiny by the official opposition, which offers itself as a government-in-waiting, and by all backbench MPs, including its own supporters.

Legislative Procedure

Primary legislation encompasses bills tabled in either House which, if passed through all the necessary stages, become Acts of Parliament. Secondary or delegated legislation refers to regulations issued by ministers (or, since Britain's accession to the EU, by the European Commission) under the authority granted by Acts of Parliament (or in the case of European legislation,

Britain's signature of the Treaty of Rome). Unless it is passed under the provisions of the Parliament Acts 1911 and 1949, all primary legislation must be passed by both Houses of Parliament. The Parliament Acts allow the Commons to override the rejection of a bill by the Lords, but only four Acts have become law in this way: two in 1914, the 1949 Act itself and, most recently, the War Crimes Act 1991. In addition, the Parliament Act of 1911 requires the Upper House to pass financial legislation within one month of its passage through the Commons. The fact that no party has an overall majority in the House of Lords does not generally cause undue difficulties for governments and the Lords normally gives way to the Commons if the Lower House persists in its views on legislation.

Bills go through a fairly elaborate procedure, basically the same in both Houses, at all stages of which (except a formal introduction) they are subject to varying degrees of scrutiny. How effective that scrutiny is undoubtedly varies. The more strongly the government is committed to a bill the less likely it is to accept any but the most limited of amendments. Few bills are subject to a formal allocation of time motion or guillotine, which is only possible in the Commons, but all are normally subject to a timetable negotiated with opposition.

Following a second reading, which deals with the principles of the bill, it goes through a committee stage in which it is debated in detail clause by clause. The committee stage may be taken on the floor of the House or by a standing committee. Up to two-thirds of all government bills each year are referred to a standing committee. Standing committees, however, are miniatures of the House both in membership and, more importantly, procedure in that they mirror the confrontation of government versus opposition. They are therefore largely devices to enable the Commons to deal with several bills simultaneously, thus freeing the floor of the House for other business. The House then debates the results of the bill's passage through the committee in what is called the report stage, which is followed by a final look at the bill as a whole in a third reading. The House of Lords follows a similar procedure, except it does not use standing committees, but usually takes the committee stage on the floor of the House.

Commons debates on government legislation are often partisan, which tends to militate against effective scrutiny, but such debates expose bills to wider examination than they would otherwise receive and force ministers to defend their legislative proposals publicly. Though less partisan than in the Commons and not subject to formal timetabling, legislative debates in the Lords are otherwise subject to similar limitations in that scrutiny is as effective as the expertise, the number of participants, and the time available allows.

Both Houses have the power to appoint a select committee to take the committee stage, which would allow ministers, civil servants, pressure groups, and independent experts to submit written evidence on the bill's proposals and be called to give oral evidence. This procedure is seldom used, however, and debate is therefore normally confined to the members of the House concerned and extra-parliamentary expertise can only be brought to bear informally.

A similar situation prevails in the scrutiny of delegated legislation, mostly in the form of statutory instruments. The House of Commons spends only some 5 per cent of the time on the floor of the House on secondary legislation, including that from Brussels, although more time is spent in committees and the Lords devotes more time to delegated legislation than the Commons. But again, with the the important exception of the Lords Committee on the European Communities, evidence from the policy-makers and people outside Parliament is not taken by parliamentary committees dealing with delegated legislation. Moreover, statutory instruments may not be amended, only rejected, and most are subject to negative procedure, that is, they will come into force unless Parliament specifically rejects them.

Non-legislative Debates

The Commons spends between a quarter and a third of its time on government legislation, but nearly twice as much debating other matters. Some of these debates take place on the initiative of the parties in opposition, although the official opposition understandably has the lion's share of such initiatives. Other debates are initiated by backbenchers on subjects of their choice, but most debates are initiated by the government, relating either to necessary business, such as the debate on the Queen's Speech outlining the government's annual programme, or on financial matters, or debates on particular policy areas. Not all debates end with a division, but those that do normally see the government prevail through its majority. All debates, however, provide MPs, whether supporters of the government or not, with the opportunity to evaluate government policy and administration and to that extent at least are an important contribution to parliamentary scrutiny. How effective they are is a matter of judgement: much depends on the quality of the input by Members, an inevitably variable factor, and partisanship sometimes obfuscates more penetrating scrutiny. A former Speaker of the House of Commons has estimated that a backbencher is likely to be called to speak four times a year and it has been suggested that formal limits be placed on the length of speeches, as is the case in the Canadian House of Commons. There has been some informal experimentation, but it should not be assumed that the number of speakers able to participate is directly proportionate to the quality of scrutiny. What is more important is to allow and encourage the participation of those who have something useful to contribute to a particular debate, an objective more easily stated than achieved.

Parliamentary Questions

The third means of parliamentary scrutiny is the parliamentary question, sometimes seen as the most potent weapon in the hands of the individual parliamentarian. Certainly, the well-judged question can be used with devastating effect, though not always strictly as a means of parliamentary scrutiny. Furthermore, Question Time in the Commons, especially the twice-weekly Questions to the Prime Minister, is undoubtedly the aspect of Parliament most familiar to the public, particularly since the broadcasting of parliamentary proceedings began, first on radio and more recently on television. The reality of parliamentary questions is, however, more complex.

In the first place those questions which receive an oral answer at Question Time constitute only the tip of the iceberg: in the 1990–91 parliamentary session they amounted to only 15 per cent of all questions tabled; the rest received a written reply. This is partly explained by the fact that there are always more questions tabled for oral reply than can be answered in the time available, but the main explanation is that most questions seek a written, not an oral, answer. All written answers are printed with the day's proceedings in Hansard. Thus, spectacular as Question Time sometimes is, it is certainly quantitatively and probably qualitatively less important as a means of parliamentary scrutiny than questions tabled for written answer. There is no doubt that the latter provide a most effective means of extracting information from the government, often information which the government would not otherwise reveal. This is sometimes simply because it has not been asked to disclose particular information, but also because governments seek to retain as much control over information as possible. Nonetheless, parliamentary questions are a major and generally effective means of scrutiny. Moreover, their use has grown considerably since the 1946–47 parliamentary session, when a total of 16 930 were answered; in 1990–91 the total had more than doubled to 38 101. The pattern of questions has also changed significantly: in 1946–47 not only were more questions answered orally, but questions put down for oral answer were twice as numerous as those put down for written answer. In 1990–91 questions for written answer outnumbered those tabled for oral answer by a ratio of nearly seven to one; in short, questions for written answer had become immensely more important as a means of parliamentary scrutiny (Franklin and Norton, 1993).

Investigatory Committees

The fourth and final means of parliamentary scrutiny is that of investigatory committees, that is, select committees which has the power 'to send for persons, papers and records' – to take oral and written evidence from anyone or any organisation they wish. In practice, this means they can question ministers, civil servants, and experts and interested individuals and organisations from outside the governmental apparatus. Oral evidence is presented by invitation and is limited by the time available, but written evidence may be submitted by any individual or organisation and provides an important channel for pressure groups to put their point of view (Rush, 1990).

In addition to select committees, the House of Commons also uses other types of committee which play a part in parliamentary scrutiny. The use of standing committees for the committee stage of bills has already been noted, but business relating to Scotland, Wales and Northern Ireland may also be dealt with by the Scottish Grand Committee, the Welsh Grand Committee, and the Northern Ireland Committee respectively, which consist principally of MPs from those parts of the United Kingdom. The second reading of some bills – five in 1990–91 – is taken in a Second Reading Committee, rather than the floor of the House, and standing committees also examine domestic and European delegated legislation. All these committees provide additional opportunities for scrutiny, but it is investigatory select committees which are the House of Commons's most systematic means of parliamentary scrutiny. However, before turning to these in more detail, a brief word should be said about the House of Lords.

The House of Lords and Parliamentary Scrutiny

The House of Lords contributes significantly to Parliament's ability to scrutinise the executive. The membership of the Lords covers a remarkable range of expertise and legislation is often discussed more thoroughly in the Upper House than in the Commons, especially where a bill has been subject to a tight timetable in the lower chamber. It is widely acknowledged that the House of Lords deals more effectively with delegated legislation emanating from Brussels, principally through its Select Committee on the European Communities. Operating through six sub-committees, the European Communities Committee issues between twenty and thirty reports a year. It differs from its Commons counterpart in two important respects: first, whereas the Commons committee concentrates on drawing attention to proposals from Brussels of legal and political importance with a view to their being debated on the floor of the House, the Lords committee produces substantive, investigatory reports; second, the Commons committee does not normally take evidence, but the Lords committee takes a wide range of oral and written evidence. Most of the committee's reports, however, are not debated, but, as Donald Shell (1993, p. 280) points out, 'work by osmosis, transferring information and ideas around the body politic'. Strictly speaking, of course, the scrutiny involved here (and in the Commons) is of the European Commission in Brussels, rather than the government in Whitehall, although the latter bears responsibility for the British response to EU policy initiatives and for those responses to the UK Parliament. Shell (1993, p. 280) concludes that the European Communities Committee provides 'a serious and well-defined response to the practicalities of Community policy-making'.

The House of Lords also plays a major part in dealing with domestic delegated legislation through the Joint Committee on Statutory Instruments and extended its role significantly in 1993 by establishing a Delegated Powers Scrutiny Committee to 'give closer and more systematic scrutiny to the delegated powers sought in bills' (House of Lords, 1991–92, para. 33). This will add a further dimension to the parliamentary scrutiny of delegated legislation, which the Commons in particular has been unable or unwilling to address effectively.

Although the Upper House has considerably fewer select committees than the Commons, those it has are regarded as effective instruments of scrutiny and, moreover, they do not normally duplicate the inquiries conducted by Commons committees. Apart from the Select Committee on the European Communities and the Joint Committee on Statutory Instruments, the House of Lords has only one other permanent select committee – that on Science and Technology, but it also makes use of *ad hoc* select committees, recent examples being those on Overseas Trade and Unemployment. In essence the Lords has developed its own distinctive committees and this applies to other forms of scrutiny. Questions for oral answer, for instance, are often more penetrating and less partisan in the Lords and may, unlike in the Commons, lead to short debates.

The House of Lords should therefore been seen as supplementing the scrutiny provided by the Commons and not as an alternative to the latter (Shell, 1992; Shell and Beamish, 1993). That parliamentary scrutiny would be seriously damaged by the abolition of the House of Lords, leaving Parliament as a single-chamber legislature, cannot be doubted. Abolition, however, seems unlikely, but the replacement of the Lords by an alternative second chamber, probably elected, raises other questions. Anachronistic and undemocratic as the Upper House may be, it is incumbent on those who propose its replacement to ensure that parliamentary scrutiny is not weakened as a consequence.

Select Committees and Parliamentary Scrutiny

Public Accounts Committee

Select committees have long been part of the parliamentary scene, but came to particular prominence during the nineteenth century when they were frequently used to investigate particular problems and to produce draft bills. The oldest surviving investigatory select committee, however, is the Public Accounts Committee (PAC), established in 1861 to examine departmental accounts and ensure that the expenditure approved by Parliament has been properly and effectively spent. The PAC has always stood apart from the other select committees, partly because it has the assistance of a full-time official, the Comptroller and Auditor-General (C & AG) and his staff in the National Audit Office (NAO) and partly because its role is one of ensuring financial rectitude and seeking value for money. Put another way, the PAC is regarded as a financial watchdog, not as a critic of the government's policy objectives. The PAC therefore epitomises parliamentary scrutiny, but in practice the line between financial scrutiny and criticising policy is less easily drawn: criticising the implementation of policy, however closely allied to its financial aspects, can frequently lead to or imply criticism of the policy itself. Nevertheless, the PAC has built up a formidable reputation, often being described in the media as 'powerful' or 'highly influential', and it is said that civil servants (including permanent secretaries) do not relish the prospect of appearing before it.

The PAC has undoubtedly produced many penetrating, sometimes scathing, reports on a wide range of government policies. Its criticisms are detailed and widely regarded as authoritative; its recommendations are invariably accepted by the government; and, through the C & AG and, if necessary, subsequent hearings, the committee checks whether its recommendations have been carried out. In the 1980s, for example, the PAC produced highly critical reports on the dispensing of drugs in the NHS, on the enforcement powers of the Inland Revenue and Customs and Excise, on government control of capital expenditure by local authorities, on the production costs of defence equipment, on home improvement grants, and on the cost of storing EC food surpluses. The NAO, of course, plays a vital role in all this: with a staff of some 850 the C & AG is able to make detailed analyses of departmental accounts and direct the PAC to those matters which merit its attention. The number of staff at the NAO has fallen slightly in recent years, but this has been compensated for by the growing use of consultants, whose expertise in particular fields can be usefully brought to bear.

Experimental Committees

The PAC apart, however, the use of select committees declined during the twentieth century until their substantial revival in the 1960s and 1970s, culminating in the establishment in 1979 of the new system of departmental select committees. As early as the 1930s select committees were seen as a major means of adjusting the balance between the executive and the legislature. That balance, it was argued, had shifted markedly in favour of the executive in the latter part of the nineteenth century and early part of the twentieth with the growth of disciplined parties in Parliament. Increasingly the initiative in parliamentary business fell to the government, most legislation that found its way on to the statute book was government legislation, and Parliament became dominated by the confrontation between government and opposition. The opposition saw itself and was seen as an alternative government and therefore had a strong incentive to cooperate with the government it hoped to replace in managing parliamentary business – the so-called 'conspiracy of the front benches'.

The period after 1945 into the 1960s could be said to mark the zenith of two-party domination in Britain: the Conservative and Labour parties were responsible for more than three-quarters of the candidates standing at general elections between 1945 and 1970, regularly secured 90 per cent or more of the votes cast, and 98 per cent of the MPs elected. Moreover, in the same period the government was defeated only eleven times on the floor of the House of Commons, none of which resulted in the downfall of the government or the calling of a general election. The late 1950s and early 1960s, however, were marked by a growing chorus of criticism of national institutions, including Parliament (Hill and Whichelow, 1964; Crick, 1964). This coincided with an influx in the general elections of 1959, 1964 and 1966 of new Members on both sides of the House who were more reform-minded than many of their predecessors. They were not content to be lobby-fodder and expected a more active role. In addition, appalled at the low level of the parliamentary salary (from which they were expected to meet most of their expenses) and the lack of services and facilities at Westminster, they demanded better pay and conditions. In the second edition of his *The Reform of Parliament* Bernard Crick (1968, pp. 66–7) bluntly stated: 'clearly a Member should be able to draw on public funds, or be reimbursed from them, for those essentials he needs to do his job properly: secretary, office, postage, telephone and travel'. Within a short time significant advances had been made on all these fronts: from 1972 a clear distinction was drawn between a Member's salary and the expenses incurred in carrying out parliamentary duties and the cost of secretarial assistance, office accommodation, postage, telephone, subsistence, and travel are now met substantially from the public purse (Rush and Shaw, 1974; Rush, 1983, 1992).

It was in this context that reformers both inside and outside Parliament regarded select committees as offering the most effective way of improving the ability of the House of Commons to scrutinise the government's activities. A survey of MPs conducted in 1967 found that Members elected in 1959 or later were more likely to support such committees than their longer-serving colleagues (Barker and Rush, 1970, pp. 378–84). A limited experiment had been started in the 1950s with the setting up of a Select Committee on Nationalised Industries, which was cited as a successful role-model. In the early 1960s the Estimates Committee, operating through a series of sub-committees, provided further evidence that select committees could usefully investigate policy and administration in a bipartisan manner without undermining the wider partisan conflict in the House of Commons. There followed more experimentation, first with a series of specialised committees, commonly known as the 'Crossman committees' after the then Leader of the House responsible for introducing them. These covered areas such as science and technology, agriculture, education, and Scottish affairs. Then, in 1970, following a major report from the Select Committee on Procedure, the old Estimates Committee and several of the Crossman committees were replaced by a Select Committee on Expenditure using specialised subcommittees to cover a wide range of government departments and policy areas. All these committees demonstrated the viability of investigatory select committees as instruments of parliamentary scrutiny, but they also showed the need for a comprehensive system of committees to cover the full range of government responsibilities. It was such a system of departmentally related committees that a further Procedure Committee report recommended in 1978.

Its recommendations were accepted by the newly elected Conservative government in 1979, which, following the rejection of devolution proposals for Wales and Scotland, added committees on Welsh and Scottish Affairs to the twelve departmental committees advocated by the Procedure Committees. The departmental select committees have therefore been in existence since 1979 and remain a vital part of the process of parliamentary scrutiny. They now number sixteen, since the former Department of Health and Social Security has been split into two departments and, after the general election of 1992, the Prime Minister created a new Department of National Heritage and a separate Office of Science and Technology headed by the Chancellor of the Duchy of Lancaster, but abolished the Department of Energy. In December 1993 the government announced its intention to set up yet another committee – on Northern Ireland.

The growth in parliamentary scrutiny by investigatory select committees can be gauged by examining committee activity in selected parliamentary sessions between 1956–57, when the Nationalised Industries Committee was properly established, and 1990–91, the last complete session of the 1987–92 Parliament.

Although the figures in Table 5.2 on the number of committees in existence are misleading to the extent that greater use was made of subcommittees before 1979, the overall picture remains clear, especially when it is noted that the number of meetings, including those of subcommittees, increased by nearly five times between 1956 and 1986, falling only marginally in 1990–91, and that the number of inquiries rose by a ratio of more than sixteen to one. In terms of meetings the PAC was a fairly constant factor – 31 meetings in 1956–57 and 40 in 1990–91, but the number of inquiries it conducted rose from three to 43. This was a consequence of a change of policy from that of conducting a small number of major inquiries to pursuing a much larger number of short, sharp inquiries, though by no means to the neglect of the former. This was further facilitated by increased staffing at the NAO.

TABLE 5.2   *Select Committee Activity, 1956–92*

Session	No. of Investigatory Committees	No. of Meetings[a]	No. of Inquiries[b]
1956–57	3	120	11
1968–69	9	371	27
1977–78	6	456	51
1985–86	16	555	148
1990–91	17[c]	469	186

Notes: [a] Including subcommittees.
[b] Including inquiries completed in a subsequent session and those not resulting in a report.
[c] Excluding the Scottish Affairs Committee, which was not set up in the 1987–92 Parliament.

Inevitably, the number of backbench MPs involved in investigatory select committee activity increased from about 70 to some 200. Last, and most important of all, this activity constituted an enormous quantitative increase in and extension of the scope of parliamentary scrutiny.

The Departmental Select Committees

Few observers have argued that the departmental select committees are a failure: MPs, such as Enoch Powell and Michael Foot, who opposed them (and the earlier specialised committees) did so mainly on the grounds that they would undermine the role of the chamber of the House of Commons and encourage consensus politics (Granada, 1973, pp. 159–60 and 193). In short, they believe that select committees are a distraction from the basic rule of Parliament as the forum for what Powell called 'the great clash of politics'. However, among supporters of the committees there are those who regard them as only a qualified success. Certainly, the exaggerated hopes of some reformers have not been realised, nor could they have been without a fundamental change in the British political system. The idea that a range of adequately funded and well-staffed select committees could emulate congressional committees in the United States reflects a failure to understand both the congressional and parliamentary systems: the separation of powers and the loosely organised American party system combine to make congressional committees extremely powerful, just as the fusion of powers and the tightly organised British party system combine to prevent select committees from becoming powerful. Indeed, media descriptions of the most effective select committee, the PAC, as 'powerful' are inaccurate in so far as its power is limited, but its influence is considerable because of the authoritative nature of its reports and the wide respect in which it is held. Select committees can do no more than make recommendations and cannot force the government to accept them: all parliamentary committees are creatures of their respective Houses and, as far as the Commons is concerned, the government normally has the last say through its majority.

Assessing the impact of select committees is no easy task: various quantitative measures can be used, but the final judgement must be qualitative. Nonetheless, those statistics available provide a crucial basis for any qualitative judgement.

In terms of meetings and reports it is clear that some committees are considerably more active than others. For example, the Treasury and Civil Service, Foreign Affairs, and Defence Committees have always been among the most active in both respects, whereas Welsh Affairs and Agriculture have been among the less active. On the other hand, some committees have varied in their level of activity over the three Parliaments, notably Education and Environment. However, the relationship between the number of meetings and number of reports is variable. For instance, the Energy Committee held 150 meetings in 1979–83 and produced eleven reports, compared with 123 meetings and 29 reports in 1983–7. What the figures suggest is that, in spite of being subject to common procedures, the committees do not operate in a uniform fashion. Each committee decides its own agenda and a great deal depends upon who chairs the committee. Committee chairmanships are shared between the parties: in 1979–83 the fourteen were shared equally between Conservative and Labour, and in 1983–7 and 1987–92 there were nine Conservative and five Labour chairmen. In the 1992 Parliament there are ten Conservative and six Labour chairmen. Who chairs a committee, however, rather than which party, shapes the level of activity and style of a committee. For example, between 1979 and 1983 the Education Committee was one of the most active committees and also ranged very widely in its inquiries (including areas beyond the scope of government responsibilities, such as the

TABLE 5.3   *Numbers of Meetings and Reports Presented by Departmental Select Committees, 1979–92*

Committee	1979–83 Meetings	Reports[a]	1983–7 Meetings	Reports[a]	1987–92 Meetings	Reports[a]
Agriculture	99	6	78	10	134	17
Defence	159	13	176	18	161	50
Education, Science and Arts	166	19	126	10	129	14
Employment	112	11	102	13	152	16
Energy	150	11	123	29	151	31
Environment	116	9	131	16	136	25
Foreign Affairs	249[b]	21	192[b]	20	203	17
Health	–	–	–	–	45	7
Home Affairs	218[b]	20	125[b]	16	145	31
Scottish Affairs	118	8	72	7	–[c]	–[c]
Social Security	–	–	–	–	44	6
Social Services	154	11	135	18	86	26
Trade and Industry	119	19	141	12	189	17
Transport	137	15	136	14	132	16
Treasury and Civil Service	226[b]	24	178[b]	30	157[b]	33
Welsh Affairs	117	6	74	5	104	17
Totals	2140	193	1789	218	1968	323

Notes: [a] Excluding special reports, mostly government responses to substantive reports.
   [b] Including meetings of subcommittees.
   [c] The Scottish Affairs Committee was not set up in 1987–92.
Sources: Gavin Drewry (ed.) (1985) *The New Select Committees: A Study of the 1979 Reforms*, 2nd edn (Oxford: Clarendon Press) p. 334 and Annex 22.2; and House of Commons Sessional Returns.

future of *The Times* supplements and of the Promenade Concerts, when both were affected by strike action). Informal subcommittees were used, chaired by another member of the committee. All this owed much to Christopher Price (Lab.), the committee's chairman, but under his successor in the 1983–7 Parliament, Sir William van Straubanzee (Cons.), the committee was less active and changed markedly in style. Other active chairmen have been Terence Higgins (Cons. – Treasury and Civil Service, 1983–92), Frank Field (Lab.–Social Services, 1987–90 and Social Security, 1991–), and Nicholas Winterton (Cons. – Health, 1991–92). In a number of cases chairmen have developed close working relationships with senior members of the opposite party and the departmental committees are noted for a high level of bipartisanship, including agreeing on reports, as are select committees generally. The number of divisions per meeting was 0.267 in 1979–83, 0.228 in 1984–85, 0.284 in 1985–86, and 0.149 in 1990–91. These figures are both low in number and remarkably consistent, invariably being concentrated on very few matters on particular draft reports and by no means always on strict party lines.

The most obvious statistical measure of the impact of the departmental committees is the extent to which their recommendations are accepted by the government.

The data shown in Table 5.4 are inevitably far from conclusive, especially given the impreciseness of the term 'main recommendations' in section (b) of the table. A favourable interpretation is that the number of recommendations accepted is surprisingly high given the dominance of the government in the British parliamentary system; a less favourable interpretation is that the proportion of recommendations accepted is very low and that 'keep under review' is a euphemism for rejection. Even if this latter view is adopted, however, the figures suggest some influence and therefore impact on the part of the departmental committees.

An alternative approach is to examine specific claims. Griffith and Ryle (1989, pp. 430–3), in their major study, *Parliament Functions, Practice and Procedure* cite twelve 'claimed successes' for the committees. These include Home Affairs and the 'sus law', Transport and the privatisation of HGV testing, Education and the new British Library building, Agriculture and animal welfare, and Energy and North Sea oil taxation. More recently the Procedure Committee pointed to other claimed successes: Foreign Affairs on the future of Hong Kong, Treasury and Civil Service on the publication of the annual reports of government departments, and Trade and Industry on the effect on overseas trade with Asian countries, particularly Malaysia, (something of an irony, given the subsequent disquiet over the Pergau Dam affair!), of the raising of overseas student fees (House of Commons, 1989–90, para. 358). On the other hand, Griffith and Ryle also provide instances of the government firmly rejecting major recommendations: by several committees on the Westland affair, by the Treasury and Civil Service Committee on the future of the Civil Service Department (abolished by the

TABLE 5.4   *Government Responses to Recommendations by
Departmental Select Committees*

(a) *The Education, Science and Arts and the Social Services Committees,
1979–83*

Response a	Education, Science and Arts %	Social Services %
Accepted	26.5	35.1
Keep under review	46.4	45.2
Rejected	27.1	19.7
Totals	100.0	100.0
	n = 181	n = 188

Note: a Excluding recommendations not directly the responsibility of the
government.

(b) *Main Recommendation of Departmental Committees Accepted by the
Government, 1983–6*[a]

	1983–84[b]	1984–85	1985–86	Total
No. of main recommendations accepted	37b	143	144	324

Sources: Michael Rush (1985) 'The Education, Science and Arts Committee' and
'The Social Services Committee', pp. 100, 249; and *HC Deb.*, vol. 101,
15 July 1986, cc. *460–78* (written answers).

Notes: a From March to March in each year.
b The figures for the period March 1983 to March 1984 were affected by
the holding of the general election in June 1983 and the delay in
reconstituting the departmental committees until December 1983.

government), by Employment on the dismissal of miners following
the coal dispute of 1984–85, by Defence on the privatisation of naval
dockyards, and by Foreign Affairs on Britain's withdrawal from
UNESCO. But Griffith and Ryle place the matter firmly in perspective: 'Select committees have not made a general impact on government policies' (Griffith and Ryle, 1989, p. 430).

These claims and counter-claims raise a further question,
however: should select committees be judged simply on their
success or failure to influence government policy? And underlying
that question is a more fundamental one: should select
committees be seeking to influence government policy? Given the
recommendatory role clearly ascribed to select committees, there

is no reason why they should not seek to influence government policy if their inquiries and deliberations suggest that it is appropriate. But influencing policy is not their sole objective, only a by-product of their scrutinising role. In assessing the impact of the departmental select committees over the 1979–83 and 1983–7 Parliaments, Gavin Drewry (1989, p. 426) concluded: 'select committees are, and can realistically only aspire to be, in the business of scrutiny, not of government'.

Judging the effectiveness of the departmental committees as instruments of parliamentary scrutiny should not be limited to assessing their influence on government policies – far more has been achieved in this sphere by the growth of backbench assertiveness since the early 1970s (Norton, 1975, 1978, 1980, 1985). Committees need to be judged by additional criteria, many of which do not lend themselves to quantification or only partly so.

First, and perhaps most important, now that the Lord Chancellor's Department and the Law Officers' Departments have been brought within the remit of the Home Affairs Committee, all government departments now come under scrutiny by the departmental committees. Second, the sheer volume of information published by the committees brings government policy and administration more fully into the public domain than ever before. Third, ministers and senior civil servants are subject to public questioning more frequently than ever before. Fourth, the longer-term impact on policy and administration is likely to be significant, especially as committees increasingly review earlier inquiries and return to particular policy areas. Fifth, more MPs are involved in select committee activity, enabling the House of Commons to develop and increase its pool of specialised knowledge and scrutinising skills. Sixth, the departmental committees are much better staffed than their predecessors: in 1990–91 the number of administrative staff was 67 and the number of specialist advisers 95. Nonetheless, problems remain, but these are best considered in the wider context of parliamentary scrutiny.

Parliamentary Scrutiny: An Overview

Ministerial responsibility is the foundation of parliamentary scrutiny, but it can also be used to blunt that scrutiny. In giving evidence to select committees, for example, civil servants use ministerial responsibility to justify a refusal to divulge what advice they have given ministers and ministers refuse to disclose details of intra- and inter-departmental discussions, unless, of course, it suits them. On occasion, in response to parliamentary questions or requests from committees, ministers refuse to disclose information on the grounds that it is not in the public interest to do so, while retaining the right to define the public interest. The role of the whips in determining the membership and, indeed, chairmanships of select committees was highlighted in the bitter wrangle over the exclusion of Nicholas Winterton (Cons.) from the Health Committee after the 1992 election, although there is little evidence that the whips play a significant part in the subsequent operation of committees.

It is undeniable that parliamentary scrutiny has increased quantitatively from the 1960s onwards, most notably in the number of parliamentary questions asked and in the range and level of select committee activity. But is it effective? Ministers and civil servants are forced to explain and attempt to justify their proposals and actions far more than their predecessors ever were. This can only help to increase the effectiveness of parliamentary scrutiny. Moreover, some of that public exposure – potentially all of it – now reaches a wider audience than ever through the broadcasting of parliamentary proceedings, especially on television. Events like the Falklands War and policies such as the future of Westland Helicopters came under much greater scrutiny than would have been the case in the 1950s; there was, for instance, no parliamentary inquiry into any aspect of the Suez Affair in 1956. More does not necessarily mean better, but the more Parliament is able to subject government policy and administration to public examination the more effective parliamentary scrutiny is likely to be.

Effectiveness, however, also needs to be measured qualitatively and that judgement is considerably more difficult to make. The predominance of party normally ensures not only the government's survival, but the survival of its policies. In circumstances other than normal retirement, the fate of leaders lies with their party rather than Parliament, as Edward Heath and Margaret Thatcher know to their cost. This is sometimes true of ministers as well, as could be argued in the cases of David Mellor in 1992 and

Norman Lamont and Michael Mates in 1993. A small government majority (or the lack of a majority as in February–October 1974 and 1976–9) can be a crucial factor, considerably enhancing the influence of government backbenchers in particular, but also increasing the potential for greater influence by Parliament. But much depends on perception: the Conservative government's majority of twenty-one after the 1992 election has increasingly been seen as fragile, especially after the subsequent loss of by-elections, but a similar majority after the 1951 election was seen as a secure base. A small majority renders the government vulnerable to pressure from its own backbenchers and therefore likely to make concessions on policy, but it also places those same backbenchers under pressure to support their government.

The party, however, is not Parliament but at national level operates largely through Parliament as one of a number of factors influencing policy and with it the scrutiny process. Ministers and civil servants are fully aware that policy is subject to parliamentary scrutiny and take it into account in its formulation; they are aware that they must explain and defend policy and administration to Parliament; and they are aware that they may later be called to account by Parliament. In the absence of parliamentary scrutiny the policy process would be less open and the government less accountable than would otherwise be the case. The fact that policy is largely formulated behind closed doors and that political accountability is far from perfect should not be used to suggest that parliamentary scrutiny is of no significance.

Parliamentary scrutiny, however, must itself be the subject of continuing scrutiny and the Procedure Committee must be prepared to take as dispassionate a view as possible of the efficacy of parliamentary procedures. The various instruments of parliamentary scrutiny need to be seen not as alternatives but as a complementary package, seeking to fulfil different types of scrutiny. Question Time and certain debates, for instance, should be seen as a form of ideological accountability, part of what Crick called 'the continuing election campaign'; questions for written answer and much of what select committees do should be seen as the extraction of information and an efficiency audit; and legislative procedure as a combination of justifying and explaining proposals and subjecting them to detailed examination. None of these is entirely effective and there remain other important gaps in the scrutiny process. The House of Commons is still a long way from providing systematic and effective scrutiny of financial policy and public expenditure; scrutiny of EU legislation has improved, but remains inadequate; domestic delegated legislation is subject to only limited scrutiny. However, it is the reorganisation of the civil service through the creation of executive agencies under the Next Steps programme that presents Parliament with its greatest challenge in parliamentary scrutiny.

Improving parliamentary scrutiny depends in turn on the attitudes of Members of Parliament. A balance needs to be maintained between the ideological confrontation of government and opposition and rendering the government accountable. For backbenchers these are conflicting roles – sustaining the government or the opposition, on the one hand, and acting as public watchdogs, on the other – and it is flying in the face of the realities of British politics not to recognise that the conflict between the parties is a more powerful behavioural factor than the demands of parliamentary scrutiny. Nonetheless, procedural and attitudinal changes in the House of Commons have resulted in a limited but significant modification of the partisan confrontation, as a comparison with the 1950s and earlier amply illustrates, and the sharper ideological conflict which characterised the 1980s should not be allowed to obscure that modification. There is, moreover, a further potential conflict between such ministerial ambitions as backbenchers may have and their watchdog role: upsetting the whips, as that latter role sometimes involves, is hardly likely to smooth the path to ministerial office.

In short, backbenchers are no longer willing to be taken largely for granted by the whips, but they, or enough of them, must also be willing to undertake the more mundane tasks of parliamentary scrutiny if the House of Commons is to maintain and improve one of its most important roles.

References

Barker, A. and Rush, M. (1970) *The Member of Parliament and His Information* (London: Allen & Unwin).
Crick, B. (1964; 2nd edn 1968) *The Reform of Parliament* (London: Weidenfeld & Nicolson).

Drewry, G. (ed.) (1985) *The New Select Committees: A Study of the 1979 Reforms* (Oxford: Clarendon Press) repr. 1989 with a supplementary chapter on the 1983–7 Parliament.

Franklin, M. and Norton, P. (eds) (1993). *Parliamentary Questions* (Oxford: Clarendon Press).

Granada Television (1973) *The State of the Nation: Parliament* (London).

John A. G. Griffith and Michael Ryle (1989) *Parliament: Functions, Practice and Procedure* (London, Sweet and Maxwell).

Hill, A. and Whichelow, A. (1964) *What's Wrong With Parliament?* (London: Pelican).

House of Commons (1989–90) *Second Report of the Select Committee on Procedure: The Working of the Select Committee System*, HC 19-I.

House of Lords (1991–92) *Select Committee on the Committee Work of the House: Report*, HL 35-I and 35-II.

Norton, P. (1975) *Dissension in the House of Commons, 1945–74* (London: Macmillan).

Norton, P. (1978) *Conservative Dissidents: Dissension within the Parliamentary Conservative Party, 1970–74* (London: Temple Smith).

Norton, P. (1980) *Dissension in the House of Commons, 1974–79* (Oxford: Clarendon Press).

Norton, P. (1985) 'The House of Commons: Behavioral Changes', in Norton, P. (ed.), *Parliament in the 1980s* (Oxford: Basil Blackwell) pp. 22–47.

Rush, M. (ed.) (1983) *The House of Commons: Services and Facilities, 1972–1982* (London: Policy Studies Institute).

Rush, M. (1990) 'Select Committees', in Rush, M. (ed.), *Parliament and Pressure Politics* (Oxford: Clarendon Press) pp. 137–51.

Rush, M. (1992) 'The Secretarial, Research and Office Accommodation and Expenses of Legislators in 13 Countries: A Comparative Survey, 1991', Top Salaries Review Body, *Report No. 32: Parliamentary Allowances*, Cmnd 1943, pp. 41–50.

Rush, M. and Shaw M. (eds.) (1974) *The House of Commons: Services and Facilities* (London: Allen & Unwin).

Shell, D. (1992) *The House of Lords*, 2nd edn (London: Harvester Wheatsheaf).

Shell, D. (1993) 'The European Communities Committee', in Shell, D. and Beamish, D. (eds), *The House of Lords at Work*, pp. 247–81.

Shell, D. and Beamish, D. (eds) (1993) *The House of Lords at Work: A Study of the 1988–89 Session* (Oxford: Clarendon Press).

6

The Political Parties

STEPHEN INGLE

Government in the UK is party government. We can only approach a proper understanding of governing in the 1990s if we take time to examine the functioning of the main political parties. In this chapter, we shall examine some of the manifest, or alleged, failings of the party system, before going on to consider intraparty developments in more details.

The Party System: Some Deficiencies

It can be argued that the UK party system has failed to fulfil a number of functions crucial to the proper running of government in an adversarial polity.

The system has failed to:

- Offer choice on key policy issues.
- Provide for an alternation of parties in government.
- Provide an opposition party competent to deliver effective scrutiny or hold government properly to account.
- Produce governments truly representative of the nation at large.

Although it is by no means necessary to accept every item of this litany of shortcomings to be convinced that the modern British party system is failing to deliver in key respects, it is necessary to explore these points in a little more detail in order to assess their validity.

131

Such an exercise will put us in a better position to make judgements on the role of parties in government today, help us more fully to appreciate that few of the certainties that buttressed arguments in the older or more traditional textbooks and which became accepted wisdom concerning the role in government of political parties can any longer be taken for granted. British party politics may truly be said to be in uncharted waters. Let us look in a little more detail at the ways the parties can be said to have failed the system of government.

On perhaps the most significant issue facing the voters in the 1992 election, each of the three major parties (and also the Nationalists) were in favour of fuller participation in the European Community: there was no clearly expressed alternative offered to the electorate. Yet the textbooks tell us that one of the principal functions of political parties in government is to simplify issues so that voters can be offered a genuine choice on major issues. A second advantage that adversarial politics is supposed to provide for government is the fairly regular alternation in power of the two parties. In 1992 Labour suffered a fourth successive electoral defeat, so if it finally forms a government in 1997 (say), it will have been out of office for eighteen years and virtually a whole generation of leading figures will have spent their most effective years in opposition. A Labour front bench will be as ignorant of the realities of holding power as the leaders of minority parties are rightly accused of being now. When the Australian Labor Party under Gough Whitlam finally came to power after 23 years in opposition, its programme provoked an unprecedented constitutional crisis. Thirdly, the adversarial system is supposed to provide Britain with an opposition which not only keeps the government in check by its vigilance but is able to offer a spirited philosophically-based alternative set of policies persuasive enough, should it be put to the test, to convince the electorate to support it. Yet for all of the 1980s the only effective opposition to Conservative governments came from the Conservative back benches and the House of Lords. When these two agents of opposition palpably failed, as in the debate on the poll tax, a profoundly damaging piece of legislation found its way on to the statute book. When eventually, in November 1990, there was a change in the premiership, and (apparently at least) a change of ideology, these changes came from *within* the Conservative Party and Labour was no more than a by-stander. Fourth, an axiomatic advantage brought to government by an adversarial party system is that a party is elected to fulfil its manifesto pledges – in theory this is why people are supposed to have voted for it (though evidence suggests that people vote *against* rather than *for* political parties). In the general election of 1992, however, Major's principal policy commitment was to the exchange rate mechanism (ERM) of the European monetary system, to a fixed exchange rate, a relatively high interest rate and a tight monetary policy. Yet within five months each of these commitments had been replaced by its polar opposite and not a single member of the Cabinet (much less the whole government) offered to resign. Finally, there is the problem of regional representation. In 1992, three-quarters of Scottish voters supported parties promising constitutional change but they continued to be governed by a party which won only eleven Scottish seats out of 72. Scottish voters heavily rejected (and resented) the policies of successive Conservative governments but their service industries were privatised, hospitals encouraged to opt out and, worst of all, Scotland was used as a 'guinea-pig' for the implementation of the poll tax. This is a crucial and disturbing question for British parliamentary democracy but its most obvious answer is even more crucial and disturbing: the Scots were no different from the majority of British voters, who did not want these policies either (if the opinion polls are to be believed). In other words the British party system has proved unable to prevent major changes in the way the country was being governed although these changes were promoted by an administration representative of only a minority of voters.

Every system has its faults but we are surely entitled to judge whether a party system falling so far short of its traditional responsibilities to government is capable of regeneration or whether we should anticipate (or even hope for) some transformation in the role of parties in government. If we are to consider this question seriously then it will be necessary to examine the state of the parties individually so as to judge how they might be expected to respond to the new situation. We shall begin with the Conservatives, the party of government since 1979.

The Conservative Party

It is worth observing that, properly speaking, the Conservative Party is that body of MPs and peers who take the Conservative whips, and the function of constituency associations and regional and national structures is to support and sustain that body. As the political system became more democratic during the nineteenth century so the relationship between the party at large and the parliamentary party changed, though Lord Randolph Churchill failed in the 1880s to democratise the relationship as he had hoped and much later Balfour was still able to declare that on matters of policy he would as soon take the advice of his valet as that of his party's annual conference.

One of the reasons that Conservative leaders were permitted such freedom of manoeuvre had been the relative certainty on the part of the faithful that they would pursue the proper objectives of Conservatism which may be briefly summarised as sound administration and tight control of the economy. Not for Conservatives the grandiose aims of their opponents – to make society more equal or to empower ordinary people. Conservatives believed in what the *Guardian*'s Edward Pearce referred to as 'chug-chug' government, or so it had always been thought. It is true that as leader Edward Heath had attempted to give the party a radical agenda with his Selsdon programme but he subsequently felt obliged to withdraw behind the ideological safety barrier of the postwar consensus. Margaret Thatcher's aim, however, was nothing less than to 'roll back the state' so that government could concentrate on its historic functions, such as defence, security and justice, thus allowing the unrestricted flowering of the nation's entrepreneurial talents. And this leader was not fur turning.

Paradoxically, in order to recreate (or approximate) the minimal state it was to prove necessary for central government to take on substantially increased powers (for example in areas of health, education and local government) and to implement a legislative programme as far-reaching as that of the most radical of left-wing governments. It quickly became clear that Thatcher was driving a wedge between the Tory and Whig wings of the party (between the 'wets' and the 'drys'). Thatcherism could be said to have brought ideology into Conservative party politics (although this is not accepted unquestioningly by some elements of the ideological right!) and in doing so helped to destroy the basis of unity, trust and loyalty which had been one of the party's most reliable (and envied) weapons.

In destroying the myth that the Conservative Party was not ideological Thatcher also put at risk the largely unconstrained power of its leader (Ingle, 1989, ch. 2). Conservative leaders, it was believed, could count upon the loyalty of all levels of the party until they had become clearly recognised as electoral liabilities. The events of the Thatcher years have largely changed the balance of the relationship within the parliamentary party. Prominent among these were the series of senior ministerial resignations and the resulting public recriminations, culminating in the fatal (for Thatcher's leadership) resignation of Sir Geoffrey Howe (Young, 1989, p. 558). Most prominent was the unseating of the leader herself: not so much a body blow to the myth of the infallible leader and the loyal party as a nuclear explosion whose fall-out engulfed her successor. Thatcher was not the first Conservative leader to be removed; indeed history suggests this to be quite a normal process, but the manner of her fall, and indeed the height from which she fell, were unusual to say the least.

The 'European' Divide

At the heart of Thatcher's disputes with her ministers, and symptomatic of the relationship between them, lay Britain's relationship with the EC, and there is no doubt that Conservative party politics continue to be revolutionised by the issue of Europe. Prime Minister Major had declared that one of his reasons for not holding an election until spring 1992 was so that he could personally negotiate the detail of the Maastricht Treaty in November 1991, which was to plot the course towards greater European unity. The implementation of the provisions of that treaty would clearly be one of the priorities of his new government after the 1992 election. In an article written in the summer of 1992 Hugo Young declared that Major was in a stronger position than any other Western leader: 'he faces no rival in his party, and no early contest outside it' (Young, 1992). Indeed the notion that opposition to Maastricht, and hence to the government, was proof of disloyalty seemed incontrovertible to that staunch Conservative paper the *Daily Telegraph*, which had taken ex-leader Thatcher to task for speaking against Maastricht in November 1991. It was nonsense, the paper argued, to present Thatcher's anti-Maastricht stance as 'standing up to Europe'; such a stance would be seen by people and markets as a sign of failure with dire consequences for economic recovery (*Daily Telegraph*, 1991).

However, the fact that the treaty was narrowly opposed in a Danish referendum and narrowly endorsed by a French referendum gave encouragement to the powerful lobby within the party opposed to closer European unity. What brought the issue into absolute prominence was the collapse in September 1992 of the government's entire economic strategy: Britain was forced out of the ERM and obliged to devalue the currency. Under such circumstances the long-term objectives of the treaty, both political and economic (though more immediately the later), seemed to many to have lost practical relevance; to go ahead with its ratification was, for them, mindless obduracy. For the resolute pro-European wing of the party it seemed to be a crucial statement of faith. Open battle was joined at the annual conference in October with powerful anti-Maastricht (and by implication anti-government) interventions from Lord Tebbit and Lady Thatcher. Indeed, when Major addressed the conference, a reference to Maastricht had filled the hall with hisses. Never had such antipathy and division shown itself at a Conservative conference. The conference of 1993 was, by contrast, an anodyne affair largely because conference managers had taken the greatest care to minimise opportunities for opposition to the leadership on contentious issues such as the imposition of VAT on domestic heating. European unity did not appear as an issue at all. Despite the cessation of open hostilities few commentators believed that peace had broken out or that Conservative conferences had returned to their traditional status of the political equivalence of Balfour's valet.

Returning to the Maastricht issue, much had happened by the time the House of Commons was to debate the treaty again. The fissures which had manifested themselves at the conference had hardened and widened. Party leader Major would discover that the party in parliament was, like the annual conference, very much its own creature. The details of the debates need not detain us; it is sufficient to state that, even in what amounted to motions of confidence, the results of the debates frequently rested on a knife's edge. That the party leader was rattled is beyond conjecture. He declared before one debate that if defeated he would call an election. The constitutional propriety and political wisdom of such a statement was highly questionable. The loyalist *Daily Telegraph* thought it unseemly that Conservative backbenchers should be herded grudgingly and irritably into the lobbies, 'merely because the alternative is the fall of the Prime Minister' (*Daily Telegraph*, 1992). The Conservative party leader's hold on the party in parliament had grown so tenuous that it was likened to that of Neville Chamberlain during the early days of the Second World War (*Guardian*, 1992a). The government won its crucial votes with the support of the unequivocally pro-Europe Liberal Democrats and the Ulster Unionists (who would certainly have hoped for some *quid pro quo*), but these were intensely close-run things.

Other Divisive Issues

Nevertheless Europe is not the only issue on which the Conservative back benches have refused to be cowed by the government. When President of the Board of Trade Michael Heseltine declared the government's intention to close 31 pits in October 1992 the furore which ensued from sections of his own back benches was so great that the government was obliged to retreat; the dissidents made their feelings too well-known for the government to risk the division lobbies. It is true that within a year the majority of the threatened pits had indeed closed, though not as a direct consequence of government action. The issues of the extension of VAT to domestic heating and the privatisation of British Rail rumbled on through 1993, with the government fighting a rearguard action in defence of generally unpopular policies. What can be said in conclusion to this section is that not since the Second World War has a Conservative leadership had such little control over the party in Parliament or enjoyed such little sympathy from activists. The disastrous by-election defeats by the Liberal Democrats at Newbury, Christchurch and Eastleigh, together with the wide losses, again principally to the Liberal Democrats, in the 1993 local government elections, indicated that disillusion with the party and its leaders stretched down to the voters.

Organisational Problems

Present discontent stretches even further: the vaunted efficiency of the party organisation and its supposed financial stability can no longer be assumed. Chiefly because of the demands she made upon party chairmen and because the inefficiencies of Central Office made it more difficult for them to respond to these, Thatcher's leadership did much to undermine senior headquarters staff. Butler and Kavanagh have outlined the problems with various chairmen, culminating in the acrimonious confrontations over strategy between Mrs Thatcher and her chairman Norman Tebbit during the 1987 campaign (Butler and Kavanagh, 1992, ch. 2). Moreover most commentators concluded that the Labour campaigns of 1987 and 1992 (and the Liberal Democrat campaign of 1992) were better organised than those of their Conservative counterparts.

After 1987, because of Cabinet opposition, Mrs Thatcher found it impossible to persuade her preferred candidate, Lord Young, to take on the chairman's job. Peter Brooke took on the post and managed to reorganise Central Office into three sections dealing with research, communications (to which he appointed a director) and organisation. The first trial of the revamped organisation was the European elections of 1989 and it proved to be disastrous. Peter Brooke made way for the more senior Kenneth Baker who retained the office until Major appointed his own man, Chris Patten, who presided over the 1992 election victory, a triumph which surprised many at Central Office as much as it did most correspondents. During the Thatcher years Central Office had, in fact, become somewhat less 'central' in party affairs. The research department had been obliged to give ground, in terms of policy development, to the Prime Minister's Policy Unit and to outside bodies such as the Institute of Economic Affairs and the Adam Smith Institute. Party communications moreover had come under the influence of the former professional public relations consultants, such as Saatchi & Saatchi's Tim Bell. This signalled a professionalisation of Conservative campaigning with experts like Bell and, earlier, Harvey Thomas, both of whom enjoyed the confidence of the party leader, shaping campaigning strategies to some extent. Neither of these is now directly involved but the fact that both the last two Smith Square communications directors,

Brendan Bruce and Shaun Woodward, left their post after election campaigns suggests that the reforms at Central Office have not restored the mystique of efficiency which once surrounded that institution.

Financial Problems

One of the major problems affecting the party bureaucracy is shortage of funds. It has been estimated that by the end of the 1993 the party will be £19 million in debt. In October 1991 the reformist constituency organisation, 'Charter', mounted a scathing attack on Central Office's 'stunningly incompetent' financial stewardship. The £1.3 million annual income from constituencies is a shrinking proportion of overall budgetary requirements (falling from 14 per cent to 7 per cent between 1987 and 1991) (*Guardian*, 1992b). 'Charter' urged proper democratic control of the voluntary donations that had come to provide the lion's share of income. 'We don't know what Central Office had to concede in return for this money, but we can be absolutely sure that the interests of party democracy are not enhanced.' Indeed, Labour accused the government of awarding 'privatisation' contracts to City firms which had contributed to party funds, though such a claim is as impossible to substantiate as it is to refute (*The Sunday Times*, 1991). It remains the case that Conservative Party accounts do not include a balance sheet and by far the greatest share of income comes from undisclosed voluntary donations. It was alleged, for example, that a Greek shipping tycoon with connections with the former military junta had donated £2 million. The party also received a donation of half a million pounds from Polly Peck, a company that later went into liquidation, and whose ex-chairman Adil Nasir, subsequently charged with theft and fraudulent accounting, had fled to Cyprus. Indeed just prior to the 1992 general election the party received £7 million from overseas backers (*Guardian*, 1993). To the party's embarrassment the issue came before a select committee in June 1993. In the face of this growing debt, the chairman planned to cut 60 jobs from the organisational structure, and regional offices were to be closed or merged. Moreover, professional party agents, paid by constituencies, were to be made redundant in growing numbers in the face of falling membership subscriptions. It is also apparent that the

Chairman is keen to end what he sees as unhelpful competition between the three sections at Central Office. All in all, it is clearly the case that the party bureaucracy, far from offering a model of well-heeled efficiency for others to follow, is in a state of disarray and certainly no longer the predictable, obedient creature of the party leader.

Taken as a whole, there seems to be no area in which the traditional strengths of the Conservative party remain undiminished. Whether it is the habit of almost unrestricted power over a long period which is finally destructive, the transformation from strong leadership to a more consensus-building approach, the corrosive issue of the United Kingdom's relationship with Europe (which all but broke a Labour government in the 1970s), the obvious and continuing recession for which government economic strategies must take some responsibility at least, or whether it is a combination of these factors, the Conservative party today is in confusion. The position of the leader is threatened from both the left and right of the party, and it has part-jettisoned the ideological ballast of Thatcherism without replacing it. It was widely asserted during the last years of Thatcher that the party has headed for the rocks – but at least the captain was on the bridge, steering her course and denying the elements. Nowadays the ship seems to be at the mercy of any unfriendly wind. The new captain appears to have little authority and his officers are in disarray. It could be argued that the party needs a spell in less tempestuous waters of opposition to address these major problems. There can be little doubt that the quality of government has suffered as a consequence of them. However, we should not deny the Conservative Party's proven capacity to strike back, even in the face of great odds, and function as an election-winning machine of real effectiveness.

The Labour Party

Following its defeat in 1987, which was attributed to unpopular policies rather than a badly fought campaign, the party leader Neil Kinnock initiated a series of policy reviews which were intended to have the cumulative effect of transforming Labour's election prospects by modernising its image. The scope of these reviews was wide and their effect in transforming the party into something approaching a modern social democratic party on the Western European model was profound (Smith and Spears, 1992). Yet the party lost again in 1992, in the most propitious circumstances. What more could be done? Labour needed to question some of the most fundamental assumptions about its nature and objectives if it was again to achieve power. Perhaps the greatest and certainly the most pervasive of these assumptions was that Labour was the party of and for the working class.

A 'Working Class' Party?

This relationship was assumed to manifest itself in terms of the membership of the parliamentary party and the party in the country, the link with the trade unions, and in the party's policies – 'socialism'. Whilst Labour would never have claimed to be *only* a party for the working class, its very *raison d'être* was to support and further the interests of that class. Yet precisely because the working class has declined as a proportion of the total population, and will almost certainly continue to do so, working-class support will never be sufficient to win elections for Labour (Curtice and Steed, 1992). Moreover in its failure to win wider support from the more affluent section of the working class (especially in the south of England), Labour demonstrated its inability even to hold on to its natural constituency (Rose and McAllister, 1990).

Labour's claim to be the party of the working class is challengeable in other respects. It is some considerable time since the parliamentary Labour party (PLP) reflected that class (Ingle, 1989, ch. 7). The 1992 Parliament comprises 271 Labour members of whom no fewer than 186 have university degrees (including 40 from Oxford and 18 from Cambridge) and 18 have polytechnic qualifications. The occupational background of current Labour MPs is equally revealing: 50 journalists or authors, 48 lecturers, 43 teachers and 46 trade union officials or party workers, 21 barristers or solicitors (*The Sunday Times*, 1992). A number of these may be the sons and daughters of workers, but that is hardly the same thing and it forces the observer to conclude that the PLP is nowadays no more representative of the working class than was the Liberal Party which Labour replaced over 70 years ago.

Similar trends are apparent in the party in the country. By the early 1990s, it was estimated that 49 per cent of activists were salaried, and only 14 per cent were wage-earners–further evidence of the 'embourgeoisement' of the party (Smith and Spears, 1992). Although working-class activists remained numerous, especially those coming from the ranks of the trade unions, many of their views would not be particularly welcome to party modernisers. For example, 51 per cent of those surveyed thought that Labour ought to 'capture the middle ground', but 61 per cent believed that the party should 'stick to its principles'. Moreover, 82 per cent were in favour of renationalisation, 68 per cent favoured unilateral nuclear disarmament and 92 per cent supported increased taxes. A stark contrast of policy preferences between leaders and activists could pose problems for an incoming Labour government.

Militancy

The conflicts during the early and mid-1980s over the activities of radical left groups such as Militant do not make headline news so frequently in the 1990s but the problem has not gone away. Indeed the suspension of MPs Nellist and Field for supporting Militant was only part of a much broader campaign which brought the expulsion of some 200 constituency members. The seriousness with which the party still takes Militant is indicated by the fact that Labour's director of organisation compiled a 132-page dossier on Nellist and Field (*Independent*, 1991). The internal politics of Militant had become explosive by this time. The majority wanted to fight Labour openly for the socialist vote but a significant minority continued to believe that 'entryism' offered the best option. At the Liverpool Walton by-election in 1991 the Militant candidate secure 2613 votes and some hailed this as a victory for socialism. Of the 18-strong breakaway Liverpool Labour group on Liverpool Council, half were Militant supporters. In Glasgow too, candidates led by Tommy Sheridan, standing under the banner of Scottish Militant Labour, won seats from Labour on the city council and the Strathclyde Regional Council. Nor is Militant the only hard left group acting within and against Labour. The Socialist Organiser group is said to have tried to rig constituency ballots for the NEC in Sheffield Brightside and Bassetlaw, becoming active in the former when the local MP David Blunkett had failed to support Nellist over his suspension.

That the Labour leadership is apprehensive about the militancy (in the general sense) of some of its activists is indicated by the part that the NEC plays in drawing up candidate shortlists for difficult constituencies.

Entryism is by no means as wide a problem as it was ten years ago but the defection of radical elements from the Labour Party in its heartland (e.g. Liverpool and Glasgow) may come to present a problem for the party; it certainly indicates grass-roots disillusion. What is clearly of greater concern is that Labour's working-class base appears to be shrinking and fracturing and all recent attempts to reverse this trend have failed. As leader, Neil Kinnock undertook a well-publicised membership drive aimed at procuring a mass membership of 2 000 000. Currently the membership stands at 279 000, though fewer than 200 000 have paid their fees, and this probably provides a more realistic idea of the true membership (*Guardian*, 1992c). Even the offer of a reduced subscription failed to prove sufficiently attractive: recruitment of new members fell each year from a high of 32 000 in 1989 to 22 000 in 1991.

The Trade Union Connection

Labour's relationship with the unions has usually been held to provide the party's main justification for considering itself the party of the working class, but even this relationship has changed and is likely to change more radically in the near future (Minkin, 1991). As far as Labour is concerned there is strong evidence of public anxiety about the extent to which the unions act as Labour's paymasters. In a detailed analysis of public opinion before the 1992 election, 61 per cent of respondents believed that unions would be given more power under a Labour government and when asked what they considered to be the Conservatives' greatest achievement in power, most thought it had been cutting trade union power (twice as many, in fact, as mentioned curbing inflation). No fewer than 32 per cent responded that Labour's union connection would make them less likely to vote for the party (*Sunday Telegraph*, 1991).

All this public anxiety has been reflected within the party. Union influence, through the block vote at annual conference, through constituency candidate selection and reselection, through the leadership elections and on policy through conference and the NEC, was seen by many to be too great. The unions themselves were, by and large, not averse to the idea of change. A *New Statesman* survey in 1992 indicated that six out of ten union leaders were willing to relinquish the block vote and eight out of ten would support 'one member one vote' for parliamentary candidates' selection and reselection and almost as many for the party leader. It was against the background that the new leader John Smith set up a seventeen-strong review group, including five members of the shadow Cabinet and with Lewis Minkin as its academic adviser, to consider the nature of the relationship. The group reported to Smith's leadership committee though no document was subsequently published. Minkin argued that the unions provided some important advantages, such as 'financial resources, a core electoral support, avenues of communication to the electorate and a broad social composition which enhances [the party's] appeal' (*Guardian*, 1992d). Minkin was strongly of the opinion that a 'contested divorce' would cause enormous damage to both parties but this clearly did not make agreement any easier. The thrust of the review group's proposal was that unions should continue to have a major role in party affairs but on the basis of a ballot of members who identify themselves as 'registered Labour supporters'. Smith made it known that he wished to see 'one member one vote' in candidate selection and no union say in leadership elections. The group was asked to reconsider some of its proposals.

At the 1993 annual conference the Labour leader promoted a compromise package of reforms of the relationship between the unions and the party. The aim was to abolish the union block vote in constituency selection and reselection ballots and to require trade unionists to pay a £3 levy to join the party before being able to vote. This reform became known as OMOV (one member one vote). Ballots for constituency and trade union representation on the National Executive Committee and for constituency delegates to conference were to be held on a similar basis. Moreover the electoral college for leadership and deputy leadership elections was henceforth to comprise equal representation of trade unions, parliamentary party (including MEPs) and constituencies. Finally, the trade union block vote at conferences was to comprise not 90 per cent, but 70 per cent of the total, with every prospect of this shrinking to 50 per cent. Of these reforms OMOV was probably the least important but it was signalled by Smith as decisive. Had the vote on OMOV been lost his leadership would have been damaged, perhaps beyond repair. Yet, having tied his flag to the mast, Smith in fact did very little to ensure victory. Although in the end he carried the day – by virtue of one union deciding to abstain and by virtue of an impassioned concluding speech by John Prescott – this was an extraordinary risk. Right to the end the outcome had been unpredictable. As a consequence of the vote Smith strengthened his hand and the party superficially at least, democratised its links with the trade union movement. As the 1990s progress, much will hinge on the leader's ability to project this arrangement as a victory for democracy; he must prove himself 'as a maker of a message that the country can understand' (Young, 1993).

Perhaps it had been entirely coincidental that in December of 1992, whilst the review group was deliberating, the Transport and General Worker's Union, one of Labour's largest benefactors, decided to cut its subscription to the party by more than £500 000. This followed a decision by the TGWU to reduce its notional party membership from 1 075 000 to 850 000 in 1993 and to 750 000 in 1994. This decision was described by General Secretary Bill Morris not as a *quid pro quo* but simply a general political refocusing by his union. After all, Labour had lost four successive general elections. Morris felt it was likely that the union would begin to sponsor MEPs and so would support fewer than the current 38 MPs. He felt confident that other unions would follow. Certainly other unions had begun to take a firmer interest in Europe. In January 1992 one major union (the General, Municipal and Boilermakers) opened an office in Brussels; others are sure to follow this trend. The despondent party treasurer feared that Labour was a dying party (*Independent*, 1992a). If this seems somewhat melodramatic it is worth observing that the NEC set up a working party in 1992, whose task was to reduce annual running costs from £11 million to £8.3 million by cutting staff at party headquarters in Walworth Road from 120 to 90 and reducing the number of regional offices from nine to six or seven. It has been argued that as the process of trade union amalgamations continues (AEU and EETPU followed by NALGO, NUPE and COHSE in 1992), perhaps by the end of the decade there will be five or six major unions not all of which are likely to retain their links with the party (Holliday, 1993).

Policy-Making

Reform of the trade union link was only part of Labour's programme of modernisation. In 1990 Kinnock initiated reforms which fundamentally changed the way the party makes policy. In that year conference agreed to the establishment of a 170-strong national policy council, elected every two years from all sections of the party. From this would come seven commissions of about thirty members covering the whole gamut of policy. These would report on a two-year rolling programme. Annual conferences would debate the reports, thus the repetitive and damaging policy rows at conference, which have tended to characterise party history, would be minimised.

One of the first and potentially most significant fruits of these new procedures was the establishment of a commission on social justice chaired by the former Director of Fair Trading, Sir Gordon Borrie. In July 1993 Borrie produced the commission's first two discussion papers, with the thought-provoking phrase: 'Social justice is important for the bottom 100 per cent.' Whilst not seeking confrontation with government ministers, nor indeed blaming the government for all Britain's ills, Borrie nevertheless made it clear that the commission wholeheartedly rejected the Thatcherite claim that there is 'no such thing as society'. Wealth and welfare went together, he claimed, and full employment should be seen as central both to economic efficiency and social justice. The commission accepted that inequalities are not necessarily unjust but argued that some certainly were, and that wherever possible these should be eliminated. Equality of opportunity, it was stressed, lay at the very heart of social justice (Borrie, 1993).

A Party of Government Again?

How successful are these reforms likely to be? Will they help to propel the party back into government? In the immediate future prospects for Labour could scarcely be less encouraging. Two pieces of research have explored this area. The first, commissioned by party campaign and communications director David Hill, *What the Electorate Think of Us*, was presented to the leadership committee towards the end of 1992. The research was based upon a series of in-depth interviews with lower-middle-class and skilled working-class voters aged 25–40 and living in the south of England. The report suggested that Labour had no clear identity with the voters. Hill noted an unprecedented disillusionment among voters six months after the 1992 election but discovered that Labour was not benefiting from this because the party was still associated with a poor economic record, trade union dominance and the so-called 'loony left'. The conclusions seemed dispiriting: 'Despite one of the most unpopular governments of modern times, despite the opposition's double-figure lead in the polls, not one of these people would vote Labour if there were an election tomorrow' (Macintyre, 1992).

The second document was prepared by Giles Radice for the Fabian Society. Entitled *Southern Discomfort* it told a similar story. Labour simply did not understand the attitudes of the 'aspirational' working classes, which were bound up with financial well-being. Labour seemed to have the worst of both worlds: it was perceived as unreconstruted – opposed to council house sales for example (not true after 1987) – or where it had reformed, as inconsistent. These studies seemed to support David Hill's own analysis of the 1992 general election defeat: 'the greater the prospect of a Labour victory the more fearful the public were of that prospect' (*Independent*, 1992b).

The first task for Labour, and for its new leader, Tony Blair, surely, is to fix its ideological lodestar. Is it primarily still a party for (if not of) the working class or is it a party with a broader social appeal? Is it still at heart a socialist party or is it in the process of redefining its goal more broadly, as social justice? Can it manage to loosen its ties with the unions without losing their essential goodwill and financial support? Is it still capable of turning itself into a true mass-membership party? Basically is it a democratic socialist or a social democratic party? Finally, is it capable of undergoing change without losing the support of traditionalists who are already appalled at what they see as the undue influence of the party's public relations consultants? These questions bear directly upon the nature of government in Britain for if they are not addressed successfully the country may never again be governed by Labour.

The Liberal Democrats

In contrast to the two major parties the Liberal Democrats have, on the whole, made solid progress over recent years. The 1992 general election result (20 seats won) can hardly be represented as a triumph but when it is remembered that the party had been decisively beaten into fourth place by the Greens in the European elections only three years earlier it was hardly a failure either. Liberal electoral strategy must always confront a paradox: it considers itself to be a progressive, even radical party, yet its support comes principally from disgruntled Conservative voters. Were it to identify itself too clearly with Labour in a general election campaign then its vote might collapse (Marquand, 1992). However, after the general election the party fought two stunningly successful by-election campaigns in 1993 at Newbury and Christchurch (where a Conservative majority of 12 357 was turned into a Liberal Democrat majority of 22 055). Party membership rose to more than 100 000, and the party's local government representation was immeasurably strengthened. In May 1993 the party returned 873 county councillors, an increase of 392. More important even than this, in 27 counties no party had overall control and Liberal Democrats were sure to have a measure of power in the great majority of these. The Liberal Democrats are particularly strong in the south-west of England, where they control Cornwall and Somerset. Throughout much of the south they pose a genuine threat to Conservative hegemony. If they manage to maintain their strong electoral performances the Liberal Democrats will be in a good position to bring about the electoral defeat of the Conservative Party. Perhaps civil servants at Whitehall should begin to look at the many hung local councils to see how they operate!

Nationalists

What finally of the nationalist parties? 'Free in '93' had been the electoral slogan for SNP and if this always seemed overambitious the party nevertheless was riding higher in the opinion polls prior to the general election than for many years. The election result, however, was desperately disappointing. Though securing 21.5 per cent of the Scottish vote the SNP actually lost one of its seats, thus leaving the party with 'three in '93'. Nevertheless, if the call to independence was rejected by over three-quarters of Scots an unreformed Union was rejected by an almost equally high number. Yet the mass demonstrations in Glasgow (and later in Edinburgh) which followed indicated not only a dissatisfaction with undiluted rule from Westminster but also an inability on the part of Labour, Nationalist, Liberal Democrat and other reformers to combine on a common programme.

In Wales Plaid Cymru, although far less vociferous, has been electorally more successful, returning four MPs on 8.8 per cent of the vote in the Principality. Neither of the nationalist parties managed to sustain a high profile after the 1992 general election.

The government's decision not to privatise Scottish water unquestionably diffused a potentially damaging issue which would have been extremely beneficial to the SNP, but the increase of VAT on domestic heating, hitting the Scots particularly hard, may also prove grist to the nationalist mill and bring the politics of devolution (and indeed independence) on to the political agenda once again. Chapter 9 contains a detailed discussion of nationalism's implications for governing the UK.

Conclusion

What does this review of relative party strengths and weaknesses suggest for party government in the United Kingdom during the next decade? Perhaps the way forward is for Labour to redefine its principal aim as social justice. Perhaps its future electability will rest upon accepting that its links with the working class need to be redefined. Perhaps its future in government will require some working arrangement with the Liberal Democrats. Perhaps none of these is true. Those within the party who despair might well reflect that the bitterness of defeat in 1992 was largely a consequence of having expected to win and it will be instructive to consider for a moment some 'might have beens'. If Labour had polled as well among women as it did among men, it would now be in office (*Guardian*, 1992e). If 1200 people in eleven marginal constituencies had voted Labour (or in two cases Liberal Democrat), John Major would have been denied a majority (*Independent*, 1992). If approximately 352 000 people who did not register for poll tax reasons had voted, eight marginals – at a conservative estimate – would have been won by Labour and the Liberal Democrats and not the Conservatives, cutting the overall majority to five. However, surely the point is not that Labour might have won in 1992 or that it might do next time. The point is to make the party or parties of the left as electable as the party of the right on a long-term basis. In modern political history, this has been the case only in 1960s and 1970s and we have to go back to the days before the First World War to discover a time when parties traditionally vied for power on almost equal terms over an extended period of time.

This brings us back to the system of adversarial government, and the problems with which we were concerned at the outset when we argued that the party system has ceased to function effectively. We have tried to indicate, too, that the two major parties have changed greatly. Although space has precluded detailed discussion of the Liberal Democrats we have suggested that they may be said to hold the key to the future. In 1992, in the immediate post-election disappointment on the left many commentators argued that only some realignment could prevent the Conservatives from ruling indefinitely. But experience clearly shows that whenever the Liberals or Liberal Democrats have drawn close to Labour they have suffered electorally as a consequence, for many of their supporters and activists regard Labour as unelectable. If Labour was once again to be considered electable however, it would presumably be at the expense of the Liberal Democrats. So the Liberal Democrats require an electable Labour party on the one hand and on the other, it is the last thing they need. Moreover, there is very little that the Liberal Democrats could offer Labour in any electoral pact: if Liberal Democrat candidates stood down in certain constituencies probably only a third of their votes would go to Labour (*Independent*, 1992d). Some have suggested that some form of proportional representation could bring the parties into an acceptable working relationship but the obvious paradox here is that if the parties of the left need proportional representation to win, they also need to win to introduce proportional representation. Moreover the lukewarm reception given by the Labour party (and its leader) to the Plant Report on electoral reform indicates that a Labour commitment to electoral reform may not be forthcoming. Perhaps Labour's interests might best be served by concentrating on rediscovering its *raisons d'être* and how best to project them and also by considering working towards local agreements in key marginal constituencies in the south and south-west of England as a means of supporting the local Liberal Democrats. Agreements on power-sharing already operate in up to ten councils, although this is without official sanction and indeed is in strict contravention of Labour's guidelines. If there is to be an anti-Conservative alliance, electoral pact, or whatever, the pressure might well come from below. Under such circumstances a Conservative defeat followed by a Labour–Liberal Democratic government pledged to introduce proportional representation would not be inconceivable. Such a government might also introduce measures of constitutional reform such as devolution, perhaps a regional tier of government in England, a reformed House of Lords, a Bill of Rights and so on (Williams, 1992).

Whether these governmental and constitutional changes are desirable or not, the odds on their being implemented are long (but not impossibly so). The pressures for change are considerable, pressures from the failure of the two-party system such as lack of accountability and the paucity of alternatives, pressures from a disenchanted Scotland and from a developing Europe. It is well to remember, too, that the world's only other first-past-the-post, two party parliamentary system, New Zealand, voted in a referendum in 1993 to change its first-past-the-post voting system for a version of the Additional Member System, favoured by many on the Plant commission, precisely because the present system of government in that country was widely considered to be unrepresentative and unresponsive.

In the United Kingdom, four successive victories have brought the Conservative party to a state of unaccustomed torpor, uncertainty and disunity; four successive defeats have obliged Labour to reconsider some of its most fundamental assumption. It is not easy to see how the governmental system could survive a fifth Conservative victory.

References

Borrie, G. (1993) *Social Justice in the Changing World* (London: IPPR).
Butler, D. and Kavanagh, D. (1992) *The British General Election of 1992* (London: Macmillan).

Curtice, J. and Steed, M. (1992) 'The Results Analysed', in Butler, D. and Kavanagh, D. (eds), *The British General Election of 1992* (London: Macmillan).

Daily Telegraph (1991) 25 November.

Daily Telegraph (1992) 26 October.

Guardian (1992a) 26 October.

Guardian (1992b) 13 December.

Guardian (1992c) 17 December.

Guardian (1992d) 9 November.

Guardian (1992e) 12 July.

Guardian (1993) 24 April.

Holliday, I. (1993) 'Organised Interests After Thatcher', in Dunleavy, P. *et al.* (eds), *Developments in British Politics 4* (London: Macmillan).

Independent (1991) 21 September.

Independent (1992a) 4 December.

Independent (1992b) 13 June.

Independent (1992c) 24 April.

Independent (1992d) 17 September.

Ingle, S. (1989) *British Party Politics* (Oxford: Basil Blackwell).

Macintyre, D. (1992) *Independent on Sunday*, 13 December.

Marquand, D. (1992) *Guardian*, 11 April.

Minkin, L. (1991) *The Contentious Alliance* (Edinburgh: Edinburgh University Press).

Rose, R. and McAllister, I. (1990) *The Loyalties of Voters* (London: Sage).

Smith, M. J. and Spears, J. (eds) (1992) *The Changing Labour Party* (London: Routledge).

Sunday Telegraph (1991) 1 September.

The Sunday Times (1991) 17 November.

The Sunday Times (1992) 12 April.

Williams, S. (1992) *Guardian*, 16 September.

Young, H. (1989) *One of Us* (London: Macmillan).

Young, H. (1992) *Guardian*, 2 June.

Young, H. (1993) *Guardian*, 30 September.

Part III

Beyond Whitehall and Westminster

7

The Mass Media: Fourth Estate or Fifth Column?

KENNETH NEWTON

The Victorian writer Thomas Carlyle called the press the 'Fourth Estate of the Realm'. By this he meant that it acted as a sort of watchdog of the constitution and, as such, formed a vital part of democratic government. Most modern writers would agree that the mass media should play a central role in sustaining and developing democracy: the media should present a full, fair, and accurate account of the news, they should inform and educate the general public, and they should cover a wide range of political opinions and positions (Keane, 1992). Many modern writers, however, are concerned that the mass media no longer play their proper democratic role. They believe that far from being the fourth estate, the media are becoming a sort of fifth column that threatens democracy from within. Some commentators believe that the threat is strongest in Britain. This chapter considers the competing views of fourth estate and fifth column writers in modern Britain.

In Carlyle's day things were simpler and easier than they are now. Newspapers and journals of news and opinion were relatively inexpensive to set up and to operate. Therefore there were many of them and they could be run by many different people with different interests and independent political opinions. The press was fragmented, pluralist, and diverse. The national press did not dominate but there was a varied and vigorous local press.

Taken as a whole, it presented the views of a fairly broad spectrum of political opinion, much of it independent from parties or other major political organisations.

The media world is now both more complicated and simpler than in Carlyle's time. It is complicated because it extends far beyond the printed words of pamphlets, journals, and newspapers to include radio and television (international, national and local), film, records, tapes, CDs, videos, and a vast array of magazines. At the same time the media market has become simpler because a pluralist and diverse array of papers and journals has been replaced by a national market in which a few papers and radio and TV stations dominate.

Because they have huge national and international audiences, the mass media have also acquired a huge potential political power. Whereas the newspapers were once limited to a role of reporting and commenting on the news – they had influence but not power – the modern mass media have become major political actors in their own right. They have power but not responsibility, it is said (Curran and Seaton, 1985). Some people fear that the mass media are inclined to use their new political power for their own particular purposes.

The fear the British media are more of a fifth column than a fourth estate is based upon three general arguments concerning the mass media in modern society:

- The concentration of ownership and control
- Systematic political bias
- Political influence

The chapter will examine these three points in the context of government and politics in Britain in the late twentieth century.

Ownership and Control of the Mass Media

In Carlyle's Victorian England there were many newspapers, mostly in small, local circulations. The capital costs of setting up a newspaper were fairly modest, and there were opportunities for many different producers reflecting a wide variety of political opinion. In our own era of national and international mass markets, however, the capital costs of setting up a newspaper or a TV channel are large and there is room only for a few producers to operate efficiently. In addition, national newspapers are dependent upon fast and efficient distribution networks, and there are few of these. The result is oligopoly – a relatively small number of producers.

Such a market does not seem to conform to the requirements of pluralist democracy in which many different producers meet the demands of many different consumers with many different political tastes and opinions. On the contrary, pluralist diversity seems to have given way to the concentration of ownership and control in which a relatively few producers dominate the media markets. In fact the growing concentration of media ownership and control seems to be composed of five different but closely interrelated aspects: consolidation and centralisation; a declining number of newspaper titles; concentration of ownership and control; the growth of multi-media conglomerates; and growing internationalisation.

Consolidation of a National, Centralised Market

Nearly 185 million newspapers are sold weekly in the UK (Peak, 1992, p. 13). Britain is also a relatively small but densely populated country. As a result there has emerged a single, large, national newspaper market. Although there are local and regional papers, two-thirds of the adult population regularly see a national paper, and about 70 per cent a national Sunday paper. In other Western nations – Germany and the USA, for example – the newspaper market is a regional one based on large cities, and the result is a larger number of papers with small circulations. Of the eleven highest-circulation newspapers in Europe, nine are British.

The electronic media (radio and TV) are also highly centralised with a few national organisations dominating. There are regional slots in national TV programming and an increasing number of local radio stations, but most viewers and listeners are still tuned to national stations and national programmes.

The Declining Number of Titles

In the same way that the market for cars has resulted in fewer and fewer giant producers, so it is with the British national newspaper market. As a large national market emerged with room for only a few efficient producers, the number of national newspapers has slowly but gradually declined. Since 1900 the number of national daily papers has fallen from 21 to eleven. Between 1923 and 1983 the number of national Sundays fell from fourteen to eight. New titles have been added in this period, but those with the biggest circulation have come from companies that already produce other mass-circulation papers.

The number of provincial and local daily papers has also declined from 134 in 1921 to 99 in 1983 and 87 in 1992 (Curran and Seaton, 1985, p. 288; Peak, 1992, p. 14). By 1975 only 18 per cent of British towns had competing papers run by different owners, half that of 1921 (Hartley *et al.*, 1977). In 1900 London had nine daily evening papers. Now it has one (Negrine, 1989, p. 69).

Concentration of Ownership and Control

A concentration of ownership and control in the British newspaper business is not new. In 1910 Lord Northcliffe controlled 39 per cent of the London morning papers. In 1987 Murdoch, the biggest proprietor, had only 35·per cent. However, there is an increasing concentration. While the top three controlled two-thirds of morning dailies in 1910, the top three in 1983 (Murdoch, Maxwell and Matthews) took a 75 per cent share of national dailies and an 83 per cent share of national Sundays (Negrine, 1989, p. 72; Curran and Seaton, 1985, p. 92). Five companies accounted for 84 per cent of national daily and 96 per cent of national Sunday sales.

The big five have also increased their control of the local and provincial press. In 1947 they controlled 44 and 65 per cent of provincial evening and morning papers respectively; by 1983 the figures had risen to 54 per cent and 72 per cent. In the same period they increased their share of the local weekly market from 8 per cent to almost a third (Curran and Seaton, 1985, pp. 92–3).

Because there is a large national market with relatively few producers, Britain's newspapers are among those with the highest circulations in the Western world. The national daily broadsheets and tabloids sell over 14 million copies a day, and the Sundays sell over 16 million. With between two and three people reading each newspaper sold, this means a daily readership in the region of 30 million, and a Sunday readership of about 35 million. The sales of most papers have been dropping steadily for a few years now, but nevertheless, the two best-sellers, the *Daily Mirror* and the *Sun* total about 6.5 million.

Multi-Media Concentration

What makes the contemporary situation qualitatively different from the era of Northcliffe and Rothermere in the early twentieth century is that concentration of ownership and control in the media now extends far beyond the press to publishing of all kinds, films, recording, radio, television, entertainment, and a wide range of other business interests besides. The following thumb-nail sketches illustrate the point:

- In 1991, when he died, Maxwell newspapers (*Mirror/Daily Record*, *Sunday Mirror*, *Sunday People*, and *Sporting Life*) had sales of close to twelve million, including a quarter of the daily tabloid market. Maxwell companies also had interests in TV (Central TV, Border TV, SelecTV, MTV, and Rediffussion Cable), books (E. J. Arnold and Pergamon Press), magazines and journals, as well as computer software, transport and plastics.
- Murdoch owns newspapers and TV stations on three continents (Europe, Australia and the USA). In Britain his company, News International, publishes the *Sun*, *News of the World*, *The Times*, *The Sunday Times*, and *The Times* supplements (total circulation over ten million, including a third of tabloid circulation and 45 per cent of Sunday broadsheet circulation). He has interests in London Weekend TV, satellite TV (BSkyB, the largest in Britain) and cable TV, books, films (Metromedia and Twentieth Century Fox), magazine and journal publishing (Collins, Fontana, and Granada Books), the Reuters news agency, and in companies involved in property, transport (TNT trucking), gas, and oil. Laws in Australia forced him to sell his TV stations to keep his newspapers, and in the USA to sell his New York and Chicago papers in order to keep his TV station.
- Associated Newspapers under Lord Rothermere publishes the *Daily Mail* and the *Mail on Sunday*, and *Weekend* (total circulation of about 5 million), and has interests in Northcliffe

Newspapers and other companies on three continents involved in publishing, broadcasting, theatre, oil, transport, and investment.

- Lord Matthews' main company Trafalgar House ran the Express Group (sold to United Newspapers in 1985) which included the *Daily Express* and the *Sunday Express*, the *Star*, the *Standard* and eleven local papers (a circulation of over 7 million). The company had interests in TV-AM, Capital Radio and in publishing companies in Britain and abroad. It also has a controlling interest in Cunard Shipping and Cunard Hotels as well as holdings in property and insurance companies.

- United Newspapers added the Express Group to its list of local and regional papers accounting for over a quarter of daily tabloid circulation, and more than 10 per cent of Sunday tabloid sales. By 1990 it published eight regional dailies, over one hundred weeklies, and controlled two large publishers of magazines and directories, as well as a news agency (Extel) and *Punch*.

Royal Commissions on the Press in 1949, 1962 and 1977 expressed concern about increasing concentration of ownership and control. As a direct result of a recommendation of the second commission a regulation was established in 1965 requiring large companies to obtain the assent of the Secretary of State before they could acquire more newspaper holdings. Between 1965 and 1977 fifty such applications were made but not one of them was turned down by the Secretary of State or the Monopolies Commission. The acid test of monopoly legislation was in 1981 when Rupert Murdoch was allowed to buy *The Times* and *The Sunday Times*, giving him a 30 per cent share of the national daily, and a 36 per cent share of the national Sunday market (Curran and Seaton, 1985, p. 293).

A second example of the failure of provisions to control the growing concentration of the media business concerns the merger in 1990 of Murdoch's Sky cable company with his main competitor, British Satellite Broadcasting, to create BSkyB. The two companies did not consult the Independent Broadcasting Authority before they acted and the merger was inconsistent with the cross-media ownership clauses of the 1990 Broadcasting Act. The merger was, nevertheless, given approval by the IBA.

A third example involved Yorkshire Television's take-over of Tyne Tees Television in 1992, when there was supposed to be a moratorium on TV mergers. The Independent Television Commission (which took over the IBA's television functions after the 1990 Broadcasting Act) agreed to the take-over.

In the autumn of 1993 the government loosened its restrictions on TV mergers, and, almost immediately, Carlton took over Central Television. During the months following, speculation mounted about further mergers, and, in February 1994, Granada took over London Weekend Television. Further mergers seemed likely, and the era of significant ownership spread in independent television appeared to be coming to an end.

In general, British provisions to maintain a pluralist and competitive media market have not worked at all well.

Internationalisation

On the international level a few huge media moguls and companies have already emerged. These include Ted Turner in the USA, Berlusconi in Italy, and the Springer Group in Germany, as well as Murdoch. Perhaps the most notable at present is the Berlusconi empire which owns three television channels in Italy and one each in France, Germany, and Spain, as well as a film company, two national papers, magazine publishers, a radio network, the largest Italian publishing company (Mondadori), and a chain of cinemas. It also has interests in insurance, finance, real estate, construction, a football team, and a supermarket chain (Keane, 1991, p. 71). As satellite and cable TV become more widely available, international media conglomerates are likely to grow. While newspapers are still organised into predominantly national markets they are increasingly owned and controlled by multi-national companies. Some weekly journals and magazines are broadening their international circulation (the *Financial Times*, *The Economist*, *Time*, *Newsweek*, and the international editions of newspapers). Other sections of the mass media (notably recording, films, and some TV) are already international.

The process of international conglomeration in Britain has reached the point where the nature of the media as a business interest has changed. For much of the twentieth century – until the 1970s – newspapers were largely in the hands of national publishing conglomerates. Now, the newspapers have been joined by other mass media, and these are, in turn, controlled increasingly by non-media business interests. As the Press Commission put it, 'Rather than saying that the press has other business interests, it would be truer to argue that the press has become a subsidiary of other business interests' (quoted in Seymour-Ure, 1991, p. 110). In short, the mass media in Britain and other Western nations have been incorporated into the world of international business capital.

There are exceptions to this general trend of the concentration of ownership and control. The first concerns the magazine market. New desk-top publishing technology, new titles and new markets have made this a highly changeable and volatile world. The result is the proliferation of small-circulation magazines covering education, art and culture, politics, and many other minority interests. At the same time, a few large companies have gained control of many of the large-circulation magazines. Between 1966 and 1974 over half the new consumer magazines with a circulation of over 30 000 were launched by four major publishing groups (Curran and Seaton, 1985, pp. 286–7). The largest of these is the International Publishing Corporation with 200 titles (Tunstall, 1983, pp. 90–1).

The second minor exception involves the national newspaper market. For a time it was felt that new computer-driven technology and production methods would open things up. Events proved otherwise. The quarter-century after 1960 saw only two new national papers, but eight were launched between 1986 and 1992. Of these, four failed and four are still in production (the *Independent/ Sunday Independent, Today, Sunday Sport,* and the weekly *European*). However, the newcomers have small or ailing circulations which make little impact, and in any case two (*Today* and the *European*) are owned by the Murdoch and Maxwell empires.

The most notable new paper is the *Independent* which set itself up with only £18 million capital. Nevertheless, with sales of less than 400 000, accounting for 2.7 per cent of the national daily circulation, the *Independent* has barely disturbed the mass-circulation oligopolies and its future in its present form is open to doubt. The brief history of Eddie Shah's newspaper is more typical. In 1986 Shah, a small provincial newspaper publisher, set out to use the latest printing technology to produce the first new national daily for decades. Amid much publicity he was hailed as a new force who would challenge Fleet Street and introduce real competition. Within weeks of the launch Shah was in financial trouble, and a few months later he sold out to Tiny Rowland's Lonrho group – a multi-media multinational. The following year the paper closed down. The person who benefited most from Shah's work was none other than Rupert Murdoch who used the new technology and a new union agreement to move News International out of Fleet Street into modern and spacious facilities in Wapping. Other national papers soon followed suit. Far from breaking up the old oligopoly, the new publishing technology has strengthened it.

Systematic Political Bias?

Fears about growing oligopoly in the media business are fuelled by claims of a systematic political bias. Here, however, it is essential to distinguish between the print and the electronic media. In theory it is possible for anyone to set themselves up in the print media business: all they need is paper, ink, a press, and some outlets; new and cheap desk-top publishing technology makes it easier than ever. The newspaper business is therefore deemed to be a free market and in no need of state regulation or control. Radio wavelengths and TV channels are different and strictly limited in number – something known as spectrum scarcity. As a result broadcasting wavelengths are regarded as part of public property and publicly regulated by means of broadcasting licenses. This is known as market regulation.

More than this, because broadcasting wavelengths are in the public domain, broadcasters are required to serve the public interest in making use of them. This is known as content regulation. The Independent Television Act of 1954 (updated in 1981) specifies a long and elaborate code of conduct for independent TV, including a ban on all political advertising and editorialising, and requiring news programmes to maintain 'a proper balance' and 'accuracy and impartiality'. The same code applies to local radio. The BBC is not legally limited in this way but it subscribes to the code imposed on independent TV. No such content regulation is imposed on the 'free market' of the newspaper business. Therefore, it is essential to distinguish between the electronic and the print media.

The Electronic Media

So far as anything can ever be fair in politics, British broadcasting seems to be reasonably so. In a stop-watch sense, the major parties get time for their election broadcasts in proportion to their votes in general elections. More than this, news and current affairs programmes are generally accurate and reasonably impartial, though it is not possible to be entirely accurate all the time, and complete impartiality is an impossibility. Compared with the print media, however, TV and radio news in Britain gets fairly close to these two impossible ideals, although the extent and type of systematic political bias in radio and television coverage of news and current affairs is hotly debated (Miller, 1991, pp. 77, 207–8; Adams, 1986; Jones, 1986; Gavin, 1992, pp. 596–611).

Surveys show that a large (but declining proportion) of viewers regard both ITV and BBC news as accurate and impartial. A small minority (15–20 per cent) think the BBC is biased towards the Conservatives, and a smaller minority (about 5 per cent) believe it shows a Labour bias. Between 3 per cent and 8 per cent believe that ITV shows a Labour bias and roughly the same believe it favours the Conservatives (for recent figures see *The Economist*, 26 October 1991, p. 39). The impartiality of TV news is important because up to eight or nine million regularly watch the evening news programmes on Channel 3 and BBC, and for an increasing number of people this seems to be the main source of political news.

In spite of the general public's faith in the BBC, it is strongly criticised in some quarters. The political left believes it has a right-wing bias, and the right thinks of it as left-wing. Politicians have become increasingly critical in the past two decades or so, especially since 1979. In 1982 Margaret Thatcher and Conservative MPs accused the BBC of biased reporting of the Falklands War. A few years later Norman Tebbit attacked the BBC's coverage of the American bombing of Libya.

At the same time there were a string of controversial incidentals in which the government attempted to control television programmes. These included programmes about Northern Ireland and the

IRA (*At the Edge of the Union* and *Real Lives*), about security and the secret service (*My Country Right or Wrong*, *Death on the Rock* and the Zircon affair), and about the MI5 admission that it vetted BBC journalists. One newspaper reported 'intense and colossal bitterness' about the BBC's treatment of the Conservative's 1992 election campaign (*The Sunday Times*, 5 April 1992, p. 3). As a result fear has been expressed about the future political impartiality of TV in general and the BBC in particular (Milne, 1990, pp. 81–2; Walters, 1989, pp. 380–98). The BBC's dependence on the government which sets the licence fee, plus its anxiety about the new charter required by 1997, adds to the fears. The initials BBC, it is said, stand for 'Be Bloody Careful'.

The BBC has also come in for academic criticism, especially from the Glasgow University Media Group, a research team which has published four books – *Bad News*, *More Bad News*, *Really Bad News*, and *War and Peace News*. In the first and probably the best volume, the team reported an elite and Conservative bias in the presentation of news about economic and industrial problems, including: the assumption that there is a direct link between wage rises and inflation; an obsession with strikes; an assumption that these were caused by trade union action rather than management failure; and a failure to interview strikers for their views on the disputes, as against managers or members of the general public for their views. *Bad News* concludes that TV news is inclined towards 'the laying of blame for society's industrial and economic problems at the door of the workforce' (Glasgow University Media Group, 1976, p. 267).

The Glasgow team has been roundly criticised in its turn by other academic writers, most notably Martin Harrison. He argues that it ignores evidence which goes against the grain of its own predetermined conclusions, and interprets other evidence in a biased way. *Bad News*, he concludes, is often wrong, or exaggerates its points, or else ignores facts which are inconsistent with its own views. In sum, it is not TV news which is biased but, on the contrary, the Glasgow Media Group itself (Harrison, 1985; Hetherington, 1985).

The conclusions of the Glasgow Media Group are supported in part by an official source, the Annan Committee Report, published in 1977. It pointed out that 'the coverage of industrial affairs [is] in some respects inadequate and unsatisfactory ...

Management representatives are often interviewed at their desks, apparently the calm and orderly representation of reason and sense, whereas trade unionists are often interviewed at the factory gates against a background of noise and disturbance, apparently the agents of disruption and trouble' (Committee on the Future of Broadcasting, 1977, p. 272; see also Royal Commission on the Press, 1977, p. 99). Yet the controversy about broadcasting bias is not resolved and it will no doubt continue for as long as the sun continues to rise.

Meanwhile, just as important is the argument that the nature of electronic broadcasting is changing. Spectrum scarcity will be eliminated by the growth and spread of satellite and cable TV and by low-power community TV. These will produce a much greater number and variety of TV channels resembling something like a free market. In some American cities fifty or more cable TV channels are available, as well as the ordinary (terrestrial) channels. To this will be added a capacity to receive satellite programmes from all over the world. As a result, it is said, there will soon be no need for state regulation of the electronic media, which should be left to the 'free market'. Critics of this view claim that arguments linking free-market economics to the news media are entirely misplaced since there are no market tests for news as there are for soap powders or motor cars (Newton, 1989, pp. 13–56). Moreover, what reason is there to believe that the result of unregulated electronic media will be any different from that of an unregulated print media? 'Tabloid television' will replace the *Nine O'Clock News*.

Nevertheless, we should be careful to distinguish between the two major branches of the media – the print media and the electronic media – in our discussion. It has been said with some truth that all statements about 'the mass media' are bound to be wrong. There is no such thing. Rather there are different medias with different properties and different qualities.

The Print Media

Unlike radio and television the national papers are most generally partisan. The tabloids are unashamedly partisan both in their presentation of opinion and in the selection of the 'facts' they report. The broadsheets try to cover the hard news, and often present a range of political opinion, even if they make it clear that they support one political party. The *Guardian* and the *Independent* are not attached to any particular party, although the *Guardian* has a left–liberal orientation. It is also notable that Britain has no fewer than four quality national dailies (five including the *Financial Times*) which is an unusual amount of choice by the standards of most countries in the West.

The tabloids are totally different. They are not only highly partisan, but they appear to make little effort to distinguish between news and opinion. On the contrary they mix fact, views, and fiction in the same stories so it is difficult to distinguish between them. The Labour *Mirror* is not so very different from the Conservative *Sun* in this respect. Indeed, it is probably safe to say that the nature and style of the political partisanship of London's tabloid press is not found anywhere else in the civilised world. The British take the tabloids for granted (like their weather!) because they are used to them, but few other countries have equivalents. It might be said that some British tabloids should not be classified as newspapers at all, but as scandal and amusement sheets.

The British press is not only highly partisan, but it is also heavily loaded towards Conservative partisanship. Of the eleven national dailies, eight are Conservative (the *Sun, Mail, Express, Telegraph, The Times, Star, Today,* and *Financial Times*), one- is Labour (the *Mirror/Record*), one expresses qualified support for Labour (the *Guardian*), and one is independent (the *Independent*). On election day 1992, however, the normally Conservative *Financial Times* advised its readers, 'by a fine margin', to vote Labour. Of the national Sunday papers, five are Conservative (*News of the World, Sunday Mail, Sunday Express, The Sunday Times,* and *Sunday Telegraph*), two are Labour (the *Sunday Mirror,* the *People*) one qualified Labour (the *Observer*), and one independent (the *Independent on Sunday*). The Tory press accounts for 67 per cent of national daily sales and 63 per cent of national Sunday sales. Labour claims 28 per cent of dailies and 34 per cent of Sundays. The Liberal Democrats have no paper of their own.

The political leanings of the national press have grown gradually stronger over time. In 1945, four national dailies supported Labour with a readership of almost 4.5 million or 35 per cent of sales. The Conservative Party also had four papers, and these

accounted for half the circulation. Since then the number and circulation of Labour papers have declined, while Conservative
support and circulation have increased (Seymour-Ure, 1991,
pp. 196–7). Nor is it simply a matter of pervasive and systematic
political bias, but also of pervasive and systematic distortion and
fabrication, particularly in the tabloids. This has been documented
at length and in depth (Hollingsworth, 1986; Snoddy, 1993).

The Conservative bias of the national press concerns – even
alarms – some people. Writing in 1984, the distinguished
columnist Hugo Young said:

> Taken as a whole the press is massively biased in one direction ... Not
> only has detachment been devalued and politicisation increased, but
> the process is all one way ... At the very time politics is becoming more
> open, fissiparous and diverse, the press becomes more monolithic and
> doctrinaire ... It fails to reflect and assist in the debate about the future
> of the British left – that is anything to the left of Mrs Thatcher. It is
> generally so preoccupied with reinforcing anything that the govern-
> ment is trying to do that all activity is assessed by its helpfulness to that
> enterprise. (Hugo Young, *The Sunday Times*, 18 March 1984)

Another journalist states:

> I have been sceptical of the constitutional claims made for Britain's
> fourth estate. Far from acting as the watchdog of the body politic, Fleet
> Street has so often served as its lapdog. However, proprietorially inde-
> pendent, it has integrated itself into the political establishment rather
> than stood over against it. (Jenkins, 1986, p. 223)

In short the tabloids show little of the pluralism and diversity required by democratic theory. Nor do they maintain high professional standards of accuracy or impartiality. Rather than appealing
to a range of different interests and political tastes, there is little to
distinguish them either in terms of content and style. They generally
lean heavily to the political right and, left or right, their bias seems
to grow stronger and stronger. They make little effort to distinguish
fact from opinion, and they mix both with cheque-book journalism,
sensationalism, triviality, unreliable reporting, even fiction.

It is a short step from these observations about poor political
quality to more general comments on the low professional
standards and unreliability of the British tabloid press. The result

is an increasing distrust of the tabloids by the public as a whole, and anger about their methods and standards. In particular, attention has been drawn to stories involving blatant invasion of individual privacy. The Calcutt Committee report of 1990 opposed statutory regulation but recommended a voluntary code of practice. As a result, the Press Complaints Commission replaced the Press Council in 1991 as a self-regulating body. However, the PCC seems to be no more effective than the Press Council, and a series of controversial incidents involving low standards have kept various proposals for statutory regulation on the political agenda, not least because many of the more scurrilous stories involve members of the Royal Family. Proposals for reform include the introduction of a Press Commission, a press complaints ombudsman, and a privacy law. The government was committed to producing a White Paper on press regulation, but this had yet to be published in the early part of 1994.

The Impact of the Media

All of this is rather beside the point if the media have little impact on mass political attitudes and opinions. If they have no impact on public opinion or behaviour then we have little need to worry. Do the media have their own independent impact? Here we get into even more complicated and difficult sets of arguments. There are two major difficulties. The first concerns extreme difficulties in untangling the effects of the media from the effects of other social agencies such as the family, the workplace, the community, schools, churches, and education. The media are only one set of influences among many, and what sorts of effects they have on what sorts of people is a tricky issue to unravel. In any case, it is unlikely that there is a single media effect rather so much as a whole set of conflicting and contradictory influences of different media – the tabloids versus the broadsheets, the Conservative versus the Labour press, the radio and television versus the print media, and so on.

The second problem concerns the cause-and-effect relationship between the media and their publics. These almost certainly flow in two directions: people pick the media which suit their tastes and opinions; at the same time, the media shape themselves to appeal to particular markets. In this way there is mutual accommodation between the media and their audiences. Besides, media influence over public opinion is not as simple or direct as might appear at first sight. People attend mainly to the messages that suit them. They often have a well-developed capacity to avoid, suppress, forget, distort, or misinterpret other messages that do get through. As the joke has it: the trouble with left-wingers is that they read too little right-wing literature; the trouble with right-wingers is that they read too little.

It is not surprising, in the light of these problems, that the experts do not agree on the power and impact of the media. There are three main schools of thought.

1. Reinforcement Theory

This theory argues that the media do not so much create and mould public opinion as reinforce pre-existing tendencies. The tendency of people to be ideologically blinkered and to use ideological filters places severe limits on the power of the media. At the same time, the forces of market competition oblige the media to attend carefully to the demands and tastes of the market they want to attract. They are adept market researchers and skilled at feeding to their audiences the very things the audience wants to see and hear in the first place. In short, the theory argues that consumer sovereignty and individual psychology render the media moguls all but powerless to influence mass political opinion. They are bound by the golden chains of the market.

The argument is weakened by the evidence that the modern British media do not necessarily operate in a free or competitive market. The electronic media are subject to both market and content regulation of the state, and the print media form an oligopoly. The argument is also weakened by the fact that citizens often have no first-hand experience against which to judge the news and opinions which bombard them. On such things as the Falklands War or the Gulf War, or on remote and technical matters like the European Monetary System, the economics of nuclear power, or argument about school and hospital opt-outs, many citizens are hard-pushed to know what to think. They may well be open to media influence where they have no first-hand knowledge or experience of the issue. This is not to say that we are all 'brainwashed' by the media.

2. *Agenda-Setting*

The essence of agenda-setting theory is its claim that the media cannot determine what we think, but they can exercise a strong influence over what we think about. In other words, agenda-setting theory agrees with reinforcement theory that the media cannot mould or determine our views on any particular matter. But the media can, and do, exert influence over what is on the agenda. Only a few items can be at the top of the agenda at any given time and the media play an important role in the constant process of sifting and sorting issues for attention. One example might be the way in which the Conservative papers concentrated on Labour's tax plans during the 1992 election campaign.

One of the more controversial aspects of the mass media's agenda-setting role concerns its capacity to keep certain matters out of sight and out of mind. One school of thought argues that the diversity of media sources ensures that most issues will get an airing. Another argues that the media are in the hands of big business whose ineluctable commercial interests cause them to maintain a narrow, capitalist agenda. A third points out that the modern mass media tend to focus on personalities and trivialise complex matters. Television, in particular, is said to concentrate on pictures and images, rather than words or ideas (for example, see Axford, 1992, pp. 17–20). Elections are presented not as a battle of ideas and programmes, but as a horse race with winners and losers, goodies and baddies. In this way the mass media are said to discourage people from thinking about politics at all – at least, in terms of issues, programmes, and party principles.

3. *Media Impact*

A third school of thought is now emerging which argues that the media, or at least British newspapers, do influence voting behaviour. First, while it is true that many people select a paper which fits their politics, a large minority do not select their paper on political grounds at all. They pick it for its sports pages, gossip columns, agony aunt, page 3, fortune tellers, TV reviews, gardening columns, recipes, women's pages, or simply because their partner or parents take it. Moreover, a large minority either do not know or misunderstand the politics of the paper they read. It has been estimated that well over 13 million readers of the *Daily Mail, Daily Express, Sun, Mirror* and *Telegraph* failed to perceive correctly the party supported by these papers. In the case of the strongly Conservative *Sun*, 9 per cent thought it supported no party, 33 per cent thought it supported Labour, 1 per cent thought the Liberals, and 25 per cent did not know (Kellner and Worcester, 1982, p. 61). The argument that newspapers simply reflect or reinforce the political views of their readers cannot apply to the 13 million.

Statistical analysis of newspaper reading and voting shows that even allowing for the fact that some people pick their newspaper for its politics, and even after allowing for the effects of such variables as social class, education, party identification, and attitudes towards key election issues, there is still a strong statistical association between reading a paper which supports a particular party and voting for that party. In other words, comparing people with exactly the same sort of social background, exactly the same party identification, and exactly the same sorts of attitudes towards the same election issues shows that those who read Conservative papers are more likely to vote Conservative than those who read Labour papers, and vice versa.

One careful and systematic panel study of the impact of the media in Britain to date (a study of the 1987 election) concludes as follows:

Even with stringent controls for partisanship and ideology, multiple regression analysis show that the press, *but not television*, had a significant influence on voters' preferences. Those who read right-wing papers proved significantly more satisfied with the Conservative Party's handling of major issues, and felt significantly warmer towards Mrs Thatcher and her party. Indeed, the ideological leanings of readers' papers had more impact than their own ideology. (Miller, 1991, p. 198)

The same writer studied the effect of newspaper reading on the 1992 election result. He found that between the second half of 1991 and election day 1992, 'the swing to the Tories was 9 per cent among *Sun* readers and 6 per cent among *Star* readers, compared with just 1 per cent among *Mirror* readers' (Miller, 1992, p. 17).

Another study carefully compares groups of voters with exactly the same attitudes towards key election issues (defence, trade unions, the NHS, and education). Those who read Labour papers are significantly more likely to vote Labour than those with identical political attitudes who read Conservative papers. Similarly, among those with the same political attitudes, those who read Conservative papers are significantly more likely to vote Conservative than those who read Labour papers, and vice versa. The study concludes that the newspaper effect is not just of statistical or academic significance, but has a substantial effect on election outcomes. The closer the race between the parties, the bigger the newspaper effect (Newton, 1992, pp. 51–74).

It should be remembered that this research finds evidence of a newspaper effect, but not a TV or radio effect. This is not surprising since radio and TV news coverage is intended to be non-partisan – politically neutral between the parties. Moreover, it is not claimed that newspapers are the only, even less the most important, single influence on voting behaviour. Nevertheless, the evidence does suggest that the effect is too big to ignore. Last, in all probability, reading a given newspaper for a short time is not likely to have much influence. The cumulative impact of this seems to be what matters, not the short-term effects of newspaper campaigns a week before an election (Harrop and Scammell, 1992, pp. 180–210).

Conclusion

This chapter has reviewed arguments about the role of the mass media in modern British democracy. It asks the question: Do the mass media represent the fourth estate – the protectors and watchdogs of the constitution and of democratic politics – or are they rather a sort of fifth column which threatens to subvert the democratic process from within?

The answer must necessarily distinguish between the electronic media and the print media. The electronic media, for reasons of spectrum scarcity, are carefully regulated by the state (both market and content regulation), whereas the print media are supposed to operate within an economic market which requires no (or only minimal) state regulation. Moreover, when discussing the print media it is also important to bear in mind the important differences between the quality broadsheets and the tabloids.

Nevertheless, several points stand out about the mass media as a whole. First, there has been a progressive concentration of ownership and control. The mass media, particularly the press, have become increasingly centralised on London, the number of newspaper titles has steadily fallen, and fewer companies control them. Whereas the newspaper business used to be largely in the hands of a few press barons, the mass media are now largely controlled by a few multi-media conglomerates. These typically have interests in books, magazines, papers, sound recording, videos, TV channels (terrestrial, cable, and satellite), films and entertainment. The multimedia conglomerates are, in turn, often incorporated into other business interests, and thus into the wider world of finance and capital. At the same time, the mass media have become internationalised, and the growing international market is likely to be dominated even more by relatively few multi-media, multinational companies. This is inconsistent with the democratic requirement that the media should not be controlled by an oligopoly, but should be competitive, pluralistic, diverse and politically mixed.

Democratic theory also states that the media should not only provide us with a full and impartial coverage of the news, but with a wide range of opinions about it. Radio and TV approach this ideal, since an obligation to serve the public interest is imposed upon them by state regulations which require political balance, accuracy, and impartiality. British newspapers, especially the mass-circulation tabloids, are overwhelmingly partisan in the sense that they pin their colours clearly to the mast of a particular political party. The *Independent* is the main exception. Moreover, the British press is overwhelmingly biased towards the Conservative Party. About two-thirds of national circulation staunchly supports the Tories. The remainder support the Labour party (though the *Mirror* and the *Guardian* are often diffident), leaving the Liberal Democrats out in the cold.

In sum, the British tabloid press does not seem to live up to the requirements of diversity and pluralist balance required by democratic theory. For the majority of newspaper readers – the tabloid readers – the British press is not open, impartial, free-ranging and dependable. It is narrow, monolithic, doctrinaire and unreliable. This, in turn, would not be so bad if the press had little or no influence over public attitudes and political behaviour. Although a strong school of thought argues that the media can do no more than reinforce political attitudes, another school also claims that the media are a powerful influence on the political agenda. The media cannot determine what people feel about any given issue, but they do exert a strong influence over what people think about. A third view is now gaining momentum. It argues that the national press does indeed exert a strong influence over voting behaviour in general elections. And it has presented some fairly compelling, though still not conclusive, evidence to support this claim.

This chapter has presented argument and evidence about the growing concentration of ownership and control of the mass media, about the political bias of the print media, and about the political impact of the press. If the argument and evidence is persuasive, and there is still plenty of room for doubt, then it seems that fears about the political importance and effects of the mass media, especially the British tabloids, are not at all groundless. There are reasons for believing that it may form a sort of fifth column which does as much to undermine democracy as to sustain and protect it.

References

Adams, V. (1986) *The Media and the Falklands Campaign* (London: Macmillan).

Axford, B. (1992) 'Leaders, Election and Television' *Politics Review*, 1, pp. 17–20.

Committee on the Future of Broadcasting (1977) Cmnd 6753, p. 272.

Curran, J. and Seaton, J. (1985) *Power Without Responsibility* (London: Methuen).

Gavin, N. (1992) 'Television News and the Economy: the Pre-Election Coverage', *Parliamentary Affairs*, 45, pp. 596–611.

Glasgow University Media Group (1976) *Bad News* (London: Routledge & Kegan Paul).

Harrison, M. (1985) *TV News: Whose Bias?* (Hermitage, Berks: Policy Journals).

Harrop, M. and Scammell, M. (1992) 'A Tabloid War', in Butler D. and Kavanagh, D. (eds), *The British General Election of 1992* (London: Macmillan).

Hartley, N. *et al.* (1977) *Concentration of Ownership in the Provincial Press*, Cmnd 6810, Royal Commission on the Press, 1974–7, Research Series 5 (London: HMSO).

Hetherington, A. (1985) *News, Newspapers, and Television* (London: Macmillan).

Hollingsworth, M. (1986) *The Press and Political Dissent* (London: Pluto Press).

Jenkins, S. (1986) *The Market for Glory* (London: Faber).

Jones, N. (1986) *Strikes and the Media: Communication and Conflict* (Oxford: Basil Blackwell).

Keane, J. (1991) *The Media and Democracy* (Cambridge: Polity Press).

Keane, J. (1992) 'Democracy and the Media – Without Foundations', *Political Studies*, pp. 116–29.

Kellner, P. and Worcester, R. (1982) 'Electoral Perceptions of Media Stance', in Worcester, R. M. and Harrop, M. (eds), *Political Communications* (London: Allen & Unwin), pp. 57–67.

Miller, W. (1991) *Media and Voters* (Oxford: Clarendon Press).

Miller, W. (1992) 'I am What I Read', *New Statesman and Society*,- 24 April.

Milne, A. (1990) *DG: Memoirs of a Broadcaster* (Oxford: Clarendon Press).

Negrine, R. (1989) *Politics and the Mass Media in Britain* (London: Routledge).

Newton, K. (1989) 'Neutrality and the Media', in Goodin, R. E. and Reeve, A. (eds), *Liberal Neutrality* (London: Routledge).

Newton, K. (1992) 'Do People Read Everything They Believe in the Papers?: Newspapers and Voters in the 1983 and 1987 Elections', in Crewe, I. *et al.* (eds), *British Elections and Parties Yearbook 1991* (Hemel Hempstead: Simon & Schuster).

Peak, S. (ed.) (1992) *The Media Guide* (London: Fourth Estate).

Royal Commission on the Press (1977) Cmnd 6810, p. 99.

Seymour-Ure, C. (1974) *The Political Impact of the Mass Media* (London: Constable).

Seymour-Ure, C. (1991) *The British Press and Broadcasting Since 1945* (Oxford: Basil Blackwell).

Snoddy, R. (1993) *The Good, the Bad and the Unacceptable: The Hard News about the British Press* (London: Faber & Faber).

Tunstall, J. (1983) *The Media in Britain* (London: Constable).

Walters, P. (1989) 'The Crisis of "Responsible" Broadcasting', *Parliamentary Affairs*, 42. pp. 380–398.

Young, H. (1984) *The Sunday Times*, 18 March.

8

The European Union Dimension

TREVOR SALMON

Analysing the processes and challenges of governing the UK in the 1990s increasingly involves coming to terms with the European dimension. The implications of the United Kingdom's membership of the European Union (styled 'European Community' until November 1993, and referred to as such in the context of discussions of the preceding period) loom ever larger. Before considering the particular challenges of the 1990s, it is important for us to understand the background to UK membership of the EU.

Pre-Entry Hesitation

The United Kingdom has acquired the reputation of being 'An Awkward Partner' (George, 1989; and Bulmer, George and Scott, 1992) for the other member states in EU matters, and this awkwardness has stemmed from deep-seated roots in British political culture.

Perhaps most important for Britain's attitude to European integration was its very different experience from that of defeated and occupied nations and states. The Second World War, far from revealing a need for a radical overhaul of the state and, consequently, of sovereignty for Britain, seemed to vindicate the value of the British state. There was thus not the same perception of the need for radical readjustments such as embracing federalism and relinquishing sovereignty. Therefore, British policy-makers firmly opposed such developments.

Many agreed with Attlee when he argued that they were 'not prepared to accept the principle that the most vital economic forces of this country should be handed over to an authority that is utterly undemocratic and is responsible to nobody' (Nicoll and Salmon, 1993, p. 248). The preferred model was strictly inter-governmental cooperation in limited fields. Her Majesty's Government would have to acquiesce before any decisions were made in the debate over the structure and powers of the Council of Europe and the North Atlantic Treaty.

This attitude was deeply ingrained and the British never really appreciated the 'depth of drive towards real unity, as distinct from intergovernmental cooperation on the continent' (Camps, 1964, p. 339). This failure was profound and enduring, although to some extent the gradual realisation that the Europeans did care, did mean business, and were making progress towards their objective, was an important factor behind the gradual movement of British policy towards applying for membership of the European Economic Community.

The first application was lodged on 10 August 1961. In the debate at that time both Prime Minister Macmillan and Hugh Gaitskell, leader of the opposition, emphasised their antipathy towards federal developments. For Gaitskell there was 'no question whatever of Britain entering a federal Europe now'. Conservative anti-marketeers agreed (Nicoll and Salmon, 1993, p. 250). In fact, entry did not occur until January 1973, as two applications (1961 and 1967) were vetoed by the French President, de Gaulle. Only after he left the political scene in 1969 could successful negotiations leading to entry begin.

Hesitant Initial Membership

Despite entry in January 1973, there was the lingering feeling that, Prime Minister Heath and a few others apart, there was no deep enthusiasm for the experiment of uniting Europe, a feeling re-inforced by the party divisions on the European question. The

British sojourn to Europe was motivated not by enthusiasm, but by the lack of visible alternatives (Northedge, in Jenkins, 1983, p. 26). This set the tone for British attitudes and policies towards the Community. Entry did not resolve the debate about the nature of Britain's relationship with the Community. In February 1974 Labour fought the general election arguing that entry on the Heath terms was a mistake, and calling for renegotiation of those terms, particularly as regards the CAP, the financing of the Community, and retention of British control over regional, industrial and fiscal policies. Labour said they would give the British people an opportunity to express their view through either a general election or a consultative referendum. If the renegotiation was unsatisfactory Labour would not be bound by the terms of the treaty, but if successful Labour would play a full part in Europe.

On 5 June 1975, in Britain's first ever national referendum, the result was 17 378 581 'yes' votes against 8 470 073 'no' votes in answer to the question: 'Do you think that the UK should stay in the European Community (Common Market)?'

TABLE 8.1   *The British 1975 Referendum*

Yes	No	Turnout
67.2%	32.8%	64%

Of 68 voting areas only the Western Isles and the Shetlands voted 'no', with a general pattern of greater support in the south than in the north.

In the campaign the government and the pressure group 'Britain in Europe' reiterated previous arguments stressing the availability of a veto and that traditional sovereignty was a chimera. Membership provided a say in decisions. Parliament would still have the right to repeal membership at a later date. The 'no' campaign was headed by the National Referendum Campaign which claimed that pre-entry promises about jobs and prosperity had proved to be false and that the British were being asked to give up ruling themselves.

Given the referendum result, Prime Minister Wilson claimed that 'the debate is now over' and called for past divisions to be laid aside (Nicoll and Salmon, 1993, p. 254). These hopes proved to be pious, particularly in his own party where many contended that the referendum had been an unfair contest, given the disparity of resources between the two sides. The Community also became an issue in the internal Labour Party divisions for the next ten years.

The Conservative Government's Policy Towards Europe 1979–90

Although after 1979 British policy towards the Community was made by Conservative governments, there was to be a continuation of the predominantly suspicious British attitude to European integration, even if it was now accepted that the question of membership was closed. The pervasive concern became, therefore, an attempt to remodel the Community in the British image, that image reflecting certain features common to both major parties and to traditional British postwar policy, although there were also distinctive Thatcherite elements.

This attempt to remodel the Community was originally hampered by the problem of the British budgetary contribution, which occupied the years 1979–84. More significant in the longer term was the fact that Britain had a different vision of the future from the one held by many of its partners. In the 1980s, for example, while Britain favoured proposals relating to improving European Political Co-operation (EPC), it opposed all reforms of the institutions that would strengthen the centre or radically alter the current institutional balance. Britain opposed the call for an Intergovernmental Conference (IGC) in 1985 in Milan, but participated in the IGC because it knew that any treaty change required unanimity. Britain had made clear earlier that it strongly supported the single market dimension of the discussions. Parts of the Single European Act (SEA) fitted in very well with the Thatcher government's emphasis upon deregulation and market forces, and reflected a British preference for measures of negative integration, that is 'the removal of discrimination as between the economic agents of the member countries', as distinct from positive integration, namely 'the formation and application of coordinated and positive policies on a sufficient scale to ensure that major economic and welfare objectives are fulfilled' (Pinder, 1968). Enthusiasm for the single market did not extend to all aspects of the SEA, not all of which seem to have been fully appreciated in 1986–87. Britain, for example, was not enthusiastic about the 'social dimension' which, as well as new measures to alleviate unemployment, gave weight to workers' rights to consultation and to participation, and about the revived notion of monetary union going beyond the EMS.

In September 1988 Mrs Thatcher articulated her vision of the future in a famous speech at Bruges. Some of this reflected the specifics of contemporary Conservative thinking on the free market, but some also reflected very traditional British policy. Britain, it was said, sought no alternative to the Community, but did not want a European super-state. Attention was to be given to specific tasks in hand, not 'arcane institutional debates' which were 'no substitute for effective action'. Mrs Thatcher went on to offer some 'guiding principles for the future' development of Europe:

- There must be 'willing and active cooperation between independent sovereign states'. It was not possible to 'suppress nationhood and concentrate power at the centre of a European conglomerate'. Europe should seek to speak with a single voice on more issues, but this did 'not require power to be centralised in Brussels or decisions to be taken by an appointed bureaucracy'. Success for Europe lay, as in Britain, in 'dispersing power and decisions away from the centre'. Britain had 'not successfully rolled back the frontiers of the state ... only to see them reimposed at a European level, with a European super-state exercising a new dominance from Brussels'. She wished to see 'Europe more united', but this had to be done in a way which 'preserves the different traditions, Parliamentary powers and sense of national pride in one's own country'.
- 'Community policies must tackle present problems in a practical way' – for example, although progress had been made in reforming the CAP it remained 'unwieldy, inefficient and grossly expensive'.
- Community policies must 'encourage enterprise' and there must be a greater awareness that the Treaty of Rome 'was in-

tended as a Charter for Economic Liberty'. The aim should be deregulation, free markets, wider choice, reduced government intervention, and freer movement of goods and services. However, it was a 'matter of plain commonsense that we cannot totally abolish frontier controls', because of problems relating to drug traffic, terrorism and illegal immigrants.

- 'Europe should not be protectionist.'
- Europe 'must continue to maintain a sure defence through NATO'.

In concluding her speech, Mrs Thatcher reiterated that it was 'not enough just to talk in general terms about a European vision or ideal', and 'new documents' were not required. It was necessary to make decisions, rather than being 'distracted by Utopian goals'. In sum, the British wanted a 'family of nations, understanding each other better, appreciating each other more, doing more together but relishing our national identity no less than our common European endeavour' (Thatcher, 1988).

The European issue continued to cause trouble for British political parties, especially now the Conservative Party. In 1989 the Chancellor of the Exchequer, Nigel Lawson, resigned over the conduct of government economic policy: particularly the management of the exchange rate and the circumstances necessary to join the ERM. The real crisis, however, was generated by the resignation of Sir Geoffrey Howe from the government in November 1990. He revealed that there were deep and continuing divisions over European policy, especially over monetary policy within the government, and that he and Lawson had only been able to persuade the Prime Minister to make a specific commitment to joining the ERM, albeit with conditions, at the Madrid European Council in June 1989 by threatening to resign. Britain had joined the ERM on 8 October 1990 at 2.95 DM (with a 6 per cent plus or minus fluctuation band and a commitment to move to the narrower band when appropriate), three weeks before Howe's resignation, but he felt that the Prime Minister was still not really committed to the idea. She clearly continued to have reservations, at least partly because she identified the pound sterling with sovereignty. At Rome in late October 1990, Mrs Thatcher had been isolated in her opposition to an early move towards the second stage of EMU and it was clear that she would resist the possible ultimate introduction of a single currency. There was a growing feeling that her trenchant negotiating style was now becoming counter-productive, both at home and abroad. Conservatives also had other concerns about the direction of the government.

The Major Government and European Integration

The new Prime Minister, John Major, shared some of Mrs Thatcher's views on Europe (*The Economist*, September 1993), and as Chancellor had made known his antipathy towards the Delors path to EMU, proposing instead a gradualist approach via the introduction of a parallel optional currency, the 'hard ecu'. He seemed, however, to believe that it was more productive to argue one's case positively by seeking to be constructive than to continually adopt negative tactics and rhetoric. He had to be mindful, however, that many in the party shared the Bruges' views of Mrs Thatcher, indeed had formed a 'Bruges group'.

Not surprisingly, Britain was adamantly opposed to the federal vocation espoused by many. John Major made it clear that reference to it had to be removed when it appeared in the preamble of drafts of the Treaty on European Union. Its deletion from the draft Maastricht text was seen as a British success. There was political hostility across the Labour and Conservative parties to the 'F-word'. The British much preferred to stress the principle of subsidiarity. For example, speaking to the European Parliament in July 1992 Douglas Hurd, the Foreign Secretary, argued that:

> In the wide areas outside the exclusive competence, the Community should ask two questions: is it necessary for the Community to act; if so, to what extent? (Hurd, 1992)

The British position was that the two questions were applicable in all areas, and should be answered in a minimalist fashion. Britain regarded subsidiarity as 'bottom up' and therefore acceptable, and 'federalism' as centralisation and therefore unacceptable.

The government welcomed the fact that the new Common Foreign and Security Policy (CFSP), and home affairs and judicial cooperation, would be on an intergovernmental basis, so that they were outside the purview of the Court of Justice and supranationalism. The government did recognise that there were advantages in the Twelve speaking with one voice but wanted unanimity to be retained for CFSP, and a right to take national decisions. It was the same with regard to defence policy. Britain continues to believe in the primacy of NATO, and that nothing must call into question the North American presence in, and commitment to, Europe. Whilst Europe could do more for its own defence, the UK strongly opposed new structures as unnecessary and even worse as duplicating and undermining NATO.

The British position on EMU was already clear by mid-1991. Britain believed in the necessity for strict convergence criteria before moving to the third stage, but would not accept the need for a firm commitment on its part to a single currency. The decisions about joining and when to join were to remain matters for separate decision by the British Parliament. When pressed by opponents to EMU as to why the government did not block this part of the treaty, the government replied by showing nervousness that the other eleven might go ahead in this area on their own, leaving Britain aside. The final Treaty on European Union did contain Protocol 11 which recognised 'that the United Kingdom shall not be obliged or committed to move to the third stage of Economic and Monetary Union without a separate decision to do so by its government and Parliament' (Treaty on European Union, 1992).

Britain also stood aside from the decision by the other eleven to proceed by agreement on social policy in order to implement the 1989 Social Charter which it had not accepted. The Conservative government felt these proposals would undo much of their labour and social policy of the 1980s, as well as costing jobs. All new policy proposals in this and other areas had to be judged in the light of the British government's own political philosophy, and against Mr Major's belief that 'We must constrain the extension of Community competencies to those areas where Community action makes more sense than national action or than action on a voluntary, intergovernmental basis' (Major, 1991). In line with traditional British thinking, the government's basic position on institutions was to support intergovernmentalism, and partly for that reason it was keen that nothing be agreed that would make enlargement more difficult.

Immediately after Maastricht, John Major described the negotiations as 'game, set and match for Britain', and on 19 December

1991 the House of Commons supported the negotiated outcome by 339 to 253. It repeated this verdict early in 1992 on the second reading of the European Communities (Amendment) Bill by a majority of 244. But this did not end the discord. On 5 November 1992 the government had a majority of only three on a motion inviting the House to proceed to further consideration of the bill, a general election (won by the government), the Danish 'no' and the narrow French 'yes', plus 'Black Wednesday' in September 1992 (when the pound was forced out of the ERM by currency speculation and devalued) having radically changed the environment. This majority was only achieved with great difficulty, and the progress of ratification faced other significant problems.

Some opposed on principle, for much the same reasons as before, some opposed because there was to be no referendum or direct consultation with the British people on what was seen as a move curtailing sovereignty, and some opposed because of the 'opt out' on social policy. Labour was ambivalent because of that 'opt out' but did not wish to see the Treaty on European Union defeated. The Gordian knot was only finally cut through in July 1993, when the government had to resort to a motion of confidence to complete the ratification process. The treaty came into effect in November 1993.

Britain has remained awkward, still concerned about the ultimate direction of the European journey, but at least officially has come to the view that the events of 1992 in Denmark, France and elsewhere, the emphasis upon subsidiarity, plus the prospect of enlargement may mean that the Community is moving in a direction favourable to the long-standing British position of antipathy to all forms of centralisation.

Impact of Membership Upon British Government

Policy-Making Competence

Despite many misconceptions, the European Union, 'Brussels' and the Commission are not ubiquitous, involved in every 'nook and cranny' of British life. The European Union can only legally act on the basis of articles contained in its treaties, although it is noteworthy that the areas covered by the treaties have significantly evolved since the Treaty of Paris in 1951, which established the European Coal and Steel Community, and the treaties of Rome of 1957 which created the European Economic Community and the European Atomic Energy Community. The Single European Act of 1986 added new areas including research and technology, as well as laying a basis for the completion of the single internal market in the Community by the end of 1992. The Treaty on European Union, agreed at Maastricht in December 1991, and coming into force on 1 November 1993, also involved innovation, on this occasion including such areas as consumer policy, education and vocational training, and most notoriously the basis of economic and monetary union.

The importance of the legal base was starkly revealed in the summer of 1993, when the Commission put forward proposals for a Working Time Directive. The Commission aimed to provide for a maximum 48-hour working week, a minimum of eleven hours' rest per 24 hours, and a minimum of four weeks' paid holiday. It also proposed limits on young people's hours. The proposal came under Article 21 of the Single European Act, which introduced a new Article 118A into the original EEC treaty. The relevant article now referred to the 'health and safety of workers' and allowed for decisions to be made by qualified majority vote. Her Majesty's Government vehemently opposed not only the proposals themselves, but also the legal basis of Article 118A, claiming that it was inappropriate. Britain abstained from the vote on the issue, because it calculated that this would best preserve Britain's position before the European Court of Justice, when Britain challenged the validity of the Commission's proposal.

The Treaty on European Union also contains provisions creating intergovernmental cooperation on a Common Foreign and Security Policy, as well in Home Affairs and Justice. Both these areas are indicative of a further complication in considering the impact of Community membership upon British government and administration since neither of these parts of the new European Union come under the same decision-making system as applies to the old Community system and neither the European Commission nor the European Court of Justice have any jurisdiction over them. In these areas nothing can be forced upon Her Majesty's Government.

This is also true to some matters covered by the Community system. Whilst the treaties lay down issues that can be decided by 'qualified majority vote', and these areas have been expanded by the Single European Act and Treaty on European Union, it still remains true that other areas require unanimity. For the most part these are constitutional or quasi-constitutional questions, but they also affect parts of other areas, such as taxation. As was seen in 1992 and 1993 any changes to the treaties themselves require to be ratified by each member state according to its own constitutional provisions, and each member state has a veto over any such changes.

To complicate matters further, different aspects of the same policy area may be subject to voting or unanimity. Thus in the Treaty on European Union, for the most part questions dealing with the environment are matters for qualified majority voting, but this does not extend to fiscal provisions, town and country planning, land use, or choice of energy sources.

This distinction is important because it means that in some areas a British minister can be outvoted by European colleagues in the Council of Ministers, even against the wishes of the UK Cabinet and Parliament. When there is a qualified majority vote Britain, along with France, Germany and Italy has ten votes. A qualified majority is 54 out of a total of 76. Conversely a blocking minority vote is 23. This means that now in a wide range of policy areas, Britain can be outvoted, unless it can gain the support of a minimum of two other states (one of the ten-vote states, plus any other member apart from Luxembourg, which only has two votes). Of course, if no large state supports Britain, then the task of mustering a legal block becomes harder. It is this possibility of a sovereign state being outvoted that makes the European Union unique.

In practice on nearly all issues Britain is unlikely to be outvoted in this way, because there is an unofficial agreement, dating from a meeting in Luxembourg in January 1966, that if a member state feels particularly strongly on what it considers to be a vital interest, the other members will not force the issue. With one exception, ironically involving Britain in 1982, this understanding has been adhered to, and it might be regarded as a convention of the Community system. Inroads, however, have been made into this 1966 agreement, which for twenty years nearly strangled the decision-making process in the Community, and states have come to accept that voting may be necessary to progress, as was highlighted in the Single European Act provisions for the creation of the single internal market by the end of 1992. Amendments to the qualified majority voting system were agreed (amidst some controversy) in the Spring of 1994, in order to accommodate the expansion of the EU.

In still other areas of policy, although under no legal treaty obligation to pursue a common policy with Community partners, a government may decide to do so. This was the position between 8 October 1990 when the UK joined the European Exchange Rate Mechanism (ERM) at 2.95 DM (with a +/–6 per cent fluctuation band and a commitment to move to the narrower band when appropriate) and its leaving the system on 'Black Wednesday', 16 September 1992, when it became clear that rate of exchange could not be sustained, and the pound was forced out of the ERM by currency speculation and devalued. Joining the ERM and leaving it had pronounced effects not only upon the British economy during this period and since, but also on British politics as it played a part in the downfall of Mrs Thatcher. Membership meant in practice that interest rates could not be moved up or down to suit the narrow requirements of the British economy alone, lest this affect the pound's position in the ERM, and so other instruments such as fiscal policy and public spending restrictions had to come into play. Yet, membership was not compulsory in a legal sense, but a matter of choice, albeit that for some that choice was determined by developments in Europe, the progress of the single market and the proposals for economic and monetary union.

Impact on Departments

The competence of the European Union, therefore, varies enormously with regard to policy-making and management and so, as a consequence, does the involvement of the British government and its departments. In some areas, like the Common Commercial Policy (CCP), the clear competence lies now with the Commission, and the major decisions on agriculture are now made at EU level, although their detailed implementation is left to the member states acting as agents of the European Union.

Other areas see less comprehensive but nonetheless significant EU involvement, an involvement which has often had to be fought for. An example is competition policy, where there is a tension between the need to create organisations large enough to be able to compete in the world market and national concerns about the effect of mergers on employment and competition. For many years most member states took the view that the issues raised by mergers were too important to be allowed into the less sensitive hands of outsiders – matters such as employment or the loss of it, location of new investment, defence industry production and industrial champions. Social policy is another contested area where the Commission is trying to maximise its role and develop the European dimension. There are still areas where EU involvement is very limited, such as health, although, as noted above, recently it has sought to move into this area as a way of circumventing restrictions which the British have sought to place on matters such as limitations on the working week. In sum, the impact of membership is now surprisingly wide and continues to spread.

In other areas such as civil law, on questions such as divorce, slander and libel, the Community has no jurisdiction at all.

Traditionally British government and politics were seen as stopping at the water's edge. Within the islands of the United Kingdom of Great Britain and Northern Ireland, the British Parliament was sovereign and unfettered by any legal or constitutional constraints on its power. Outside actors or states might seek to influence British decisions, but that influence was indirect and had to be mediated through the British political system and policy process. Since 1973 in certain areas covered by the treaties of the Communities, as has been seen, the European Union is now legally and constitutionally entitled to make decisions, even against British wishes.

Britain joined an organisation with the potential to be more than purely intergovernmental. Intergovernmentalism is a mode of action which preserves the authority of the member states by providing each with the right to say no and to stop a measure of which they disapprove, and where agreement is consensual or non-existent. By contrast, it is now a well-established legal principle and fact that domestic British law is subservient to European Union law in those areas covered by the treaties. It can be argued that 'Community membership, and the fulfilment of obligations arising from it, are no more than exercises of – not limitations on – sovereignty', since each member state 'freely chose to join; each can leave at will' (Adonis, 1990, p. 11). In reality, however, this is extremely difficult to do. Just as an individual may jump off a rising escalator, at first relatively painlessly but with the passage of time and height increasingly painfully, even suicidally, so a state that has been in the Community for nearly forty years, or twenty or more in the British case, would find the pain associated with jumping off prohibitive.

In addition, there is now clearly a new dimension to British policy-making as the government and administration are involved in a wide range of decisions which now have a European dimension, and which, therefore, require that EU law and policy be taken into account. Europe 'has become a major institutional influence' on British policy-making, setting 'boundaries of acceptable policy options'. The 'EC framework is essential to effective policy *implementation* in a widening range of areas' such that the 'sheer ubiquity' of the Community dimension 'constitutes a powerful influence on the policy process, for it constantly shapes and reshapes the implementation framework within which British officials have to operate' (Clarke, 1992, pp. 161–2).

This influence has become routine and reaches deep into departmental life, limiting the freedom of action of British policy-makers. Whereas it could be argued that the British government used to take decisions which ended the matter, now on many matters the British 'decision' is only a negotiating position. On the positive side, that EU involvement means that Britain is now able to have direct influence over the policies of other states. An interesting example of this is the 'infamous' story of the alleged Brussels imposition of a maximum lawn mower noise, and prohibitions on the use of noisy lawn mowers by innocent British citizens. In fact, this was a case where British industry was facing problems as several member states have laws on noise levels of grass-cutting machines, in some cases to keep out British lawn mowers. This industry therefore approached the British government and the Commission to resolve their export problem. Involvement in this type of decision affecting others, and in taking collective action, has led to the term 'pooled sovereignty'.

The pervasiveness of the European dimension is exacerbated by the fact that many of the issues cut across the traditional divisions and boundaries of British departments. Thus the Ministry of Agriculture and Fisheries now plays an international role over which the Foreign and Commonwealth Office (FCO) has relatively little influence. The Common Agricultural Policy (CAP) touches upon very sensitive questions of domestic politics, involving large sums of money and transfer of resources. This in turn puts a premium on interdepartmental coordination. Very rarely will the British position be self-evident. Usually there will not only be differences of political viewpoint, but within the administration itself there will be competing bureaucratic viewpoints and interests, resulting in competition for influence over outcomes and control over policy-making. The Treasury is particularly well-placed in this competition because of its central role in approving all financial aspects of policy, whether the policy entails Community expenditure or, directly or indirectly, British expenditure.

Since 1973 there has been competition in the UK system for influence and control of Community policy. There was some initial expectation that there might be a Department of European Affairs or that the Foreign and Commonwealth Office (FCO) would hold the key coordinating position, but this was challenged on two grounds. The Prime Minister at the time of entry, Mr Heath, was determined that membership should not be seen in terms of participating in some foreign body, but that the involvement in the Community should permeate every department, even those that traditionally had had little to do with 'foreign affairs', so that they all would become imbued with the Community spirit or awareness. Thus, to some extent, a system has evolved wherein every government department may conduct relatively low-level negotiations or exchange technical information with similar departments in other member states. Each major department now has its own foreign, international, or European division or divisions, although these divisions have not become international ghettoes. In the Department for Education for example, while there is an international branch, the routine matters of dealing with EC fees reimbursement or ERASMUS educational exchanges are dealt with by the same officials who would deal with such issues on the domestic front (James, 1992, p. 24).

Great challenges are now posed to the achievement of coherent policy in particular areas and in terms of overall British strategy towards the European Union, especially since progress in one area may well require concessions in another, and care must be taken to avoid a line in one area which is inconsistent with what the government is trying to do in another. Many of the predominantly domestic departments feared that the FCO could not be trusted to uphold and defend British interests with sufficient vigour, since it was perceived to be too pro-European. As a result of such concerns the European Secretariat of the Cabinet Office acquired a central position in British policy coordination towards the Community. This secretariat, with a staff of less than twenty, is not so much involved in the making of policy, but in the coordinating process, pulling together a response from departments through a network of official committees. It may often take a lead in bringing departments together and its role in coordinating policy and trying to engender coherence can influence the nature and shape of policy, as well as advise on strategy and tactics. Its neutrality was the reason why some domestic departments, especially Agriculture, have favoured it to be a convenor of committees when policy is being thrashed out. The secretariat holds a watching brief over areas where problems may occur, and keeps an eye on long-running issues, such as the budget dispute which dominated the early 1980s. It performs a managerial function. Its staff are seconded from the departments which deal most often with Brussels.

Also influential is the group of deputy secretaries, which meets several times a week and shadows the ministerial European Questions committee. In addition, the Cabinet Office European Secretariat, the FCO and the UK Permanent Representative meet regularly to consider what issues are coming up and what needs to be done to prepare for them. Most of the work is performed inside this network of officials and departments.

It should be noted that the UK Permanent Representative (UKREP) in Brussels plays a key role in contributing to the coordination process. The basic principles of the coordination system are the same as for domestic policy, namely, a great deal of interdepartmental correspondence and meetings, feeding official committees and headed by the Cabinet committee on European questions. Given the highly technical nature of much EU business, there is a premium on the system producing as much agreement as possible at the lowest level possible, but running counter to that imperative is the fact that the contentious nature of European business within UK politics, and the contentiousness of much of it between the member states, means that even detailed and technical issues may have to be resolved at senior political level.

Another element in the system, is, of course, the Cabinet, which receives a weekly briefing on European Union matters, although the real work is done by the Committee on Defence and Overseas policy (OD) or its subcommittee on European questions. Whilst the OD is chaired by the Prime Minister, the OD(E) is chaired by the Foreign Secretary, and other members recently have included the Chancellor of the Exchequer, the Home Secretary, the President of the Board of Trade, the Transport Secretary, the Lord President of the Council, the Minister of Agriculture, Fisheries and Food, the Welsh, Scottish and Northern Ireland Secretaries, the Employment Secretary and the Attorney-General, as well as a few junior ministers. Other ministers are invited to attend depending on the nature of the business being discussed, and the UK's Permanent Representative to the Community is also in attendance. Its terms of reference are to consider questions relating to the UK's membership of the European Union and to report as necessary to the OD. Other committees, such as the Committee on Legislation and the Committee on European Security, will also discuss matters as appropriate. Given the pressures of time these committees will only examine the key questions.

The workload entailed by this is very heavy for senior politicians. In addition, the European Council, will meets twice a year in the capacity of supreme arbitrator of disputes unresolvable by others and the motor of future developments in the Community, brings the Prime Minister into EU decision-making at the very highest level. Agreements made or not made at such meetings set the whole tone for several months.

The FCO is also heavily involved in the handling of European Union matters. It has responsibility for the Office of the Permanent Representative in Brussels and for communication between London and Brussels. This provides it with an overview of a range of matters. The FCO is responsible for the overtly political questions which arise, such as the political implications of proposals, providing negotiating expertise, and institutional questions. Recently in connection with the IGC on Political Union the FCO played a crucial role, and one of its ministers, Tristan Garel Jones, played a decisive part in the British Presidency of the Community, which culminated in the successful Edinburgh European Council of December 1992.

The FCO has functional departments for dealing with the EU. One, European Community (Internal), takes an interest in questions relating to such things as the internal market, its negotiation and implementation, and the other, European Community (External), focused on European Political Cooperation, now the CFSP (Common Foreign and Security Policy), and its Political Director plays a central role in that process. CFSP is now a vital part of the environment of British foreign policy, and the FCO has developed a European 'reflex' on a number of questions. This is not to say that Britain always agrees with its partners, but it is now commonplace to automatically consult them and be consulted by them on all aspects of foreign policy. Indeed, it is important to note that the European dimension is now both a formal and informal part of the decision network.

It is these units of the FCO, the European Secretariat and UKREP that are the key actors in shaping overall UK Community policy, but the functional departments are jealous of their own spheres of policy and are thus keen to emphasise the technical aspects of policy and, in so doing, their own unique expertise on those matters. This is particularly so for a major player like the Ministry of Agriculture, Fisheries and Food, given the importance of the Common Agricultural Policy (CAP) to both Britain and the Community. Some other departments are less centrally involved, and it is these departments that have to rely more on the expertise of others. A central department, like Agriculture, can expect to send officials to over a thousand EU meetings a year.

Impact of Membership Upon the British Parliament

In order to fully understand the implications of EU membership for governing the UK, consideration must be given to the role of Parliament. The British Parliament has found it even more difficult than the institutions of government to adjust to Britain's membership of the European Union. It was originally expected that parliamentary roles in the Community area would largely wither away, and be replaced by input from the European Parliament. National parliaments, however, still play an important role in EU affairs, although not always well-equipped to play that role.

Parliamentary consent is still needed for any treaty amendments to the founding treaties of the Community that have an impact upon British domestic law. Thus the Single European Act of 1986 required parliamentary consent, as did the Treaty on European Union, although as noted earlier this was only achieved by the government moving a vote of confidence on Friday 23 July 1993 'in the policy of the Government on the adoption of the Protocol on Social Policy'. Faced with a vote of confidence even the rebels decided not to defeat the government in their own quest for a rejection of the treaty. The British Parliament was also involved in the enabling and detailed legislation for direct elections to the European Parliament in June 1979, having passed the European Assembly Elections Act 1978, which created the constituencies and determined the electoral system. Interestingly, Clause 6 of this Act stated that: 'No treaty which provides for any increase in the powers of the Assembly shall be ratified by the United Kingdom unless it has been approved by an Act of Parliament.'

This clause became one of the three issues of contention raised by Lord Rees Mogg's challenge to the government's ratification of the Treaty on European Union since he argued that there was doubt whether the whole treaty had been so approved. It was claimed that Parliament had not voted for the Social Protocol opt-out, and since the protocol would have the effect of increasing the powers of the European Parliament it was contrary to the 1978 Act. Ratification would also alter the Treaty of Rome, which again required parliamentary consent, but again this had not been given to the whole Treaty on European Union since Title V on Common Foreign and Security had not been put before the House. The High Court rejected these arguments, saying in effect that Parliament had ratified the whole treaty, and that in response to the argument that Title V was *ultra vires* ('beyond the powers') in transferring Crown prerogative, the Court held that to the contrary it was an exercise of prerogative. The Social Chapter was contentious because in July 1993 the House of Commons rejected the policy of opting out, and even a government motion that it 'take note' of the government's position. The government had only managed to secure parliamentary approval for the European

Communities (Amendment) Bill, which legitimised those parts of the treaty having domestic effect, by making it a matter of confidence in government.

Parliament is involved in translating much European legislation into effect, especially with respect to directives in which the EU lays down the objective to be achieved, but leaves a degree of discretion as to how they are achieved. Some international agreements cross the boundary between what the European Union has the competence to do on its own and what requires the consent of individual members, so-called '*accords mixtes*'. More generally, it remains true that the national government is accountable to Parliament for its policies in general and on the EU and must retain the support of its own party and of a majority in the House of Commons, although as noted earlier this is somewhat undermined in theory by majority voting.

In practice British parliamentary involvement is sporadic and isolated. Apart from the interminable two hundred hours in debate on the Treaty on European Union, it is rare for there to be major debates on EU matters. Part of the problem is the technicality and specialist nature of much of what emanates from the institutions of the European Union and the related problem that MPs often do not see any significant political mileage in these issues. Traditionally the Commons has regarded foreign affairs as a matter of Crown prerogative and has only been intermittently interested. Many of the agreements reached by ministers in the Council of Ministers are 'package deals', which by definition are difficult to unscramble. Even more importantly, although ministers are accountable, this is limited by the nature of the Community process. The Council is a negotiating forum of a relatively secret nature. Proposals evolve during negotiations and there is give and take. Even a parliament which has sought to mandate a minister, like the Danish Folketing and its Market Relations Committee, has found it difficult to enforce its position. Ministers can always refer to the circumstances prevailing in the Council at the time of decision. Periodically it has been argued in Britain that no major Community decision should be made without Parliament's explicit approval but this runs counter to the 1972 European Communities Act and the whole basis of the EU's decision-making. Moreover in 1973 Sir Geoffrey Howe encapsulated the position when he wrote that 'Parliament intends to refrain (as is required by the treaties) from exercising its own legislative power' (Howe, 1973, pp. 1–13). The Labour government in the 1970s did undertake to seek to ensure that no important Council decision would be taken unless Westminster had debated it, but this proved difficult to adhere to given the time pressures on the Commons and the unpredictability of Community business. In the summer of 1989 the Commons Treasury Select Committee complained not only about what had been agreed at the Madrid European Council meeting on economic and monetary union, but also about the lack of prior parliamentary consultation. Somewhat acidly it noted that 'If the government attaches significance to arguments about the sovereignty of Parliament, it ought not to be selective in its attachment to them' (Adonis, 1990, pp. 179–180).

More recently, in the context of the debate about Maastricht and subsidiarity this issue has returned to the agenda. It remains the case that some decisions taken by the Council, as long as the due processes have been gone through, are directly applicable and have direct effect. They cannot be unilaterally renounced, and can only be changed if the whole decision-making process is gone through again. It is also the case that Parliament is often presented in effect with *faits accomplis* in this area, and faced with the simple choice of accepting or rejecting but not reopening the decision.

The House of Commons initially also suffered in terms of scrutiny of Community matters because of the lack of a tradition of specialist committees in the House prior to the reforms of 1979. This was exacerbated by the continuing political division over membership, and the debate that has continued for over twenty years on that matter. The Commons response was to create a scrutiny committee, the Select Committee on European Legislation, although as seen above, other select committees do become involved on matters in their area. The main function of the European legislation committee is to consider Commission proposals to the Council and to report on their legal and political implications. These reports have been factual and may include a recommendation that the whole House should consider the issue, but often they are *post hoc* and only cover a small proportion of proposed EU legislation. This committee does not, however, consider the merits or otherwise of proposals. It is rather a filter to alert the House to potential problems. It has had only limited direct impact, and if its reports are debated, which is infrequently (about twenty a year), these debates tend to take place late at night, after 10 p.m. in front of a sparse audience of *cognoscenti*. The Committee has sixteen members, six Labour, (including a Labour chairman), nine Conservatives (including William Cash, one of the Tory rebels throughout the ratification process), and one Scottish Nationalist.

The House of Lords has a much better reputation and record on the Community, partly because it has more time available and partly because the EU has been a less contentious matter there so their Lordships have been freer to discuss more substantive matters. Its key committee's remit is to report on Commission proposals which raise important questions of policy or principle, or other questions which the committee believes the whole House should consider. The Lords Select Committee on the European Communities has produced a number of substantive reports, for example on the European Monetary System (EMS), which have been widely read and influential not only in the UK but elsewhere too. Its reports are usually debated in the whole House. The Lords committee is larger and makes more use of subcommittees. These are: (a) Finance, Trade and Industry, and External Relations; (b) Energy, Transport and Technology; (c) Social and Consumer Affairs; (d) Agriculture and Food; (e) Law and Institutions; and (f) Environment. It also occasionally creates *ad hoc* subcommittees, these having covered such issues as European Union, fraud in the EC and EC staffing. Twenty peers are on the committee but another 60 or so are involved in the subcommittees. The committee and its subcommittees take expert evidence, and take advantage of the expertise found in the House given the previous work experiences of some of its members. Even when its reports are not debated, the Lords committee has influence because its reports are widely read and held to be authoritative.

Many of these difficulties faced by Parliament in dealing with the European Union are not unique to the sphere of the EU but reflect some of the general inadequacies of Parliament, such as the in-built government majority and the information gap which exists between ministers and others. They are part of the wider debate in the Union about its 'democratic deficit'.

Conclusion

There remains an awkwardness about Britain's relations with the European Union and also about how the UK deals with the EU at the governmental and parliamentary level. This awkwardness reflects the continuing deep ambivalence that exists in the British body politic about Britain's position in Europe and the lingering perception, reinforced by the experience since leaving the ERM in September 1992, that *Great* Britain can somehow or other still be a significant independent international actor on the wider international stage. Those with governmental responsibility are more aware, however, of how real the constraints are on independent decision and action in today's world.

References

Adonis, A. (1990) *Parliament Today* (Manchester: Manchester University Press).

Bulmer, S., George, S. and Scott, A. (eds) (1992) *The United Kingdom and EC Membership Evaluated* (London: Pinter).

Camps, M. (1964) *Britain and the European Community 1955–1963* (London: Oxford University Press).

Clarke, M. (1992) *British External Policy-making in the 1990s* (Basingstoke: Macmillan).

George, S. (1989) *An Awkward Partner: Britain in the European Community* (Oxford: Oxford University Press).

Howe, G. (1973) 'The European Communities Act 1972', *International Affairs* 49(1), pp. 1–13.

Hurd, D. (1992) *European Parliament News,* July.

James, S. (1992) *British Cabinet Government* (London: Routledge).

Jenkins, R. (1983) *Britain and the EEC* (London: Macmillan).

Major, J. (1991) *House of Commons,* November.

Major, J. (1993) *The Economist,* 25 September.

Nicoll, W. and Salmon, Trevor C. (1993) *Understanding the New European Community,* 2nd edn (London: Harvester Wheatsheaf).

Thatcher, M. (1988) Speech at the opening ceremony of the 39th academic year of the College of Europe, Bruges, September.

Treaty on European Union (1992) (Luxembourg: Office for Official Publications of the European Communities).

9

Governing Scotland, Wales and Northern Ireland

ROGER LEVY

Since the upsurge of political nationalism in Scotland and Wales in the late 1960s, and the onset of 'the troubles' in Northern Ireland in 1969, the territorial dimension has been a perennial feature of UK government and politics. There is little agreement even about what generic to use to describe the three areas. The government's Official Handbook of the UK favours the term 'national regions' for Scotland and Wales, or simply 'lands' to designate the four parts of the United Kingdom (England, Northern Ireland, Scotland and Wales) (Crick, 1991; Kellas, 1991a). 'National region' recognises nationality while denying a separate statehood, but leaves the door open to a share in a common statehood with the other constituent parts of the UK. Most Scots and Welsh nationalists reject such a designation, arguing that Wales and Scotland are nations without states. For them, the UK is essentially an 'English' state. Paradoxically, Northern Ireland is often referred to by Irish nationalists and their allies as a 'state'; (namely, 'the Northern Ireland state'), which does not have a nation (or at least a 'legitimate' one), attached to it.

The concept of nationality as a homogeneous cultural entity is problematic when applied to Northern Ireland, although this difficulty is not without echo in Wales. Of the three, Scotland is probably the most homogeneous culturally, which is not to say that Scottish national identity is unambiguous. The Highland–

Lowland divide, for example, has deep cultural, ethnic, economic and political roots. But this is symptomatic of the general internal diversity of each of the three territories.

This chapter has three principal objectives. The first is to identify and analyse common factors shaping the governmental and political background in what Hechter (1975) terms the 'Celtic fringe' of the United Kingdom. The second is to examine the system of territorial management (Kellas, 1991a) by central government of these 'national regions' and the third is to review the recent history of and prospects for legislative devolution in Northern Ireland, Scotland and Wales. The assumption throughout is that governing the UK in the 1990s necessarily involves paying particular attention to the component parts of the state.

The Social and Political Fabric

The process of incorporation of Ireland, Scotland and Wales into the British political system is an obvious point of departure for understanding their subsequent development and administration. They all lay on the margins of the Roman conquest of Britain, were the repositories of Celtic social organisation and culture as it was driven north and west, and all suffered varying degrees of colonisation by the Anglo-Normans.

Hechter's 'internal colonial' model (1975) of the building of the British state is one of the few attempts to provide a common explanatory framework for this process. In Hechter's view, the countries of the 'Celtic fringe' were brought into the United Kingdom as 'internal colonies', and exploited subsequently for the benefit of the English 'core'. While his neo-Marxist arguments are well-made, his account of the incorporation of Scotland and Wales in particular are significantly at variance with events according to other scholars (Bulpitt, 1983; Evans, 1991). Neither Smout's (1972) nor Mackie's (1978) authoritative accounts of the background or actuality of the Union of Scotland and England support Hechter's thesis, and even Adamson's (1991) Marxist interpretation of class and nation in Wales specifically refutes Hechter's economic arguments. As Evans suggests, Ireland provides the best (but by no means perfect) 'fit' with Hechter's interpretation. Northern Ireland is still a British colony in many people's view.

In the context of what is now Northern Ireland, the situation was substantially, and perhaps tragically, complicated by the importation of Scots Presbyterian settlers into the north at the beginning of the seventeenth century, to act as an anchor to the renewed English occupation of the whole island. This created a quite distinct cultural and religious tradition alongside the indigenous community in the north, wedded to some form of British rather than Irish identity and allegiance. Thus, national identities abound among the population of Northern Ireland (Whyte, 1990), rather than exist in a duality as they do in Wales and Scotland.

In institutional terms, Scotland had a well-developed state tradition stretching back to the eleventh century (similar to England), although continuity was punctured over the succeeding centuries by inter-clan wars and invasion. The inability to decide the issue on the field of battle is one key to the voluntary nature of the agreement to unite England and Scotland politically, and is arguably quite unlike the wholesale incorporation of Wales and Ireland into the English/British state system. The Act of Union abolished the two separate parliaments of England and Scotland, creating a successor 'Imperial' parliament at Westminster. The nature of the deal struck between the contracting parties has been fiercely debated ever since. As the Union guaranteed the retention of the separate legal, religious and educational systems in Scotland, it is not paradoxical that the institutional base of Scottish nationality is also the bedrock of the system of territorial management of Scotland.

The developed administrative framework present in Northern Ireland stems from the partition of the island in 1920. Although the 1920 Government of Ireland Act gave self-government to Northern Ireland, it was under circumstances which separated Irish nationalists in the north from participation in an all-Ireland polity while simultaneously putting them under the domination of the majority Unionist forces. Thus, ownership of the institutions created by the 1920 Act has never been shared by both sides of the community.

The institutional base of Welsh nationality is much weaker historically, as what remained of it was wiped out in the sixteenth century. Welsh nationality has existed essentially as a cultural/linguistic phenomenon until recently. As Thomas (1991) observes, this has changed quite rapidly since the advent of the Welsh Office in 1964. From the nationalist perspective, central government is acting as its own grave-digger by creating 'Welsh' institutions.

Distinctive patterns of religious belief have played a major role in cementing national identities and influencing politics and administration in all three territories. Wales is least different from England as there is neither a separate established Welsh church nor a large Catholic minority. The Church of England used to be the established church in Wales (until 1920) and the Church in Wales as it is now called encompassed 49 per cent of the electorate in 1979 (Balsom *et al.*, 1982, p. 12).

This is where the similarity ends. The next major denominational grouping is Nonconformist ('chapel') Protestantism, which tends to be strongest in the remoter areas, and takes in about 35 per cent of the Welsh population. Chapel Nonconformism acted as a bulwark for the Welsh language over many generations, and the decline of this tradition in the twentieth century was coterminous with the decline of the Welsh language itself. As Wales is now predominantly (although by no means exclusively) secular, the preservation of Welsh can no longer depend on this connection alone.

At the other end of the continuum is Northern Ireland, with its extremely high level of religious affiliation, and a uniquely virulent confessional divide between Catholic minority (over 40 per cent of the population), and Protestant majority. The majority itself is divided between Presbyterians, Church of Ireland and an array of fundamentalist sects, the largest of which is the Methodist church (Whyte, 1990). Unlike in other parts of the UK, religion plays a predominant role in determining both political affiliation and national identity. In general, Roman Catholics support Irish nationalist parties and identify themselves as Irish, while Protestants support Unionist parties and identify themselves as British, Ulster or both.

Scottish religiosity is neither Welsh fish nor Northern Irish fowl. On the one hand, it most closely resembles Northern Ireland in so far as there is both a large Catholic minority (especially in the west), and a non-Anglican Protestant majority. Indeed, Scotland is unique among the three areas in having an established church (the Church of Scotland), preserved in perpetuity by the Act of Union. Thus, the Catholic minority is excluded from a key totem of national identity while Protestants are included, and Brand

(1978) has found some evidence of an 'Orange' vote for the SNP which may reflect this.

Scotland is a relatively secular society where religion has a low influence on political behaviour, although there are some exceptions. As in some of the Welsh rural counties, Sunday observance is still a major local issue in the Hebrides, where the influence of Protestant fundamentalism and the Gaelic language is strongest. Protestant sectarian parties enjoyed limited success in Glasgow until the 1930s, and the Orange Order is still active. On the other side, there is plenty of evidence showing well above average support for the Labour Party among Catholics in Scotland, reflecting traditional Catholic aversion to both the Conservative Party and to political separatism, which in their different ways are perceived as threats to privileges won (e.g. in the field of education). However, the Labour–Catholic coalition may be breaking down as Labour becomes increasingly secular, and is losing its ability locally to influence the pattern of state support for schools.

Language has also played a part in shaping the political destiny of the British periphery. The common ground is the outlawing and discouragement of the Celtic languages by Westminster over the centuries. However, it is not an issue which affects all three areas equally, as English has been the language of the dominant communities in Scotland and Northern Ireland for many generations. The situation is entirely different in Wales, where the minority language was once a majority language and clung on with some vigour. Here, the demand for language rights in schools, at work and in public places has been coterminous with the nationalist movement itself. In this sense, Welsh nationalism shares a common root with Quebec, Flemish, Basque and Catalan nationalisms. The Welsh language is no longer the sole basis of Welsh identity, as Welsh identifiers are now also found among English speakers (Balsom *et al.*, 1982). On the other hand, the nationalist movement in Wales preoccupied itself with the language issue for decades, and still has difficulty in appealing to English speakers. The contemporary significance of the Welsh language may be more in helping to create separate Welsh institutions in government and society.

As elsewhere economic conditions have a critical bearing on both political behaviour and public policy. The agricultural sector is relatively more important in all three areas compared with the UK as a whole. There are similar patterns of farming, with settled lowland agriculture common to parts of Scotland and much of Northern Ireland, and the cultivation of marginal hill areas common to the Scottish Highlands and large parts of rural Wales. Given the generally lower level of agricultural incomes, this is one factor depressing average earnings and per capita GDP compared with the UK as a whole.

This profile is reinforced by problems within the industrial sector. The densely populated areas of all three territories have a legacy of heavy traditional industry based on coal, and iron and steel producing and using. While this made Clydeside, Belfast and industrial South Wales areas of relative prosperity in the nine-teenth century, it left them with outdated economic structures. This is reflected in the prevailing levels of unemployment, which in themselves have the biggest impact on per capita GDP. As can be seen from Table 9.1, despite great regional differences within, England generally outperforms the other three parts of the UK, although most recent figures show some convergence with Scotland and Wales. Indeed, in 1992, the unemployment rate in Scotland dipped below that in England for the first time since 1945.

As Table 9.2 shows, all three areas show similarities of below UK-average earnings and GDP, and above average levels of public expenditure (in this case, measured by identifiable social benefits payable in cash). On the other hand, the figures for England show above average earnings and GDP, and below average public expenditure per head.

Over the long term, the biggest change in fortunes has occurred in Northern Ireland. It is the poorest UK region with the highest

TABLE 9.1   *Unemployment Rates, 1981–91 (% of workforce)*

	1981	1983	1985	1987	1989	1991
UK	8.1	10.5	10.9	10.0	6.3	8.1
England	7.7	10.0	10.4	9.4	5.6	8.4
Wales	10.4	12.9	13.6	12.0	7.3	8.7
Scotland	9.9	12.3	12.9	13.0	9.3	8.7
N. Ireland	12.7	15.5	15.9	17.0	14.6	13.7

Source: Employment Department.

TABLE 9.2   *Average Earnings, GDP and Public Spending Per Capita*

	Male Average Earnings (£s p.w.)	GDP Per Capita (% UK total)				Public Spending (£s on benefits p.a.)
	1991	1981	1986	1989	1990	1989–90
England	322.8	102.0	102.0	102.4	102.5	693.7
Wales	280.1	83.8	83.7	85.4	84.9	745.9
Scotland	299.5	96.7	95.6	92.7	92.6	743.6
N. Ireland	272.4	78.7	79.6	76.4	75.4	801.3

Sources: Department of Employment, Central Statistical Office, Department of Economic Development Northern Ireland, Department of Social Security, Department of Social Security Northern Ireland.

per capita public expenditure, the highest rate of unemployment and the lowest average earnings. These crude figures do, however, mask difference in relative purchasing power and hide inter-communal differences in economic well-being. Whyte concludes that there is a substantial deficit on the Catholic side, although 'the fit between social class and religion is very far from perfect' (Whyte, 1990, p. 65).

In terms of political behaviour, the economic indicators might be expected to have a mixed effect. In the UK generally, rurality tends to favour the Conservative Party, while urban areas afflicted by high unemployment and declining heavy industry tend to favour the Labour Party. These patterns are also affected by housing tenure, with greater levels of owner occupation being associated with increased support for right-of-centre parties. Scotland stands out as having the lowest rate of owner occupation in the UK (51 per cent in 1990), with both Wales (72 per cent) and Northern Ireland (66 per cent) close to the UK average (67 per cent) (HMSO 1992). Taking these factors into account, above average levels of Labour voting with pockets of Conservative voting in the rural heartlands might be expected.

Table 9.3 shows deviations from the UK pattern with well below average support for the Conservative Party, well above average support for Labour (especially in Wales), 'third' party support shared between the Liberal Democrats and the nationalist parties and virtually no support for any UK party in Northern Ireland.

TABLE 9.3   *Party Support in England, Wales, Scotland and Northern Ireland, 1987 and 1992 General Elections (% vote)*

	1987				1992			
	E	*W*	*S*	*NI*	*E*	*W*	*S*	*NI*
Conservative.	46.3	29.6	24.1	–	45.5	28.6	25.7	5.7
Labour	29.5	45.1	42.4	–	33.9	49.5	39.0	–
Liberal/SDP/								
Liberal Democrat	23.8	17.9	19.2	–	19.2	12.4	13.1	–
SNP/SDLP	–	7.3	14.0	32.3	–	8.8	21.5	34.3
Plaid Cymru								
Official Unionist/								
Democratic Unionist	–	–	–	54.0	–	–	–	50.4

Sources: *The Economist*, 20 June 1987 and 18 April 1992; *The Times*, 13 June 1987.

According to Hechter, the Conservative Party has traditionally represented the 'core' ethnic group (i.e. the English), and has always done less well in the Celtic fringes, with voters supporting a variety of other parties, not necessarily nationalist ones. While the historical evidence is not conclusive on this (Scotland, for example, recorded a vote of 50.1 per cent for the Conservative Party at the 1955 general election), recent general election results lend support to the argument that the Conservative Party does poorly in the periphery. Whether this is because the Conservative Party is either 'English' or perceived to be English, is a different matter.

The Northern Irish case is exceptional because historically, Ulster Unionism was closely allied to the Conservative Party, always seen as the best guarantor of the Union. Thus, until 1992, the Conservative Party did not contest elections in Northern Ireland. Since the onset of 'the troubles' in 1968 and the imposition of direct rule since 1972, Unionists have found Conservative governments less than 100 per cent reliably 'British' from their point of view. Thus, Conservative governments no longer enjoy unconditional Unionist support as they did up until the 1970s. However, it is doubtful whether the Ulster Unionism of old was ever the same as British Conservatism, a fact exemplified by the split in the Unionist camp between the Official Unionists (OUP), and the more populist Democratic Unionist Party (DUP) in the early 1970s. Working-class Protestant voters tend to support the DUP, and the DUP takes the most uncompromising line on the Union. On the other side, the Catholic-based parties (the SDLP and Sinn Fein) fit the anti-Conservative vote model quite well. Opposed fundamentally to the Union, and invariably siding with the Labour Party in the House of Commons, the SDLP could have no other designation than 'anti-Conservative'. Sinn Fein's MPs have refused even to take their seats in the Commons.

It is doubtful whether Hechter's theory of anti-Conservative voting applies in Wales. After all, the 1979 devolution package offered by the Labour government was overwhelmingly rejected there. The low Conservative vote is principally accounted for by a lack of support in the rural areas. This was traditionally correlated with high levels of religious nonconformism which has been associated with Labour voting. Thus, Labour not only regularly won over 50 per cent of the votes in South Wales, but also picked up a significant number of rural seats. However, the influence of chapel on votes has declined, and the outcome of elections in rural constituencies has become less predictable as party competition has intensified. This enabled the Conservatives to do much better with only a slightly larger share of the vote in both 1979 and 1983, but to slip from fourteen to only eight Welsh seats in 1987 with a marginally reduced vote (down from 31.0 per cent in 1983 to 29.5 per cent in 1987).

In terms of third party support, the Liberal Democrat and Plaid Cymru vote together is not significantly different from the Liberal vote in England. However, as it is geographically concentrated in the sparsely populated rural fringes which are also evenly balanced politically, it produces more seats for these parties pro rata. The strongest support for the nationalists is concentrated in the Welsh-speaking areas, and it remains difficult for Plaid Cymru to break into urban politics. So, while it has not been able to achieve the levels of support enjoyed by the Scottish National Party (SNP), Plaid Cymru currently holds more seats (four) than the SNP (three).

Scotland is a more questionable case. Scots show a strong sense of Scottish identity, with the strongest identifiers being more likely to vote SNP or Labour. It is significant that the nationalist vote has not dipped below 12 per cent at any general election since 1970, and the issue profiles of SNP and Labour voters grow ever closer. The social profile of the SNP vote is showing some change, although its broad base is still closer to the Scottish Liberal Democrats. Thus, the SNP has not yet made a breakthrough in the heavily populated central belt, with its support remaining highest in rural and semi-rural areas in the east and north. On the other hand, the nationalist vote grew fastest in the industrial west of Scotland between 1987 and 1992. With the Conservative vote showing a spectacular decline since the 1960s, and not rising above 30 per cent since 1979, the Scottish electorate is evidently in a state of transition.

Since the mid-1980s, the Scottish and Welsh nationalist parties have also proclaimed themselves as socialist, a development not unrelated to the high Labour vote in both countries. They take slightly different positions on the self-government issue, with the SNP adopting the more uncompromising stance (i.e. 'Independence-nothing else'). The UK-wide parties (Conservative, Labour and Liberal Democrat) have separate Scottish and Welsh organisations with varying degrees of autonomy from, and different priorities to, their UK counterparts. In their different ways, the regional arms of the major parties all seek to exploit nationalist sentiment, incorporating Scotland and Wales into their titles and issuing separate Scottish and Welsh manifestos. In Scotland, for example, the Labour Party has taken on an increasingly nationalist hue since 1979, and has gained a greater measure of autonomy from the party nationally (Geekie and Levy, 1989).

The final aspect of the political fabric deserving attention is the extent to which regionally-based interest group activity is present. There are some very obvious and successful territorially-based vested interests, such as the legal and educational professions in Scotland and Northern Ireland, and language groups in Wales, which have a high local profile, are narrow in focus and are well-organised. The aim of such sector-specific groups is simply to defend and promote the degree of local autonomy and to resist assimilationist tendencies.

The role of trade union and business lobbies is more difficult to assess, as they have broad purpose which often go well beyond territorial boundaries. Both the unions and industry have regional organisations in all three areas (the Scottish and Welsh TUCs, the Northern Ireland Committee of the Irish Confederation of Trade Unions, and the Scottish, Welsh and Northern Irish councils of the Confederation of British Industry), which sometimes have common interests – for example, in seeking more government funds for

economic development. In so doing, the enter into a broad alliance with locally-based public agencies, politicians, the local
media, and churches, to form territorial lobbies. On the other
hand, much of their activity concerns economic issues which have
nothing to do with territoriality (for example, labour market regulation). On other territorial issues – most significantly, the constitutional debate in Scotland and Wales – employers' organisations
and trade unions have lined up on opposite sides.

Territorial Management by Central Government

Within the central administrative machinery of the British state are
three almost self-contained units which defy the usual principles of
unitary government. The Northern Ireland Office (NIO), the
Scottish Office (SO) and the Welsh Office (WO) are unique in their
genuine multi-functionality based on definable territorial units. At
the political level, the three Secretaries of State and their ministerial 'teams' are similarly unique. They are often depicted as mini-
governments headed by a prime ministerial or governor-general
figure (depending on your view of the role of the Secretary of
State), with their own mini-'parliaments' in the House of Commons
in the form of the territorial committees ('grand' and select). The
territorial management of Scotland, Wales and Northern Ireland
within central government has a well-defined structure therefore.

Rhodes (1988) provides a useful summary of the functions of
the three ministries based on UK departmental jurisdictions.
Using this starting point, we can identify the degree of involvement of the territorial ministries by UK Cabinet ministerial jurisdiction. Taking into account recent changes in ministerial
portfolios – the addition of Heritage, the splitting of Health from
Social Security, the combining of Trade and Industry and the
deletion of Energy as a separate department (now part of
Industry) – we get the breakdown shown in Table 9.4.

The level of involvement does not necessarily imply a commen-
surate level of control or influence over policy. Britain is a unitary
state. In most cases, the territorial ministries are administering nationally determined policies, often using elected local authorities
as their agents. Many scholars have nevertheless identified territorially-based 'policy networks' which have made an impact in

TABLE 9.4 *Functional Involvement of the Territorial Ministries*

UK Jurisdiction	Territorial Ministry Role?		
	Scotland	*Wales*	*Northern Ireland*
Agriculture	Most	Some	Most
Civil Service	None	None	Most
Defence	None	None	None
Education and Science	Most	Most	Most
Employment	Some	Some	Some
Environment	Most	Most	Most
Foreign and Commonwealth	None	None	None
Health	Most	Most	Most
Heritage	Most	Most	Most
Home Office	Most	None	Some
Industry	Most	Most	Most
Law Officers	Most	None	Most
Social Security	None	None	Some
Transport	Some	Some	Most
Treasury	None	None	Some

Source: Rhodes, 1988, p. 144.

policy areas such as economic development. This allowed, for example, a greater degree of state interventionism during the Thatcher years than was possible in England.

The current structure shows some significant variations, with the WO being the least developed. Unlike Scotland and Northern Ireland, separate legislation is not normally required for policies affecting Wales. The WO has the fewest internal units, most of which are designated as divisions and groups rather than separate departments (there are three of these – Industry, Agriculture and Education), essentially involved in administering policies which apply equally in England.

There are significant exceptions to this reactive model, particularly in the fields of industrial development and cultural affairs and some aspects of education. There are some 250 free-standing government-sponsored agencies outside the formal confines of the WO, such as the Welsh Development Agency (WDA) and a host of arts/heritage bodies. This has not always resulted in good coordination according to the House of Commons Committee on Welsh affairs.

At the other extreme is the NIO, which sits atop a separate Northern Ireland Civil Service (NICS), and six major Northern Ireland Departments (NIDs) – Agriculture, Economic Development, Education, Environment, Health and Social Services, and Finance and Personnel. It is much more like a separate governmental machine, which indeed it was until 1972. Each department has a complex structure, with Agriculture for example having no less than 36 divisions. Compared to the WO, the NIO has more responsibilities, including social security and social security appeals, the police, the courts and the administration of justice generally, local taxation, recruitment into the NICS and housing via the Northern Ireland Housing Executive (NIHE). In contrast to the WO, it is often claimed that the NICS is very well coordinated despite its departmental structure (Connolly, 1990).

The SO is the largest territorial ministry, but structurally represents the intermediate case in the system. Thus, while the SO operates via five large, well-defined departments (Agriculture and Fisheries, Education, Environment, Home and Health, Industry), these departments are integral to the SO. There is no separate Scottish civil service. The SO departments cover much the same ground as the NIDs (including housing via Scottish Homes), with the exception of social security. On the other hand, in common with Wales, there is a range of government-sponsored agencies outside the formal departmental structure of the SO dealing with economic development – Scottish Enterprise (formerly the Scottish Development Agency) and Highland Enterprise (formerly the Highlands and Islands Development Board) – and heritage/environment/culture (e.g. Historic Scotland, Scottish Natural Heritage, the National Galleries of Scotland and the Scottish Arts Council).

This system has not developed in a planned and coordinated way but there are some common explanations underlying its growth. The first of these is based on the interface between territorial peculiarity and administration, and argues that the system of territorial management is a response to the special needs and problems experienced in these areas. In the second model, the growth of territorial administration is viewed as one consequence of the expansion of the state generally. It is argued that organisational and functional imperatives peculiar to services such as education, health and housing have resulted in differing degrees of administrative decentralisation.

A third explanation is that the territorial departments and the ministerial posts attached to them have been created and/or expanded as a response to nationalism or national sentiment, while a final and related argument is based around the issue of accountable and responsible government. Territorial ministries, ministers and parliamentary committees bring government closer to the citizen and elected representatives. In the absence of elected national/regional legislatures, these arrangements guarantee a degree of transparency between the government and the governed. Thus, the accountability argument can equally be advanced by supporters of devolved assembly government such as J. P. MacKintosh (1968), and indeed were (and still are) made by the supporters of the Stormont regime in Northern Ireland.

The Northern Ireland Office

Of the three territorial ministries, the NIO is the most recent and most unusual. Created in 1972 following the suspension of the Stormont government, it has been grafted onto a preexisting administrative structure. With the imposition of direct rule, the NIO and the Secretary of State for Northern Ireland took over all responsibility for the operation of the NIDs and the NICS from the control of the elected executive at Stormont.

Certainly a product of special territorial circumstances, the NIO was also a perverse creation of national sentiment, or rather the clash of two opposing national sentiments. It would be fanciful in the extreme to imagine that the establishment of the NIO produced any extra votes for its creators. It is debatable whether it has increased accountability either, even for the minority community opposed to the former Stormont regime. Neither the Secretary of State for Northern Ireland nor any of his ministerial team have ever represented Ulster constituencies, and the NIO itself was initially dominated by the Home (UK) Civil Service. As Connolly (1990) remarks, this did not always produce harmony and understanding between the NIO and the NIDs in the early days. However, the impracticality of integrating either the NIDs or Northern Ireland's special problems into Whitehall departments made the NIO an inevitability once it had been decided to suspend Stormont. The continuing lack of consensus about an alternative to direct rule in Northern Ireland makes its continuance equally inevitable.

In March 1994, the government announced its intention to enhance the accountability of the NIO by establishing a Commons Select committee on Northern Ireland. This was widely perceived as partial compensation to the Unionists in the wake of the Downing Street declaration (see below).

The Welsh Office

The Welsh Office and the post of Welsh Secretary were created in 1964 after lengthy if sporadic agitation. Unlike Northern Ireland, their establishment can be directly linked to the pursuit of partisan advantage (for Labour). The growth of the underlying administrative machinery, however, was characterised by functionally-driven incremetalism over the course of this century. Between 1907 and 1919 separate Welsh departments in the fields of education, insurance, health and agriculture were created, while a Welsh Office in the Ministry of Housing and Local Government, the post of Minister for Welsh Affairs as part of the Home Secretary's brief (1951), the advisory Council for Wales and enlarged responsibilities for the Welsh Board of Health were added.

As in Northern Ireland, the accountability focus is ambiguous. Since 1964, Wales has always returned a Labour majority, but more often than not, the Secretary of State has been a minister in a Conservative government. Moreover, while it has been the practice for Labour Secretaries of State to represent Welsh constituencies, this has only happened once during periods of Conservative government (Nicholas Edwards (Pembroke), 1979–87). The Select Committee on Welsh Affairs was established in the wake of the 1979 referendum result, and charged with the specific task of improving accountability. Barry-Jones and Wilford's (1986) study suggests that the anti-devolution near-consensus of the committee when first established enabled it to pursue this role and to exercise an influence over policy. On the other hand, despite the committee's early criticisms, the WDA was still plagued by serious managerial and financial problems at the end of 1992. The experience of fourteen years of one-party rule and its associated system of patronage has not enhanced the image of accountable government in Wales, and there is now a pro- rather than anti-devolution consensus on the Welsh Select Committee.

The Scottish Office

Created in 1885, the SO is the most venerable of the three territorial ministries. The post of Secretary of State has an even longer provenance, dating from the Act of Union itself. The SO's origins go back to the middle part of the nineteenth century, and according to Mackintosh (1968), its growth was directly related to functional imperatives. On the other hand, Midwinter *et al.* (1991) argue that the primary impulse came from dissatisfaction within Scotland at the way the country was being governed by distant Westminster and Whitehall ministries. As Kellas (1989) suggests, the truth probably lies somewhere in the middle.

At the political level, the Scottish Office represents another variation. It has a ministerial team of five, and so long as the Secretary of State has been chosen from the House of Commons, he has always represented a Scottish constituency, lending weight to the argument that the SO represents 'Scottish' interests. On the other hand, critics would say that the main problem with this arrangement is the persistent Labour majority in Scotland and successive Conservative Secretaries of State since 1979. Where the majority of MPs represent opposition parties which are wholeheartedly committed to either devolution or independence, the government's tenuous parliamentary position in Scotland (currently eleven out of 72 MPs) is a stick with which it is constantly beaten by the opposition in its quest for self-government.

The latter also has a major effect on the functioning of the Scottish committee system. As the biggest of the territorial ministries, the SO is arguably in the greatest need of parliamentary oversight. There is a well-established committee structure composed of the Scottish Grand Committee, the Scottish Standing Committees and a Select Committee on Scottish Affairs (the first two are essentially legislative, the latter is investigative), which should carry this out. However, in the context of the government's poor representation in Scotland, it has proved difficult to run this system without coopting Conservative MPs representing English constituencies, a practice to which some opposition MPs have become increasingly hostile.

The Select Committee on Scottish Affairs established in 1968 has had a chequered history. It failed to meet at all during either the 1974–9 or 1987–92 Parliaments, in the first instance as a result of the preoccupation of the government's legislative programme with devolution itself, and in the second because of the depletion in the number of Scottish Conservative MPs from 21 to ten at the 1987 general election. This made it difficult for the government to staff the SO ministerial team of five and leave a suitable number to sit on the Select Committee. As for the Scottish Grand Committee, it can only function so long as no votes are taken, thus saving the government from the embarrassment of defeat. The nationalist solution to this problem is for all the opposition MPs to withdraw from Westminster completely, as the Irish Home Rulers did in the 1880s. Naturally, this tactic did not find favour within the Labour party owing to the large Scottish contingent within the ranks of the PLP and the shadow Cabinet, including the late leader John Smith himself.

Finance

The arrangements for the financing of the territorial ministries are at the heart of the system. According to Likierman (1988) and Parry (1991), public expenditure per head in Scotland and Wales is about 20 per cent and 10 per cent respectively above the UK average, while the figure for Northern Ireland is in excess of 40 per cent above the average. These variations result from a combination of differential needs and demographic and employment patterns which feed into the make-up of the public expenditure programme. The recent figures for Northern Ireland, for example, can be largely explained by the much higher levels of unemployment there, the cost of the security forces in the province and the rectification of previous underfunding of services.

Added to these baseline considerations in the cases of Scotland and Wales is the effect of the so-called Barnett formula for allocating extra funds. The formula is based on the relative population shares of Scotland and Wales compared with the total for England as of 1978. Covering about 95 per cent of the funds under SO and WO control, this stipulates that Scotland should receive 10/85ths and Wales 5/85ths of any change in funding of a comparable programme affecting England. Given that these proportions now exceed the actual population shares of Scotland and Wales compared with the English total, there is an in-built tendency for SO and WO funding to maintain itself above the UK average in these spending areas. However, Parry notes that there has been a substantial differential in growth, with the SO not faring as well as the WO and NIO in the latter part of the 1980s (Parry, 1991, p. 181). In the government's autumn 1992 financial statement, the formula was readjusted to take account of the relative population decline, causing a loss to the SO of some £12 million in the first year of operation.

The degree of actual discretion open to the SO and WO in allocating funds is a matter of debate. As most of the funds (Likierman estimates about 90 per cent in the case of Scotland) go directly to local authorities and health boards for the provision of services, it can be argued that discretion is limited. But, the SO and WO do have discretion over the not inconsiderable remaining chunks, and can alter the formulae allocating funds to local authorities, so making changes to the flow of funds over a period of time (Midwinter, 1984). Moreover, the area of discretion is likely to increase, as the powers of local authorities are curtailed and taken over by the territorial ministries and their quangos.

The Northern Ireland situation is much more complex, as the NIDs carry out a public expenditure survey similar to the one conducted by the Whitehall departments. The result is submitted to the NI Department of Finance and Personnel (i.e. the NI 'Treasury'), which then negotiates with the UK Treasury. While the UK Treasury uses a population formula to calculate two-thirds of the total allocation for the NIDs (the remaining third is for social security payments which are demand-driven), the Secretary of State has a great deal of discretion about which NID gets what. Moreover, unlike the SO or the WO allocations, the NI allocation is kept in a separate Consolidated Fund account, so keeping it apart from the main UK accounts.

Policy

The influence of the territorial ministries on policy-making varies greatly. According to Rhodes (1988), they often appear in support of UK functional departments, while at the same time injecting a territorial perspective and sometimes establishing policy autonomy. With reference to the Scottish case, Parry (1981) distinguishes between three groups of subject areas: those which relate to UK departments exclusively (such as defence, foreign affairs and economic policy), those relating to the SO more or less exclusively (such as health, social work and education), and those where responsibility is shared (for example, industry, agriculture). Midwinter *et al.* (1991) use this as a baseline to establish the degree of policy autonomy possessed by the SO in each functional area, it being high in areas of exclusive SO control and low to non-existent in areas of exclusive UK department control. There is no reason why this analytical framework could not also be applied to the NIO and the WO.

Policy autonomy is relative however, and functional responsibility is not always a good guide to the amount of autonomy (for example, social security benefit levels prevailing in Northern Ireland). Similarly, the effect of policy 'spillover' from England in policy areas where there is a need for consistency across the UK to prevent overly large economic distortions or gross inequalities in opportunity has been noted by many authors. Thus, while education and health policies may vary considerably in detail, they must provide a certain basic minimum to satisfy such criteria. Variation can be considerable, as in the case of Scottish education, where the pattern of teacher training, secondary schooling and higher education are quite distinctive in comparison with England.

The policy autonomy model is also useful in focusing on implementation. In pursuing either their own or those national (UK) goals partly under their jurisdiction, the territorial ministries have great power to influence through this process which can lead to distinct patterns of policy development. This is perhaps particularly well-demonstrated in the area of economic restructuring. Although the achievements directly attributable to territorial agencies are fiercely debated (see the discussions in Day and Rees, 1991, for example), there is at least quite a lot to argue about. The role of the WDA and the old SDA both before and during the Thatcher years have been held up as successful examples of regional economic intervention, not least by some of the disadvantaged English regions which lack such agencies. To many, the greater 'dirigisme' of Scottish and Welsh sub-government enabled these regions to avoid the worst excesses of Thatcherite economic policies. Indeed, the government has confirmed this recently: the White Paper *Scotland in the Union* (1993) details the success of the 'Locate in Scotland' agency in attracting inward investment into Scotland during the 1980s.

Legislative Devolution?

It is impossible to understand the debates about devolved government in the 1990s without placing this in a slightly broader context.

From the time of the Irish 'home rule' controversy in the 1880s, there have been few periods when the constitutional status of the periphery has not been an issue. It is now most obviously signified by the presence in the House of Commons of MPs representing territorially-based parties and, more depressingly, by the continuing campaign of violence by terrorist organisations in Northern Ireland.

'Devolution' is but one facet of that debate. Sitting somewhere between the constitutional status quo and outright independent statehood, it involves setting up legislative assemblies which would have control over an unspecified range of subjects in the territories concerned without threatening the overall integrity of the UK.

The Stormont Example

While there have been repeated attempts to secure some kind of home rule for Scotland (and for Wales to a much lesser extent) since the 1880s, the only experience in the UK of such an arrangement is the now suspended Stormont Parliament and executive in Northern Ireland, operative between 1921 and 1972. The Government of Ireland Act allowed Stormont to legislate for 'the order and good government' of the province, a phrase which cropped up in the British North America Act of 1867 establishing the Canadian confederation, and related in particular to the powers of the federal government.

Notwithstanding the formal legal position embodied in the Act, Bogdanor (1979) argues that the relationship between Stormont and Westminster was an essentially federal one. Thus, Westminster did not intervene in matters falling under Stormont's legislative jurisdiction, nor did it exercise its rights to invoke constitutional safeguards to protect the minority community. Under the Ireland Act of 1949, the Stormont Parliament gained the sole right to decide whether Northern Ireland should continue to be part of the UK, and within the Stormont government, it was generally perceived that a federal relationship prevailed between London and Belfast.

As both Bogdanor and Connolly (1990) point out, however, none of this applied in the area of public finance as Stormont never had the resources to sustain itself, and was subsidised by the Treasury on a parity (with the rest of the UK) principle. Thus, in those policy areas which were expenditure-driven, Stormont was left with limited discretion. Nevertheless, by the time direct rule was introduced in 1972, Stormont had managed to build up a distinctive array of policies and practices, not a few of which were directly responsible for 'the troubles' and Stormont's own suspension in 1972, and then abolition in 1973.

Scotland and Wales

Thus, whatever the intention of the 1920 Act, the reality turned out quite differently, especially with regard to the safeguarding of minority rights and finance. It may be argued that the root of the problem lay in Westminster's inaction and lack of interest, and that the imposition of direct rule ultimately proved that the relationship between London and Belfast was never federal. At all events, present-day supporters of devolution for Scotland and Wales rarely use the Stormont example to support their case. The Royal Commission on the Constitution report (the Kilbrandon Report) published in 1973, which served as the basis for the abortive devolution proposals of the 1974–9 Labour Government, drew extensively on the Northern Ireland experience however. It argued that many of the provisions of the 1920 Act were 'equally applicable' in other parts of the UK and that the Commission's own scheme for legislative devolution for Scotland and Wales had 'much in common' with the (by then suspended) Northern Ireland system. Thus, although Stormont itself had gone, its institutional image lived on in the Kilbrandon proposals.

Although there was dissent within the Commission, the majority report proposed proportionally-elected legislative assemblies for Scotland and Wales with executive powers over the range of functions currently exercised by the Scottish and Welsh Offices. While Westminster would retain the ultimate right to legislate on all matters, it would not do so on transferred matters without the consent of the assemblies (as had been the convention in the Stormont case). As for expenditure, an Exchequer Board independent of both Westminster and the assemblies themselves would decide on total funding after taking into account the assemblies' requests and the views of the UK Treasury. The assemblies would then be at liberty to allocate these funds in accordance with their priorities. At the wider UK level, the consequences would be a reduction in the number of Scottish and Welsh constituencies at Westminster, and the abolition of the post of Secretary of State and his ministerial team.

Given their current orientations, it is interesting to see how the major parties lined up on the issue at that time. In evidence submitted to the Commission, both the Scottish Council of the Labour Party and the Scottish Trades Union Congress (STUC) opposed a legislative Assembly for Scotland, expressing themselves well satisfied with the status quo. The Conservatives, on the other hand, had expressed support for a limited form of devolution. This situation was to change rapidly after the result of the February 1974 general election, when the SNP gained a total of seven seats (increased to eleven at the October election). With some arm-twisting from London, the Labour Party in Scotland reversed its position in July 1974, so bringing it into line with the Labour government's commitment to devolution (and indeed the views expressed by the Welsh Council of the Labour Party).

Although the first government White Paper on devolution (*Democracy and Devolution: Proposals for Scotland and Wales*, Cmnd 5732) was overtaken by the October 1974 general election, it embodied the essence of the government's approach – namely, a watered-down version of the Kilbrandon Report. The second White Paper (*Our Changing Democracy: Devolution to Scotland and Wales*, Cmnd 6348) published in November 1975 proposed the creation of elected assemblies for both Scotland and Wales with powers over SO and WO functions and financed by a block grant from Westminster. However, the plan retained the position of Secretary of State for Scotland in a kind of governor-general role with a linked power to veto legislation, denied the Welsh Assembly legislative powers and retained the first-past-the-post electoral system. It reasserted the integrity of the UK and the ultimate sovereignty of Westminster, and proposed the retention of all 107 Scottish and Welsh MPs at Westminster with no diminution in their current powers.

This scheme was modified between 1975 and the eventual passage of the Scotland and Wales Acts in 1978, although the basic structure and philosophy were retained. Some concessions were made to greater devolved authority (a reining-in of the Secretary of State's powers and assembly control over the newly created Scottish and Welsh Development Agencies, for example), but these did not address the problems of financing the assemblies (still no taxation powers or guaranteed sources of revenue), or the future role of Scottish MPs in formulating 'domestic' legislation for England and Wales after the establishment of a developed assembly in Edinburgh (the 'West Lothian question'). The precise allocation of functions between London and Cardiff and Edinburgh remained confused in some areas, as did the powers of the Judicial Committee of the Privy Council which was to adjudicate on laws passed by the Scottish Assembly and subsequently disputed by the Secretary of State.

The biggest change was the introduction of a clause requiring referenda to be held in Scotland and Wales after the passage of bills through Parliament. Under pressure from anti-devolutionists on the government side, this provision was further modified to require a minimum of 40 per cent of the Scottish and Welsh electorates to vote in favour for the respective schemes to go through (the so-called Cunningham amendment). The referendum set for 1 March 1979 afforded an opportunity for pro- and anti-devolutionists to put their case, but it inevitably became judgement on the government itself.

As Table 9.5 shows, the proposals were decisively defeated in Wales and only marginally accepted in Scotland; in neither case was the 40 per cent barrier broken.

The studies by Bochel *et al.* (1981) and Foulkes *et al.* (1983) confirm that the 'Yes' sides were both divided and defensive, sometimes showing little enthusiasm for their cause. The referendum result was greeted almost triumphantly by the SNP's National Council, as the party now felt unconstrained either to keep the government in office or to mouth support for a

TABLE 9.5   *Referenda on the Scotland and Wales Acts, 1 March 1979*

% of Electorate	Voting Yes	Voting No	Not Voting
Scotland	32.5	30.7	37.1
Wales	11.8	46.5	41.7

devolution package many in its ranks did not believe in. The 'No' campaigners proved to be far more effective, with the Conservative Party in particular uniting in its opposition to devolution. Thus, the government fell in a motion of no confidence at the end of March when the SNP MPs withdrew their support. With the election of a Conservative administration under Margaret Thatcher in May, devolution for Scotland and Wales was put into effective cold storage for the foreseeable future.

While the issue has suffered severe frostbite, it has not died completely in Wales and Scotland. If opinion polls are to be believed, support for independence for Scotland topped 50 per cent for the first time in 1991, although this figure fell back subsequently. In Wales, the Campaign for a Welsh Assembly has continued a low-key campaign for a developed assembly to ensure the greater accountability of the WO and in the mid-1980s, Plaid Cymru supported a plan for the creation of a 100-member elected senate (Y Senedd) with control over WO functions.

In Scotland, a determined band of acolytes in the shape of the Campaign for a Scottish Assembly (CSA) kept the issue alive, pressing their case through the Labour Party, its trade union affiliates, the STUC and any other organisation which would listen. Pointing to the consistent majority of the Scottish population (in opinion surveys at any rate) apparently in favour of more self-government, the CSA message found an increasingly ready audience in the Labour Party in Scotland, excluded from power at Westminster by dint of the collapse of the Labour vote in England, especially after 1983. Thus, Labour in Scotland united itself around increasingly strident devolution proposals, claiming simultaneously that the Conservatives had no mandate to govern in Scotland and predicting dire consequences if they should continue to do so (the 'Doomsday' scenario). By 1984, Labour's position was indistinguishable from that taken by the SNP in its pro-devolutionary phase of the mid-1970s. Fundamentally, this meant the jettisoning of Westminster sovereignty in favour of the sovereignty of the 'Scottish mandate', the rejection of the 1707 Act of Union and the advocacy of extra-parliamentary action to achieve a Scottish Assembly.

Following on from the SNP by-election victory over Labour in Glasgow Govan in November 1988, this development reached its apotheosis with the formation of the Scottish Constitutional

Convention in early 1989. Comprising all the Scottish Labour and Scottish Liberal Democrat MPs, Scottish MEPs and representatives from the local authorities, churches, trade unions and other interested organisations, it endorsed the nationalist 'Claim of Right' which 'acknowledge[d] the sovereign right of the Scottish people to determine the form of government best suited to their needs' (Scottish Constitutional Convention, 1990). Despite the self-imposed absence of the SNP, the Convention produced a scheme for Scottish devolution going way beyond the Scotland Act 1978, which would have radical implications for government of the UK as a whole (Levy, 1992). As the delivery of this scheme was essentially dependent on the election of a Labour government in the 1992 general election, it is now of limited significance except for the SNP, which can use this failed and flawed initiative to argue its case for 'Independence in Europe', and to goad the other opposition parties into withdrawal from Westminster.

The government's response was a 'taking stock' exercise (promised by the Prime Minister at the general election), which resulted in a White Paper, *Scotland in the Union*, published in March 1993. While outlining the benefits of the Union to Scotland, it also proposed a number of reforms to improve accountability and give greater Scottish control. Within Parliament the scope of the Scottish committee system will be widened and there will be more question-time opportunities for Scottish backbenchers. Citizens will be able to benefit from greater access to the Scottish Office via an enquiry line, improved local government through local government reform (already subject to fierce debate), and the extension of the 'Citizen's Charter' programme into new areas. Practical measures to relocate more civil service jobs to Scotland and Scottish control in the arts and training are also proposed. It is questionable whether this will do much to defuse public support for some form of self-government, although this remains a very low priority for most Scots. The measures have predictably been rejected by opposition parties as 'cosmetic'.

Northern Ireland: Post-Stormont

If the one-eyed man is king in the land of the blind, direct rule must surely qualify for a regal title in Northern Ireland. Since the imposition of direct rule in 1972, numerous attempts have been made to reconstruct some form of devolved government for the province. None have secured the simultaneous consent of the major constitutional parties, let alone the paramilitary organisations. As Hadfield (1992) observes, the principles the government has tried to follow have not wavered from the provisions of the Northern Ireland Constitution Act of 1973. These included the abolition of the Stormont Parliament and its replacement by a Northern Ireland Assembly elected by proportional representation, the creation of a power-sharing executive drawn from the assembly and headed by a chief executive, and a constitutional guarantee of Northern Ireland's status, subject to the consent of the electorate in a referendum. Added to this has been the attempt from the outset to create an intergovernmental structure involving Irish, British and Northern Irish representatives. Thus, while Unionists object to the idea of power-sharing with the minority and to the link with the Republic, nationalists object to the Unionist veto over the future status of Northern Ireland.

The first attempt initially succeeded in creating an Assembly and a power-sharing executive after elections held in June 1973. Considerable pressure was exerted on some Unionist politicians to join the executive, although the majority of the Unionists elected refused to participate. Talks were then held between the British and Irish governments at Sunningdale in December 1973, where it was agreed to establish an all-Ireland Council of Ireland. This proved the catalyst which united opposition to the plan in the Unionist community, and in the February 1974 UK general election, anti-Sunningdale Unionists won eleven of the twelve Northern Ireland seats. The Ulster Workers' Council strike of May 1974 finally destroyed both the Assembly and the power-sharing executive.

In May 1975, elections were held for a consultative Constitutional Convention, but the majority report proposing a virtual return to the Stormont system was rejected by the government and the nationalist Social Democratic and Labour Party (SDLP) alike. A further inconclusive attempt was made to bring the two sides together in early 1980 (the 'Atkins Conference'), so attention then switched to an intergovernmental solution bypassing the elected politicians in Northern Ireland altogether. In 1982, a new Northern Ireland Act was passed providing for an elected assembly which would gradually take back functions from Westminster ('rolling devolution'). The assembly was boycotted by nationalist and republican politicians from the start, and was wound up in 1986. Meanwhile, the New Ireland Forum (a group of nationalist politicians from the North and representatives of the main parties in the Republic) published a report in 1984 outlining possible solutions, all of which were rejected by the British government.

The only enduring innovation has been the Anglo-Irish agreement signed at Hillsborough Castle in 1985, which gave the Irish government some consultative role in the affairs of Northern Ireland via the Anglo-Irish Intergovernmental Conference, much to the chagrin of the Unionists. In 1989, the then Secretary of State, Peter Brooke, launched another initiative to get the constitutional parties talking about devolution, but these faltered in 1991. After the general election of 1992, the twentieth anniversary of direct rule and with the number of deaths related to 'the troubles' exceeding 3000, the province was seemingly no nearer to self-government than it had been in 1974.

However, in December 1993 the Anglo-Irish consultations led to a new development on a broader front. John Major and Albert Reynolds, the Irish Taoiseach, put their signatures to a document designed to bring an end to the campaigns of violence in Northern Ireland. This Downing Street declaration offered the right of participation in future talks about the constitutional future of the province to all who renounced violence and laid down their arms.

The British government stressed that it had 'no selfish strategic or economic interest in Northern Ireland', but would uphold the democratic wishes of the majority of the people in the province, whether they wished to remain part of the Union or join a united Ireland. For its part, the Irish government accepted that it would be wrong to impose a united Ireland in the absence of the freely given consent of the majority of people in Northern Ireland.

While the Democratic unionists, led by Ian Paisley, immediately denounced the declaration as a 'betrayal', the Official Unionists simply expressed cautious scepticism. The nationalist SDLP enthusiastically supported the declaration, pointing to its broad similarities with the Hume/Adams proposals (the latter had emanated from discussions between John Hume, the SDLP leader, and Gerry Adams, the President of Sinn Fein). While there was no open acceptance of the declaration by Sinn Fein and the IRA, the latter declared a 'complete cessation of military operations' from

1 September 1994, and there were renewed hopes of a lasting settlement.

On the evidence of this brief summary, legislative devolution for Northern Ireland, Scotland and Wales cannot be judged as one of the great policy successes of the recent British governments. It is one subject which is seemingly impervious to the British talent for finding a consensus.

References

Adamson, D. L. (1991) *Class, Ideology and the Nation: A Theory of Welsh Nationalism* (Cardiff: University of Wales Press).

Arthur, P. (1984) *The Government and Politics of Northern Ireland*, 2nd edn (London: Longman).

Balsom, D. (1979) *The nature and distribution of Support for Plaid Cymru* (Glasgow: Centre for the Study of Public Policy).

Balsom, D. and Burch M. (1980) *A Political and Electoral Handbook for Wales* (Farnborough: Gower).

Balsom, D. Madgwick, P. and Van Mechelen, D. (1982) *The Political Consequences of Welsh Identity* (Glasgow: Centre for the Study of Public Policy).

Barry-Jones, J. and Wilford, R. A. (1986) *Parliament and Territoriality: The Committee on Welsh Affairs 1979–83* (Cardiff: University of Wales Press).

Bew, P. and Patterson, H. (1985) *The British State and the Ulster Crisis: From Wilson to Thatcher* (London: Verso).

Bochel, J., Denver, D. and Macartney, A. (eds) (1981) *The Referendum Experience: Scotland 1979* (Aberdeen: Aberdeen University Press).

Bogdanor, V. (1979) *Devolution* (Oxford: Oxford University Press).

Brand, J. (1978) *The National Movement in Scotland* (London: Routledge).

Bruce, S. (1992) *The Red Hand: Protestant Paramilitaries in Northern Ireland* (Oxford: Oxford University Press).

Bulpitt, J. (1983) *Territory and Power in the United Kingdom: An Interpretation* (Manchester: Manchester University Press).

Cabinet Office (1992) *Civil Service Yearbook 1992* (London: HMSO).

Connolly, (1990) *Politics and Policy Making in Northern Ireland* (London: Allen).

Connolly, M. and Loughlin, S. (eds) (1990) *Public Policy in Northern Ireland: Adoption or Adaptation?* (London: Policy Research Institute).

Crick, B. (ed.) (1991) *National Identities: The Constitution of the United Kingdom* (Oxford: Basil Blackwell).

Dalyell, T. (1977) Basic *Devolution: The End of Britain?* (London: Cape).

Darby, J. (ed.) (1983) *Northern Ireland: The Background to the Conflict* (Belfast: Appletree).

Day, G. and Rees, G. (eds) (1991) *Regions, Nations and European Integration: Remaking the Celtic Periphery* (Cardiff: University of Wales Press).

Drucker, H. and Brown, G. (1980) *The Politics of Nationalism and Devolution* (London: Longman).

Evans, N. (1991) 'Internal Colonialism? Colonisation, Economic Development and Political Mobilisation in Wales, Scotland and Ireland', in Day and Rees (1991), pp. 235–64.

Flackes, W. D. (1983) *Northern Ireland: A Political Directory 1968–83* (London: Ariel/BBC).

Foulkes, D. Barry-Jones, J. and Wilford, R. A. (1983) *The Welsh Veto: The Wales Act and the Referendum* (Cardiff: University of Wales Press).

Geekie, J. and Levy, R. (1989) 'Devolution and the Tartanisation of the Labour Party', *Parliamentary Affairs*, 42(3), pp. 399–411.

HMSO (1974) *Democracy and Devolution: Proposals for Scotland and Wales*, Cmnd 5732 (London: HMSO).

HMSO (1975) *Our Changing Democracy: Devolution to Scotland and Wales*, Cmnd 6348 (Edinburgh and Cardiff: HMSO).

HMSO (1993) *Scotland in the Union: A Partnership for Good*, Cmnd 2225 (Edingburgh: HMSO).

Hadfield, B. (ed.) (1992) *Northern Ireland: Politics and Constitution* (Buckingham: Open University Press).

Hechter, M. (1975) *Internal Colonialism: The Celtic Fringe in British National Development 1536–1966* (London: Routledge).

Hughes, E. (ed.) (1991) *Culture and Politics in Northern Ireland* (Oxford: Oxford University Press).

Keating M. and Midwinter, A. (1983) *The Government of Scotland* (Edinburgh: Mainstream).

Kellas, J. (1989) *The Scottish Political System*, 4th edn (Cambridge: Cambridge University Press).

Kellas, J. (1991) 'The Scottish and Welsh Offices as Territorial Managers', *Regional Politics and Policy*, 1(1), pp. 87–100.

Kellas, J. (1991) *The Politics of Nationalism and Ethnicity* (London: Macmillan).

Kenny, A. (1986) *The Road to Hillsborough: The Shaping of the Anglo-Irish Agreement* (Oxford: Pergamon).

Levy, R. (1990) *Scottish Nationalism at the Crossroads* (Edinburgh: Scottish Academic Press).

Levy, R. (1992) 'The Scottish Constitutional Convention, Nationalism and the Union', *Government and Opposition*, 27(2), pp. 222–34.

Likierman, A. (1988) *Public Expenditure* (Harmondsworth: Penguin).

Mackie, J. D. (1978) *A History of Scotland*, 2nd edn (Harmondsworth: Penguin).

Mackintosh, J. P. (1968) *The Devolution of Power* (Harmondsworth: Penguin).

Midwinter, A. (1984) *The Politics of Local Spending* (Edingburgh: Mainstream).

Midwinter, A. Keating, M. and Mitchell, J. (1991) *Politics and Public Policy in Scotland* (London: Macmillan).

Miller, W. (1981) *The End of British Politics?* (Oxford: Clarendon).

Morgan, K. O. (1981) *Rebirth of a Nation: Wales 1880–1980* (Cardiff: University of Wales Press).

Osmond, J. (ed.) (1985) *The National Question Again: Welsh Political Identity in the 1980s* (Dyfed: Gomer).

Parry, R. (1981) 'Scotland as a Laboratory for Public Administration', Paper presented to PSA UK Politics Group Conference (Glasgow).

Parry, R. (1991) 'The Scottish Office in the 1980s', in Brown, A. and McCrone, D. (eds), *The Scottish Government Yearbook 1991* (Edinburgh: Edinburgh University Press) pp. 174–87.

Randall, P. J. (1972) 'Wales in the structure of Central Government', *Public Administration*, 50, pp. 352–72.

Rhodes, R. A. W. (1988) *Beyond Westminster and Whitehall: The Sub-central Governments of Britain* (London: Unwin Hyman).

Royal Commission on the Constitution 1969–73 (1973) *Report*, Cmnd 5460 and 5460-1 (London: HMSO).

Scottish Constitutional Convention (1990) *Towards Scotland's Parliament* (Edinburgh).

Smout, T. C. (1972) *A History of the Scottish People 1560–1830* (Glasgow: Fontana).

Thomas, D. E. (1991) 'The Constitution of Wales', in Crick (1991), pp. 57–67.

Watson, M. (ed.) (1990) *Contemporary Minority Nationalism* (London: Routledge).

Whyte, J. (1990) *Interpreting Northern Ireland* (Oxford: Oxford University Press).

10

Elected Local Government and Central-Local Relations

DAVID WILSON

Despite the fast-moving changes which have characterised contemporary local government, local authorities retain two major roles. First, they are important as instruments of democratic self-government: local authorities are the only governmental units beyond the centre that are *directly elected* by the local population and *directly accountable* (via elections) to the local electorate. Second, local authorities still remain significant providers (both directly and indirectly) of a wide range of community services.

The massive scale of local authority activity is illustrated by the fact that service expenditure by local government in 1992–93 was £70 billion, representing over a quarter of the country's total government spending of £260 billion. Kent County Council, for example, serves a population that makes it bigger than 40 of the member states of the United Nations. With a turnover in excess of £1 billion, some 50 000 employers and 1 400 service points, the authority is not only the biggest single employer in Kent, but larger than many national and international companies such as the Beecham Group, Unigate and Burmah Oil (see Kent County Council, 1992). Even a 'middle range' county, Leicestershire, budgeted to spend some £728 million in 1993–94. So, despite the pressure upon local government in the early 1990s it remains big business. Indeed, a document published in August 1992 by the Department of the Environment outlining local government services in England ran to 165 pages! (See DoE, 1992.)

Notwithstanding the extent of its functions, local government, as a *direct* provider of services, is currently facing a number of threats (or challenges!), notably compulsory competitive tendering (CCT), structural reorganisation, internal management changes and sources of finance. This has prompted some commentators to speak of a 'crisis' in local government, with extinction being prophesied as fewer and fewer services are *directly* provided by elected authorities. Such calls are not new. In 1966 William Robson wrote *Local Government in Crisis* lamenting the possible demise of elected local government, and this was itself an update of earlier texts in 1926 and 1947!

An 'Enabling Context'

Service provision in contemporary local government is far from simple. From a situation fifteen years ago when most services were *directly* provided by local authorities we are entering an era when an increasing number of services are provided *indirectly* by other agencies such as private business enterprises and voluntary bodies. The *Citizen's Charter* (HMSO, 1991, p. 34) encapsulates the government's outlook:

> Local authorities have historically seen the direct provision of services to the community as one of their major tasks. However, we believe that now is the time for a new approach. The real task for local authorities lies in setting priorities, determining the standards of services which citizens should enjoy, and finding the best way to meet them.

The development of this *enabling* role for local government, in which the local authority is seen not as self-sufficient but as working through a range of other agencies to achieve its purposes, is at the heart of government thinking. To quote from the *Policy Guidance to the Local Government Commission for England* (DoE, 1992b, p. 3):

There should be no presumption that each authority should deliver all its services in-house; where it is efficient and cost-effective to do so, the Government encourages authorities to buy in services from the private and voluntary sectors.

The view of *enabling* espoused by the government has meant that UK local authorities are becoming increasingly important as organisers and contractors and less important as *direct* service-providers. But this does not mean that local authorities, as direct service providers, are dead and buried. They are not.

The government's definition of enabling, as outlined above, is particularly narrow. Comentators such as Clarke and Stewart (1992) have a very different view of enabling. It implies a liberation from present restrictions; their model sees councils taking on board responsibility for local social and economic issues and using all the means at their disposal to meet the needs of those living in the community. Local government thus becomes community government, freed from a preoccupation purely with service delivery and possessing broader powers to act in the interests of the whole community.

Enabling is a concept of 'infinite elasticity' with a wide range of possible interpretations. As Leach (1993, p. 32) notes, the discussion of enabling in the *Policy Guidance to the Local Government Commission* particulary falls down

in its failure to recognise that local authorities are not merely 'service-providing' agencies (the function to which the enabling concept is more directly applicable). They are also currently endowed with the important functions of regulation, strategic planning and promotion and advocacy. Enabling as an idea is much less applicable to each of these three functions. Its imprecision makes it fallible as a central tenet for moving local government forward in a coherent manner.' (See also Leach and Stewart, 1992.)

Service Provision

The introduction outlined the extensive service provision which still characterises local government. In very general terms in the non-metropolitan areas the top-tier authorities (county councils in England and Wales; regional councils in Scotland) provide those services which are most suitably administered on a large scale, e.g.

strategic planning and education. The second-tier authorities (district councils) provide more local services such as housing and refuse collection. In metropolitan areas the position is somewhat different in that metropolitan district councils control the major service areas: education, social services and housing. Police, fire and public transport are run by *joint boards* of councillors constituted from the metropolitan districts but *not directly elected* to these boards.

In Northern Ireland the 26 local authorities, district councils, have very few executive powers. Their powers do, however, include:

(a) Regulatory services, e.g. licensing of cinemas, dance halls, and street trading, building regulations, health inspection.
(b) Provision of services such as street cleaning, refuse collection and disposal, burial grounds and crematoria, public baths, recreation facilities and tourist amenities. (See Connolly, 1992, p. 37.)

In Northern Ireland *appointed* boards deal with major services such as personal health, education, housing, roads – these boards are in effect accountable to central government departments. Hence, local government's share of public expenditure in the region is relatively insignificant (about 2.5 per cent of total public spending in Northern Ireland).

The wide range of services provided by local authorities in England, Scotland and Wales means that classifications are fraught with difficulty – a situation exacerbated by the differential progress of contracting out services to voluntary bodies and commercial organisations. Nevertheless, Table 10.1 presents a useful starting point, based on a division into four major groups of services.

Compulsory Competitive Tendering

The introduction of compulsory competitive tendering (CCT) into local government needs to be seen as one element of the privatisation strategy of successive Conservative governments. Three pieces of legislation are particularly central:

TABLE 10.1   *Classification and Relative Scale of Local Government Services: % of Total Net Expenditure on All Local Government Services in 1990–91 in England and Wales*

Need Services %		Protective Services %		Amenity Services %		Facility Services %	
Education	48.6	Police	12.9	Highways	5.0	Libraries	1.5
Personal		Fire	2.7	Street Cleaning	1.0	Museums	
Social						and Art	
Services	12.4					Galleries	0.3
		Courts	0.8	Consumer			
				Protection	0.3	Refuse	
Housing		Probation	0.8	Refuse Disposal	0.6	Collection	1.4
Benefit	0.6			Environmental		Housing	0.8
				Health Services	1.1		
						Recreational	
				Parks and Open		Centres	1.3
				Spaces	1.7		
				Economic		Cemeteries	0.2
				Development	0.3		
				Town and			
				Country Planning	1.2		
				Other Services	2.4		
				Administration	2.1		
	61.6		17.2		15.7		5.5

Source: G. Hollis *et al.*, (1990) *Alternatives to the Community Charge*, p. 12.

(a)   The 1980 Local Government, Planning and Land Act, which introduced CCT for construction, building maintenance and highways.

(b)   The 1988 Local Government Act, which introduced CCT for building cleaning, ground maintenance, vehicle maintenance, school meals, other catering (e.g. staff canteens), refuse collection, street cleaning, plus sports and leisure management (added in December 1989).

(c)   The 1992 Local Government Act, drawing on the 1991 consultation paper *Competing for Quality*, which extended CCT to professional, financial and technical services. It also enabled the Secretary of State to add other services at a later date. By summer 1992 housing management had moved into the frame with the publication of *Competing for Quality in Housing*, and in spring 1993 the government set out a timetable for the introduction of 'white collar' CCT. As Table 10.2 shows, the first contracts are scheduled to start by October 1995 and the rest are set to be in place no later than April 1997.

TABLE 10.2   *Contract Start Dates for 'White Collar' Services*

Legal	October 1995
Construction-related	October 1995
Computing	October 1996
Finance	April 1997
Personnel	April 1997
Corporate/Administrative	April 1997

Some 75–80 per cent of first-round competitive bids were won 'in-house' by the local authorities themselves and later rounds reflected similar proportions. Indeed, the LGMB's seventh survey report (summer 1993) showed that local authorities had won, in the eight areas of activity covered by the Local Government Act 1988, between 51.4 per cent (building cleaning) and 90.6 per cent (catering (education and welfare)) of current contracts awarded by CCT. In terms of the value of contracts awarded, local authorities won an even higher proportion, ranging between 74.2 per cent (refuse collection) and 97.1 per cent (catering (education and welfare)).

The extensive nature of the 'white collar' list inevitably means that questions are being asked about the continuing role of local authorities as vehicles of *direct* service provision. Can local authorities effectively govern without themselves *directly* providing services? Hampton (1991, p. 76) sees CCT as 'part of a restructuring of the role of local government in a post welfare society, and of a reduction in the significance of the local democratic process'. An extreme public choice model would see local authorities as little other than contract-awarding bodies; some authorities (e.g. Wandsworth, Rutland) are already well along this road but many others have barely set out.

Party Politics

Party politics is a central feature of contemporary local government across most of the UK. In the metropolitan areas, in most of the English counties and in the larger shire districts there are fully developed party systems. In the more rural areas there tend to be weak party systems or non-partisan authorities. In 1993 the Labour Party's local government standing was statistically higher than at any time since re-organisation in the mid-1970s. As Stewart and Game note (1993, p. 18):

> For the first time, the party controls all four principal local authority associations. It has more councillors across Great Britain (some 9,300) than do the Conservatives (7,900), and majorities on more councils (165 to the Tories' 99) than ever before.

Yet, as the same authors remind us, for every Labour council there was also (in 1993) one with no single party in overall control: 163 – or nearly one in three – authorities that were technically hung or balanced, including 26 English and two Welsh counties.

The Labour Party's local strength is rooted in its urban strongholds but it is also the by-product of the Conservatives' unprecedented dominance of the national parliamentary scene since 1979. A party in power nationally invariably expects to lose seats in local elections, but with only one English county (Buckinghamshire) controlled by the Conservatives in 1993 the anti-Conservative swing has gone much further than anyone could have predicted. For better or worse the comprehensive party-politicisation of local government is here to stay and could become even more widespread given the likely development of larger unitary authorities.

Structural Change

Structural change is nothing new for local government – in fact it is almost continuously on the agenda. There was a wholesale reorganisation in 1974; in 1986 the Greater London Council and the six English metropolitan counties ceased to exist. The Inner

London Eduction Authority was abolished with effect from March 1990. At present the Local Government Commission is engaged in a major structural review programme for non-metropolitan *English* local authorities. In Scotland and Wales the respective Secretaries of State are charged with overseeing structural reorganisation without the assistance of a Commission. Indeed, in March 1993 the Welsh Secretary recommended the creation of 21 new unitary authorities to replace the eight Welsh counties and 37 districts with effect from April 1995. In July 1993 the Scottish Secretary produced proposals to replace the existing 65 local authorities by a system of 28 unitary authorities. The three all-purpose islands authorities would stay as they are; 25 single-tier authorities would replace the existing regional and district authorities. The White Paper, *Shaping the Future – The New Councils*, envisaged the existing authorities being wound up on 31 March 1996 and the successor authorities assuming full control on 1 April 1996.

By June 1993 the Local Government Commission had produced draft recommendations for its first tranche of reviews. This tranche covered 74 local authorities – ten counties and 64 districts. Out of these the Commission *recommended* that there should be 22 unitary authorities, with Lincolnshire County Council and the seven districts in the county staying as they were (i.e. a two-tier county). In the new unitary authorities (if the Commission's draft recommendations are accepted by the government) the number of elected councillors is set to fall dramatically. For example, in Derbyshire there was a total of 477 elected members on the county and district councils in 1993; under the Commission's draft proposals there would be only 172 – a net loss of 305. The 'democratic deficit' associated with this and similar proposals for change requires careful evaluation before any proposals are finally adopted.

Given the government's preference for *unitary* authorities with an *enabling* orientation there is much to be learnt from the introduction of unitary authorities in metropolitan England in 1986 following the abolition of the metropolitan counties. The metropolitan districts spawned networks of joint boards and joint committees (which are not *directly* elected) to run various services – a development which has been widely criticised, particularly from the standpoint of local democracy. Leach *et al.* (1992, p. 169) have shown that the handing over of local authority functions to joint boards. (e.g. police, fire) has had negative implications for local accountability. They also argue that it has been very difficult for those district councillors nominated to serve on joint boards to establish any real political control – something which is particularly unsatisfactory given the massive budgets allocated to these boards. Leach *et al.* (1992, p. 169) conclude: 'We are ... left with the inescapable conclusion that on any criteria of accountability, based on any conception of democracy, there has since abolition been a marked reduction in accountability.' Disquiet from a *democratic* perspective has also been accompanied by *financial* disquiet since the promised financial savings associated with the creation of joint boards have also proved to be largely illusory. Tiered local government (albeit disguised) is set to remain in England whatever the recommendations of the Local Government Commission. Given that a continuing a role (although not one incorporating increased legal powers) is envisaged for parish/town councils (community councils in Wales and Scotland) such tiering will remain overt in non-metropolitan areas. Any new 'most purpose' authorities will be only one part of the patchwork quilt of local community government which includes an increasing number of non-directly elected bodies such as Urban Development Corporations (UDCs), Training and Enterprise Councils (TECs) and City Challenge initiatives. It is the *directly* elected element, with *direct* accountability to the local population, which gives local government its uniqueness.

Unfortunately, the current round of structural change has preceded meaningful debate about the *role* and *purpose* of local government. This is akin to putting up a building without first determining its use. The separation of finance, structure and internal management by the 1991 Heseltine Local Government Review itself represented a missed opportunity for an integrated evaluation of the purpose of local government. Likewise, the whole area of central–local government relations was ignored. Change seems set to precede, not follow, reasoned debate.

Internal Management

While local authorities are constantly reviewing their internal patterns of management (invariably to streamline operations and produce economies) new impetus was given to the process in July 1991 by Michael Heseltine's publication of a consultation paper, *The Internal Management of Local Authorities in England*. Central to this document was the premise (outlined earlier) that local authorities are set to become less the direct providers of services and more vehicles enabling services to be provided for a local community. The consultation paper argued that such an enabling role demanded new skills – hence the need to rethink internal organisational patterns. The consultation paper argued that the existing committee and sub-committee structure was often 'time consuming and cumbersome' (DoE, 1991b, para. 23); likewise the decision-making role of back-bench and minority party councillors was perceived to be very limited. Against this backcloth the paper outlined the objectives of any changes in internal management (para. 24):

- to promote more effective, speedy and business-like decision making
- to enhance the scrutiny of decisions
- to increase the interest taken by the public in local government
- to provide scope for councillors to devote more time to their constituency role.

These rather selective objectives appeared in isolation from any debate about the role and purpose of local government (see Wilson, 1991). There was also an artificial divide between the constituency and decision-making roles of councillors – in practice such distinctions are often difficult to draw. Additionally there was an assumption that speedy decisions are the best decisions; in fact, the insights provided by a range of perspectives in committees and subcommittees (although often time-consuming) can frequently enhance the end product. In practice the current delegation of policy matters to officers in many local authorities ensures speedy decision-making over a wide range of detailed issues – something seriously underplayed by the Heseltine paper.

Having been critical of the existing system, the paper states (para. 27) that the government does not believe 'that all local authorities need to change their internal management arrangements'. It also emphasises that local experimentation is desirable: i.e. it is not necessary to adopt a uniform pattern throughout England. In this context six options were outlined for consideration:

1. *Retention of the present system*: a no-change scenario is possible if local authorities see their existing system as fully meeting their needs.
2. *Adaptation of the committee system*: this might involve allowing councils to delegate decision-making to committee chairs. Some reconsideration of the need for minority representation on committees is also mooted with a recognition that changes of this nature would necessitate reconsideration of the safeguards for minority parties.
3. *Cabinet system*: in this option an executive of elected members would be chosen from the council as a whole. The executive would take responsibility for the majority of the council's functions although the whole council would retain responsibility for certain matters, such as approving a budget submitted by the executive. In this option the bulk of councillors, whether in the ruling or opposition parties, would take no part in day-to-day decision-making.
4. *Council manager*: here the council would appoint an officer to take over the day-to-day running of the authority. While the council would retain overall policy responsibility it would have little involvement in day-to-day decision-making.
5. *Directly elected executive*: a radical change from present arrangements because it would involve separate elections to the council and to the executive. Otherwise this option would operate in the same way as the Cabinet model.
6. *Directly elected mayor*: this is similar to the previous option except it would involve the election of an *individual* to take over the council's executive responsibilities. This individual would be elected separately from the council.

Of all the options outlined in the consultation paper, option 6 has attracted most attention from the media although local authorities, almost without exception, are unenthusiastic about it. Heseltine had long canvassed the idea of elected mayors and they could provide a powerful political voice for local government. Stoker and Wolman (1992), drawing on US experience, argue that such mayors in the UK could provide a focal point and driving force for a more dynamic and influential local government. The system produces a high-profile figure whom the public can identify and hold to account – but in such contexts scandals over letting of contracts and use of public funds are not uncommon. Option 6 would, however, lead to far more elitist local government with relatively few councillors having any real policy-making significance. The 'representative' nature of local government could thereby suffer a body blow; fewer people with less detailed knowledge of a local community taking decisions might mean more streamlined but less sensitive community government. Local government could thus become more 'high profile' but less representative of grass-roots interests, unless the scrutiny role of the full council were to be strengthened.

The Heseltine consultation paper advocated experimentation with alternative models of management. In a similar vein, *Community Leadership and Representation: Unlocking the Potential* (July 1993) advocated experimentation. This report emerged from a working group established by the Secretary of State at the DoE. It noted (para. 2.10):

> We deliberately do not identify an ideal internal management model and recommend its application as a blueprint to all local authorities. We recognise that different approaches will be appropriate for different authorities, and that it is for them and not central government to choose which arrangements to adopt.

Where experimental models emerged they would be subject to annual review and the Environment Secretary would be able to suspend or modify experiments if the nominated panel of advisers reported they were failing. Given volunteer 'guinea-pig' authorities, radical internal change could become a reality. Indeed, in September 1993 Birmingham City Council came out in favour of a Cabinet system – possibly the first of many proposals for limited experiments.

Finance

Rhodes (1992, p. 51) argues that there were three objectives running through the Thatcher government's policy on local government finance during the 1980s:

1 The first objectives was to control local expenditure as part of its broader strategy of reducing public expenditure.

2 The second objective was to strengthen local accountability by introducing a clear link between the provision of services, paying for them and voting in local elections.
3 The third and implicit objective was 'to bury socialism'.

Rhodes also questions the dominant centralisation thesis, arguing that during the Thatcher years the centre's relations with local government were characterised more by unintended consequences than by revolutionary change. While there was centralisation, the most important consequence of the Thatcher years was the creation of a 'policy mess in which neither level of government achieved its objectives'.

Central to Thatcher's policy was the abolition of the rating system and the introduction of a new form of taxation. In April 1990 a new local tax, the Community Charge (poll tax), was introduced in England and Wales (one year after its introduction in Scotland). Less than one year later, in March 1991, the decision to abandon the Community Charge was made. A consultation paper, *A New Tax for Local Government*, was issued and from April 1993 a new Council Tax came into operation. Three different taxes in three years, the net result of which means that local domestic taxation meets barely 15 per cent of local revenue expenditure.

As Stoker (1992, pp. 67, 68) notes, the new tax combines elements from both its predecessors. 'Like the rates, it is a tax of

TABLE 10.3   *Council Tax Valuation Bands in England (Based on Market Values at 1 April 1991)*

Band	Value	Relative Tax
A	Up to £40 000	6/9ths
B	Up to £52 000	7/9ths
C	Up to £68 000	8/9ths
D	Up to £88 000	1
E	Up to £120 000	11/9ths
F	Up to £160 000	13/9ths
G	Up to £320 000	15/9ths
H	Over £320 000	2

Source: Doe (1992) *Council Tax – A Guide to the New Tax for Local Government.*

property, but it is to be levied on capital values rather than a national rental value.' Houses are not given an exact value but are placed in one of eight bands, from below £40 000 to £320 000 and over (English figures only). See Table 10.3 for details.

Each band is subject to a different relative amount of Council Tax, with band D set as the norm. The tax payable by properties in each band is relative to the tax in band D. The most expensive house cannot be taxed at more than three times the amount levied in the cheapest. The government claims that this is to prevent excessive bills falling on a minority of properties, but opponents maintain that it is a political tactic to keep down the bills of Conservative supporters living in the most expensive properties. A single adult householder receives a discount of 25 per cent but, unlike the poll tax, a system to provide full rebates where appropriate operates.

Goverments, of course, face a political dilemma with any form of local taxation. Interestingly, as Rhodes (1992, p. 58) shows, the aggregate level of local expenditure was not cut in the 1980s. For the government, 'this oft-stated and brutally simple policy objective was not attained. Between 1979 and 1988 local current expenditure rose at 1980 prices by 15 per cent in real terms.' Intervention is relatively straightforward; control is rather more elusive. The particular unpopularity of the poll tax led to further intervention by central government, notably even tighter controls on local capital and revenue expenditure. Greater centralisation seems set to remain a fundamental feature of the financing of local authorities although greater central control does not automatically produce uniform expenditure patterns nor does it always produce intended outcomes. Party-political, socioeconomic and other factors can still give rise to local distinctiveness.

As Stoker (1992, p. 69) notes, in order to get themselves out of trouble in relation to the poll tax, 'the Conservatives announced in the 1991 Budget that they would increase VAT from 15 per cent to $17\frac{1}{2}$ per cent in order to provide additional central government support to local authorities and dramatically reduce the level of poll tax bills'. Alongside this were announcements that further education and sixth form colleges were to be removed from local authority control. Subsequently (July 1992) we saw the publication of an Education White Paper, *'Choice and Diversity: A New Framework for Schools',* followed by an Education Act which reduced the role of local education authorities. To quote Stoker (p. 69):

Increased central funding is also to be a feature of the new Council Tax regime. The business rate is to remain nationalized with central government setting its level and distributing its bounties to local authorities. The increased level of centrally-provided funding and the removal of functions from local government solves some problems but creates others.

With the maximum level of expenditure in each local authority (Standard Spending Assessment – SSA) determined by central government, there is relatively little room for local manoeuvre. In financial terms the dominance of the centre is clear with less and less freedom for individual local authorities to engage in imaginative new ventures without partnership with either private enterprise or voluntary bodies. Authorities which breach the SSAs are liable to be capped. From a financial perspective local democracy has lost out to central direction. The Council Tax has not ushered in a new financial dawn for elected local authorities.

Analysing Recent Developments in Central–Local Relations

There is no simple, universally accepted model for analysing central government/local authority relationships. This is partly because of the complexities involved. For example, virtually all government departments interact with local authorities even though (in England) the focus of activity is the Department of the Environment. Within each central department there are numerous sections (or Commands) and hence many different networks develop between particular sections of Whitehall departments and specific departments inside local authorities. As Rhodes (1981, p. 18) has observed, 'It is misleading to talk of central control. Rather there are different types of control exerted by the various constituent units of central government.' A mass of networks exists; looking for any simple pattern is illusory, particularly as by no means all local actors are drawn from *elected* local government.

A number of models have been developed to facilitate greater understanding of central–local relationships. From the mid-1970s onwards probably the most widely used has been the *agency* model since it emphasises the increasing power of the centre. In the sphere of finance this currently has considerable credibility given the intensity of the pressure upon local authorities. Yet despite its obvious attractions, a simple agency model, with local authorities seen to be implementing national policies with little or no discretion, has severe limitations. There remain considerable variations in spending patterns, albeit within broad financial parameters set down by the centre. For example, in 1991–92 Westminster proposed to spend £47 per capita on libraries while Mid-Glamorgan assigned only £6.50 per capita for the same service (CIPFA, 1992, *Local Government Comparative Statistics*). Such wide variations mean that a simple agency model is a less than fully satisfactory representation of central–local relationships.

Chandler (1988) provides a variation of the agency model. He argues that the term 'agent' is not entirely appropriate since the centre has always been prepared to allow local authorities a considerable measure of discretion. He maintains (p. 185) that a more appropriate metaphor would be *stewardship* in the sense that the steward 'is delegated considerable authority by his master to order his estates'. Chandler continues (1988, p. 186):

> The steward will, from time to time, consult with his employer on how best he should manage his estate ... A capable landlord will listen to the advice of his expert manager and may often be persuaded by his arguments. The master, nevertheless, will always retain the power either to accept or reject the advice. Should the steward fail to obey these orders he will be compelled to change his conduct or, like the councillors of Lambeth, Liverpool and Clay Cross, be removed from office.

The most frequently utilised alternative to the various agency models is the *partnership* model which sees central government and local authorities as more or less co-equal partners in providing services. The most sophisticated form of partnership model is R. A. W. Rhodes' *power-dependence model* which postulates that both central government departments and local authorities have resources which each can use against the other and against other organisations as well. It is a model that pays particular attention to *bargaining*; it also argues that, while there are likely to be inequalities in the distribution of resources, they are not necessarily cumulative. Rhodes (1979, pp. 29–31) observes:

> The fact that a local authority or a central department lacks one resource does not mean that it lacks others. One resource could be

substituted for another. For example, a central department lacking the constitutional/legal resources to prevent (or encourage) a specific local initiative can attempt to get its way by withholding (or supporting) financial resources. Conversely, a local authority which has been refused financial resources can attempt to reverse this state of affairs by embarrassing the central government. Press and television reports on the adverse consequence of the centre's desicion may lead to the decision being reconsidered.

To some extent the Rhodes model has rather too much of an inter-organisational focus; changing political and economic circumstances receive insufficient attention. According to Rhodes and Marsh (1992, p. 11), the 'most significant weakness of the power-dependence model is its failure to distinguish clearly between micro-, meso, and macro-levels of analysis; consequently the relationship between them is not adequately explored'. This said, power-dependence remains a most useful perspective. Its insights are considerable and must not be undervalued.

Utilisation of a variety of analytical perspectives is invariably helpful. No single model is able to provide a complete frame of reference for what is a complex and diverse set of relationships. Indeed, the very term 'central–local relationships' is open to question and, according to Rhodes (1986, p. 28), suggests a bias towards the analysis of *institutional* relationships and 'does not always provide an adequate account of policy systems ... Intergovernmental theory with its emphasis on fragmentation, professionalisation and policy networks is more appropriate'. The complexity of the networks, both elected and non-elected, between the central machinery of government and sub-central governmental units needs to be clearly recognised. Simple uniform patterns applicable throughout the UK do not correspond to reality. At a very basic level it is important to recognise that a variety of relationships occur within the UK. In Scotland, Wales and Northern Ireland distinctive patterns operate.

Scotland and Wales

The Secretaries of State for Scotland and Wales, via the Scottish and Welsh Offices, are responsible for a wide range of policy matters relating to their particular territories – including crucial services such as housing and education. So, for local authorities in Scotland and Wales, their 'centre' is either Edinburgh or Cardiff, not London. Because of the smaller size, relationships have traditionally been relatively informal and policy networks are consequently on a smaller scale (e.g. Convention of Scottish Local Authorities (COSLA); Welsh Association of Community and Town Councils). But even here one must beware of generalisations. Carmichael (1992, p. 30) maintains that the 'last decade has revealed, if anything, a breakdown of the previous political conventions in Scotland, typified by the increasing strain under which the informal ties between the Scottish Office and COSLA have been subject'. The lack of trust which characterised central–local relations in England since the mid-1970s has permeated the more informal networks of the Celtic fringe, especially in the context of the proposals of respective Secretaries of State for structural reorganisation.

Northern Ireland

As noted earlier, the 26 local authorities in Northern Ireland have relatively few executive functions. It was in March 1972 that Westminster took direct responsibility for governing Northern Ireland through the Secretary of State. Hence, as Connolly (1986, p. 15) has argued, 'the range of interactions between central and local government is considerably less than in the rest of the UK. In turn this means that central–local relationships in Northern Ireland are less complex, with fewer central government departments involved and the range and degree of bargaining and negotiation a good deal smaller'. In Northern Ireland, then, central dominance has been exacerbated by direct rule. The networks of non-directly elected boards which provide services such as housing, education, libraries, health and social services have been increasingly squeezed by the centre.

There are, therefore, diverse political systems in England, Scotland, Wales and Northern Ireland. Goldsmith (1986, p. 169) argues that the territorial offices utilise their discretion when London sees fit or when their respective Secretaries of State can win concessions in Cabinet. 'Such concessions can only be won infrequently: otherwise the core will see its periphery as a problem and will take action to deal with it accordingly.' For any discussion of central–local relations to make sense in a UK context there needs to be some recognition that generalisations from an English perspective have little credibility. Scotland, Wales and Northern Ireland are distinctive territorial communities – this distinctiveness is replicated in the diverse patterns of central–local relations.

The Framework of Central–Local Relations

There is no formal constitutional settlement delineating the relationship between central government departments and local authorities. There are, nevertheless, a number of constituent elements which together comprise a framework within which activity takes place.

Legislation is of paramount importance since Parliament has the powers to create, abolish or amend the powers of local authorities as it determines. Recent examples include the 1985 Local Government Act which abolished the GLC and the six metropolitan counties with effect from 1 April 1986 and the 1988 Local Government Act which abolished the ILEA with effect from 1990. There were some 143 legislative enactments either directly or indirectly relating to local government in the years 1979–92. For recent Conservative governments, legislation has been a major vehicle for *intervention* (if not always *control*) and this pattern distinguishes our period from earlier eras. As Goldsmith (1986, p. xv) notes: 'This rather formal approach contrasts neatly with more informal approach generally adopted by central governments in their relations with local authorities in the years up to 1979.' The pace of legislative change has not slackened. Central intervention via legislation has become an increasingly important fact of political life.

Alongside legislation, *judicial review* is of central significance in shaping relations between levels of government. At the heart of this is the concept of *ultra vires* (beyond the powers). Local authorities have no powers except those conferred upon them by statute and when they take action which is not sanctioned by the law they are said to be acting *ultra vires*. This is clearly a restrictive doctrine and contrasts with much of contemporary continental practice. Unlike most other Western European and

Scandinavian countries British local authorities have no *power of general competence*. In, for example, France, Germany and Sweden local authorities have a general right to undertake any activities which they believe to be in the interests of their citizens unless such activities are specifically assigned to other bodies. They can, in other words, do anything they are not expressly forbidden by law to undertake.

While the general competence power which applies in Western European countries might not actually mean that, in practice, local government does much more, it nevertheless 'legitimises its status as a level of government addressing all community affairs' (Batley and Campbell, 1992, p. 2). To adopt it in the UK would have enormous symbolic value as a statement of the importance of local government. Instead of arguing amongst themselves on almost every issue imaginable the local authority associations should work together to establish a more favourable legal status for *all* local authorities.

While legislation and judicial review provide the substantive part of the formal framework, statutory instruments, circulars, default powers and inspectors also come into play (see Greenwood and Wilson, 1989, ch. 10) as well as, of course, the financial arrangements established by central government. Meaningful consultation with local authorities was minimal in the 1980s and early 1990s. It was replaced, in most policy areas, by 'a pattern of authoritative pronouncements by the centre' (Rhodes, 1992, p. 63). Bodies like the hitherto important Consultative Council on Local Government Finance (CCLGF) became facades (the CCLGF increasingly *received* policy statements from government ministers rather than engaging in meaningful consultation), while the Audit Commission loomed large as an 'enforcer' in the drive for value for money. In this context, as Rhodes (1992, p. 63) notes, 'given the ease with which local authorities ignored or evaded Government policy, the phenomenon of restrictive legislation, the frequency of legal challenges to Government policy and the search for the judge-proof legislation, the price for not consulting was high'. In the 1980s and into the early 1990s central direction replaced meaningful consultation. The top-down model utilised by successive governments did not sit easily with the diversity of British local authorities; effective two-way communication became the exception rather than the rule.

There were, however, some signs in 1992–93 that the animosity between central and local government could be subsiding. In October 1992 Michael Howard, then Secretary of State at the DoE, argued that 'the old image of eternal central–local conflict is out of date'. He maintained that ministers 'have taken an entirely fresh look at the way in which we bring local authorities into the Whitehall decision making process' (Howard's speech was reported in *Local Government Chronicle,* 13 November 1992). Writing in the Centenary Souvenir Issue of the *Municipal Journal* (September 1993, p. 3) Howard's successor, John Gummer, wrote:

> You have seen new functions, new methods of financing, new relationships with national government forged and broken. Now a more constructive relationship between local and central government has developed. The smooth introduction of the council tax is a striking example. I am determined to build on that ... Central government should not make decisions best made locally.

Genuine consultation *could*, perhaps, become a reality once again.

Conclusion

As Bulpitt (1989, p. 57) reminds us, central–local relations used to rank as one of Oakeshott's subjects of 'unimaginable dreariness'. It was also one of no great party-political significance. Today the topic is neither dreary nor unimportant. Local government has become high-profile and extremely contentious. Despite facing many pressures it remains big business. Massive *intervention* by the centre has not produced the desired *control* in all policy areas although the intensity of current financial controls on both revenue and capital expenditure is very real. Conservative government policies have polarised central–local relations in recent years as Rhodes (1992, pp. 61–2) indicates:

> The focus on grant cuts for 'overspenders', the abolition of the GLC and MCCs, and the choice of local authorities for rate capping were all seen as partisan policies and provoked a suitably intemperate response. The Labour Party controls a substantial proportion of local councils. Local government was the area in which the electoral fortunes of the party were revived, the test bed for socialist policies and

the main source of opposition to the Government. In sum, local government was a pawn in an increasingly polarized national political game.

Finance is, of course, only one, albeit particularly important, policy area. Relationships between central government departments and local authorities are not standardised and uniform. They vary from policy area to policy area; they also vary over time. Outlooks towards local government frequently vary between the different organisational units inside a single government department. The diversity of local government in the UK (with what are, in effect, 540 miniature political systems) ensures variety in policy outputs. Intervention by the centre is massive; control remains rather more ambiguous.

References

Batley, R. and Campbell, A. (1992) 'Introduction', *Local Government Studies*, 18(1), Spring.
Bulpitt, J. (1989) 'Walking Back to Happiness?', in Crouch, C. and Marquand, D. (eds), *The New Centralism* (Oxford: Basil Blackwell) pp. 56–73.
Carmichael, P. (1992) 'Is Scotland Different? Local Government Policy under Mrs Thatcher', *Local Government Policy Making*, 18(5), May, pp. 25–32.
Chandler, J. A. (1988) *Public Policy-Making for Local Government* (London: Croom Helm).
CIPFA (1992) *Local Government Comparative Statistics* (London: CIPFA Statistical Information Service).
Clarke, M. and Stewart, J. (1992) *The Enabling Council* (Luton: LGTB).
Connolly, M. (1986) 'Central–Local Government Relations in Northern Ireland' *Local Government Studies*, 12(5), September/October, 15–24
Connolly, M. (1992) 'Learning from Northern Ireland: An Acceptable Model for Regional and Local Government', *Public Policy and Administration*, 7(1) (Spring), pp. 31–46.
Department of the Environment (1991a) *A New Tax for Local Government* (London: HMSO).
Department of the Environment (1991b) *The Structure of Local Government in England* (London: HMSO).
Department of the Environment (1991c) *The Internal Management of Local Authorities in England* (London: HMSO).

Department of the Environment (1992a) *The Functions of Local Authorities in England* (London: HMSO).

Department of the Environment (1992) *Policy Guidance to the Local Government Commission for England* (London: Department of the Environment).

Department of the Environment (1993) *Community Leadership and Representation: Unlocking the Potential*, Report of the Working Party on the Internal Management of Local Authorities in England (London: HMSO).

Goldsmith, M. (1986) *New Research into Central–Local Relations* (Aldershot: Gower).

Greenwood, J. and Wilson, D. (1989) *Public Administration in Britain Today* (London: Unwin Hyman).

Gummer, J. S. (1993) 'Introduction', *Municipal Journal Centenary Souvenir Issue 1893–1993*, September, p. 3.

Hampton, W. (1991) *Local Government and Urban Politics*, 2nd edn (London: Longman).

Hollis, G. *et al.* (1990) *Alternatives to the Community Charge* (London: Joseph Rowntree Trust/Coopers & Lybrand Deloitte).

Kent County Council (1992) *Facing the Challenge: Making Strategic Management Work* (in conjunction with Coopers & Lybrand Deloitte).

Leach, S. (1993) 'Local Government Reorganisation in England', *Local Government Policy Making*, 19(4), pp. 30–5.

Leach, S. and Stewart, M. (1992) *Local Government: Its Role and Functions* (York: Joseph Rowntree Foundation).

Leach, S., Davies, H., Game, C., Skelcher, C., (1992) *After Abolition* (University of Birmingham, INOLGOV).

Rhodes, R. A. W. (1979) 'Research into Central–Local Relations in Britain: A Framework for Analysis', unpublished paper, Department of Government, University of Essex.

Rhodes, R. A. W. (1981) *Control and Power in Central–Local Government Relations* (Farnborough: Gower).

Rhodes, R. A. W. (1986) *The National World of Local Government* (London: Allen & Unwin).

Rhodes, R. A. W. (1992) 'Local Government Finance', in Marsh, D. and Rhodes, R. A. W., *Implementing Thatcherite Politics* (Buckingham: Open University Press).

Rhodes, R. A. W., and Marsh, D. (1992), 'Policy Networks in British Politics', in Rhodes, R. A. W., and Marsh, D. (eds), *Policies Networks in British Government* (Oxford: Clarendon Press).

Robson, W. (1966) *Local Government in Crisis* (London: Allen & Unwin).

Stewart, J. and Game, C. (1993) 'Labour lets it all hang out', *New Statesman and Society*, 10 September, pp. 18, 19.

Stoker, G. (1992) 'Local Government', in Terry, F. and Jackson, P. (eds), *Public Domain 1992* (London: Chapman & Hall).

Stoker, G. and Wolman, H. (1992) 'Drawing Lessons from US Experience: An Elected Mayor for British Local Government', *Public Administration*, 70 (Summer), pp. 241–67.

The Citizen's Charter (1991) (London: HMS0).

Welsh Office (1993) *Local Government in Wales: A Charter for the Future*, Cm 2155 (London: HMSO).

Widdicombe Report (1986) *The Conduct of Local Authority Business*, Cmnd 9797-9801 (London: HMSO).

Wilson, D. J. (1991) 'Making Local Councils Work: A Flawed Prescription?', *Local Government Policy Making*, 18(3), pp. 16–20.

11

The Other Governments of Britain

CLIVE GRAY

The majority of the governing and administering of Britain occurs away from the confines of Whitehall and Westminster in a large number of non-central government organisations that can be found throughout Britain. These organisations, as with the rest of the political–administrative machinery of the state, have undergone a number of distinct transformations over the past fourteen years. The extent to which these changes constitute a real revolution, and the implications of them for the management and administration of the services that the people of Britain receive, are important issues not only in their own right but also in terms of the possible shape and direction that these parts of the governmental machinery will assume in the future.

The purpose of this chapter is, first, to outline the nature of the changes that have taken place in government beyond Westminster and Whitehall and, second, to discuss what the future is likely to hold in store for the entire sphere of non-central government in Britain.

Sub-National Government in Britain

Government beyond the centre in Britain is made up of four distinct organisational *types*, each of which has its own structure, sets of functions, independence and relationships with the centre. The structure of these arenas of governmental action is complex and cannot be simply described, even if the organisational types that make it up can be. The four types of organisation that are involved in government beyond the centre are: local government; the National Health Service (NHS); quangos, qualgos and quappos; and outposts of the centre.

Whilst local government is dealt with in more detail elsewhere (see Chapter 10) it is important that all of these types of government are discussed together as there are key themes and issues that unite them all in terms of the changes and futures that they have confronted and are due to face in the coming years. Before undertaking this discussion, however, a brief outline of what is involved in each of these types of sub-national government (SNG) is necessary.

Local Government

Local government is, quite simply, the collection of county, regional, island, district, parish and community councils that provide the bulk of the goods and services that are directly received by the population. Apart from central government itself, local authorities are the largest component of the public sector in terms of the money that it spends (approximately 25 per cent of all public expenditure is accounted for by local government). Local authorities have a large number of functions to undertake, through their statutory or discretionary powers, covering everything from parks and crematoria to education and social services.

The National Health Service

The NHS provides, on the other hand, a single function (health care). To do this, however, the NHS employs more people than any other part of the public sector and is, in fact, the second largest employer of staff in the world – after the Chinese railway system. The organisations that are used to provide health care have multiplied during the 1980s through the introduction of NHS Trusts, which are effectively semi-detached parts of the overall NHS system. Alongside these Trusts there are also Regional and District Health Authorities. Family Health Service Authorities, which have managerial responsibilities for General Practitioner services, and Community Health Councils, which act as the voice of the general public within the NHS.

Quangos, Qualgos and Quappos

These are bodies that have only a semi-official existence as part of the public sector. They are, respectively, the creations of central and local government or are the joint creations of the public and private sectors. The reasons for their existence vary considerably, from the direct provision of services to removing administrative burdens from the centre (see Hood, 1978), but in general terms they are administrative devices that have been created for specific purposes that, it is usually claimed, require a removal of them from the political arena of direct governmental control. Such organisations are normally dependent for at least some of their finances on the public sector and are usually managed by appointed members. In contrast with 'national' quangos (such as the Arts Council) these bodies have a role to play in a limited part of the nation state as a whole (such as the Regional Arts Boards).

Outposts of the Centre

This category incorporates all of the offices and bodies that are formally headed by a minister but which are located away from the centre of the administrative machinery. This ensures that such organisations have at least a certain amount of independence from direct managerial control and a scope for making their own independent decisions and choices. The bulk of these bodies are to be found in the regional and local offices of central government departments, such as the local offices of the Department of the Environment. In addition to these, however, there also exist the territorial ministries of the Scottish, Welsh and Northern Ireland Offices, with their associated departments and quangos. This difference is important as these latter organisations form part of a distinctly different set of relationships with Westminster and Whitehall from those of the local and regional offices of national departments (see, for example, Midwinter *et al.*, 1991, on the Scottish Office).

The Dimensions of SNG

The size of SNG can be assessed in different ways. Organisationally, it includes over 16 000 separate units of government and administration; financially, it is responsible for approximately two-thirds of all public expenditure; in employment terms it accounts for over three-quarters of the public sector (Gray, 1994, Introduction). On whichever basis is chosen, however, it is apparent that SNG is a massive operation. The sheer size of SNG would be enough to make it important by itself, but the complexities of providing goods and services give it an extra importance over and above that which stems from size alone.

The overlapping nature of functions between the parts of SNG and the multiple interrelationships that exist both within SNG and between SNG and central government make it an inescapably political arena of action. The provision of goods and services is not simply concerned with matters of technical efficiency, effectiveness and economy but also depends upon matters of political calculation and choice. Given the impossibility of creating totally subservient organisations away from the centre (Rhodes, 1981) it is no surprise that these questions of political calculation and choice are of great importance for understanding how SNG operates in practice. Apart from the relative practical independence of the organisations of SNG there are a number of areas where the status of these organisations allows them a political significance that cannot be simply ignored by the centre, thus ensuring that a complex game of politics between the centre and the organisations of SNG will be a fact of everyday life as far as this part of the governmental system is concerned.

In effect the politics of SNG has a number of dimensions that lead to the creation of different problems for both central government and for SNG itself, with each of these dimensions being engrained into the structure of the overall system of government and administration within Britain in such a way that they can only be removed by abolishing SNG itself. As this is unlikely to occur politics will continue to form a significant part of the overall system for the foreseeable future.

The dimensions that form the overall pattern of the politics of SNG are four-fold:

- *party politics*, involving competition between party groups;
- *organisational politics*, involving conflicts within and between organisations;
- *economic politics*, involving the financing of the organisations of SNG; and
- *citizenship politics*, involving access to, and participation in, the decision-making process by the general public.

Each of these dimensions has been affected by the actions of the Conservative governments since 1979 and has served to set the scene for the contemplation of the future shape of government beyond the centre. How these have actually been reshaped as the result of central government activity needs to be considered in terms of the areas of SNG that the centre has attempted to change.

SNG in Britain has undergone a continuing, and accelerating, process of reform and change since long before the election victory of 1979 saw Mrs Thatcher become Prime Minister (see Gray, 1994, ch. 3). Since that date, however, there has been a process of change that has affected five key areas in particular. These areas and the nature of politics in SNG form the basis for the next section of this chapter where the impact of the Conservative governments on SNG is discussed.

The Changing System: 1979–94

The five areas where the Conservative governments have attempted to introduce effective change into SNG since 1979 have been in terms of:

- the *control* of the system;
- the *accountability* of the parts of SNG;
- *participation* within SNG;
- the *financing* of the organisations of SNG; and
- how the system is *managed*.

Each of these has involved the use of different forms of politics by both central government and SNG itself. How this has been the case, and what the results of this activity have been, will now be considered.

Control

The Conservative governments since 1979 have attempted to intervene in the system of SNG in such a way as to provide a system that operates in a manner that is acceptable to the centre. This has been attempted through both *organisational* and *functional* means. The former involved introducing new organisations into the system and attempting to reform those already existing. In the case of the latter there has been some shuffling of the pack, with the new organisations that have been introduced taking on the responsibility for providing certain functions that had previously been associated with, in particular, local government and the NHS. (See Table 11.1 for a listing of some of these new organisations.)

The *bypass* strategy that this has represented has been only partially successful. In some areas, as with the Urban Development Corporations, new approaches and attitudes have been introduced into the system (Stoker, 1989), but in many others the attempt to impose change has led to the creation of 'policy messes' (Marsh and Rhodes, 1992, p. 180) that have actually worsened the prospects for central control. The actions of the centre have created unintended consequences that it has been unable to resolve, thus weakening the chances for its intentions to be fulfilled. Further, the fact that the remaining organisations of SNG

TABLE 11.1 *New Organisations in Sub-National Government*

Organisation	Numbers
Training and Enterprise Councils	82
Local Enterprise Companies	22
Driving Standards Agency	10
Training Agency Regional Offices	10
Office of Electricity Regulation:	
Electricity Consumers Councils	10
Regional Arts Boards	10
Urban Development Corporations	10
Audit Commission	8
Family Health Service Authorities	98
Residuary Bodies	3

Source: Adapted from Gray, 1994, ch. 1.

still have autonomy over their own internal practices and organisation has meant that the attempt to persuade them to change has run into a great deal of resistance, and has helped to create a new form of public management ethos that runs counter to the ideas of the centre (Ranson and Stewart, 1989).

Accountability

The extremely limited success that the centre has had in achieving control over the system has been matched by the limited impact that government policies have had on the *accountability* of the organisations of SNG. In this case it could be argued that the consequences of intervention by the centre have still to be fully worked through and that the meaning of accountability in SNG *will*, eventually, change.

The mechanisms that are leading to a reappraisal of the meaning of accountability in SNG are threefold: first, the switch from democratic to economic accountability (exemplified by the Community Charge or poll tax (Barker, 1992)); second, the fragmentation of SNG as a result of introducing new organisations into the system; and, third, the introduction of various forms of 'Citizen's Charter' into SNG that emphasise the switch from a concern with people as citizens to a concern with people as consumers.

As yet, none of these developments have had a significant effect on SNG, but the potential for them to do so is immense. The consequences of this potential change are many, and will be returned to in the next section.

Participation

This is concerned with the openness of the system of SNG to inputs from the public, either directly, through elected or appointed members of the organisations concerned, or indirectly, through other forms of citizen involvement, such as pressure groups. The government would certainly claim that in both cases the quality (and quantity) of citizen involvement has been improved through the creation of new relationships between people and organisations and through the introduction of market-based, economic, ties into the system. The extent to which either of these claims is justified depends upon which policy areas and organisations are looked at.

Some policy areas, for example, *have* seen an increase in involvement (such as education (Thody and Wilson, 1988)), but other areas have seen a major *decrease* in openness as a result of the introduction of new organisations into the system and the general fragmentation of SNG that has resulted from this. Both of these serve to be de-politicise certain areas of SNG by effectively insulating them from public involvement (such as the Water Authorities after their privatisation). Many of the new organisations that are involved have actually actively attempted to *limit* direct public involvement in their work to allow them a freer hand to pursue their objectives (Thornley, 1991).

In general there has been a contradictory process at work in terms of participation. The reforms that the centre has instigated have increased participation in some areas but have reduced it in others. In practice it could be argued that the *amount* of participation has decreased as a result of central policy initiatives while the *demand* for it has increased. Some parts of SNG, such as local government, have taken active steps to attempt to improve their links with the public (Gyford, 1991) and thus encourage participation, while the actions of the centre have increasingly meant that certain key areas of activity have been taken away from local authorities and given to organisations that would rather not be bothered by importunate members of the public.

Finance

This has been a continuing issue of major concern for SNG for most of its history. *How* SNG is to be paid for, and *who* is to pay for it are questions that have long exercised the minds of politicians, academics, commentators and members of the general public. The recent past has seen such questions receive a new lease of life, particularly with the inglorious failure of the Community Charge in local government.

Attempts by central government to reform the financing of the major parts of SNG over the past fifteen years can best be characterised as being disastrous, both as practical reforms and as political events. In the case of local government, for example, the large number of reforms to its financing system have consistently failed to achieve the goals of the centre (Rhodes, 1992) and have created a massive amount of political fall-out that helped to contribute to the resignation of Margaret Thatcher as Prime Minister in 1990. Equally, the introduction of the 'internal market' into the NHS produced many problems and was extremely unpopular with medical and administrative staff within the service. The fragmentation of the NHS into separate Trusts with their own budgets, for example, has made financial planning and pricing much more complex than was previously the case.

The attempt to reform the financing of SNG has been unsuccessful as it has failed to resolve the central issues that underlie this area, and the policies pursued have often been short-term expedients which attempted to resolve problems that were largely created through the centre's own policies in the first place.

Management

Finally, the centre has attempted to lead SNC towards a *management* style that is based upon a market model. The attempt to do this has been undertaken by persuasion rather than by direct action, largely as a consequence of the fact that this area, concerned as it is with the internal organisation and management of the organisations of SNG, is almost entirely outside the direct control of the centre. In practice there is little that the centre can do directly in this area and it has to rely on SNG itself to fall into line with its wishes if success is to be assured.

Once again, the impact of the desires of the centre has been very varied, with some areas of SNG embracing market models of management with open arms whilst other areas have refused to have anything at all to do with such an approach. Quangos and the outposts of the centre have been the most supportive of the movement towards market models, largely because the centre can more easily manipulate these than it can local government and the NHS.

In the case of these latter parts of SNG the NHS has been affected as a consequence of the establishment of the 'internal market', which places a greater emphasis on 'management' than the previous system that was dominated by the medical profession (Klein, 1989), but management reform has been largely a secondary matter here when compared with the financial reforms that are also currently being undertaken. Local government has been highly active in introducing managerial reforms, but these have not been greatly influenced by the market model except in the case of those authorities that are controlled by the *New Suburban Right* wing of the Conservative Party (Holliday, 1991, 1992). For the rest of local government new management styles have been introduced that have been based around a *public sector orientation* (Clarke and Stewart, 1991) that runs counter to much of the market model.

In terms of these five areas of concern it is apparent that the centre has been far less effective in changing the basis of SNG than might have been expected. Despite the blizzard of legislative activity that has taken place since 1979 SNG as a whole has not been significantly reformed. Parts of the system, it is true, are now very different from what they once were, but large parts of it have hardly been touched by change or have successfully resisted the pressures for change that the centre has exerted. The reasons for this can be found in the nature of the political activity that has been associated with the attempts to change the system.

The four types of politics referred to earlier have all had their relevance for understanding both what has been taking place in terms of SNG and how reform has been managed and adapted to by the organisations of SNG themselves. The reform process itself has been inescapably political but has been undertaken through a variety of means involving different types of political activity.

In practice the period since 1979 has, in some ways at least, simply seen a continuation of previously existing forms and patterns of political interaction, even if these have taken place in the context of a much more heated political atmosphere. Thus, the *organisational* and *economic* politics of the SNG system have both been marked by a new intensity and bitterness, but the issues, problems and questions that are involved have been the same for many years prior to 1979 (Gray, 1994, ch. 2). To this extent there has been no significant change to the system, even if the conflicts that been generated have become more vicious and lack the common framework of consensus that they had for many years after 1945.

In the case of both of these forms of politics the essential nature of the activity that is involved has not been greatly altered. In the case of *organisational* politics the pattern of interdependence between the centre and the organisations of SNG (Rhodes, 1981) still remains the key factor, with the latter using the resources that are available to them to modify and escape from central domination. In the case of *economic* politics, the attempts by the centre to remake the financial system have been stymied by the fact that there is an in-built inertia in the system and that the centre finds great difficulty in controlling precisely what the outcome of such changes will be.

The case of *party* and *citizenship* politics, on the other hand, do show deeper changes taking place in the pattern of political activity that is involved in SNG. The discussion of *participation* has indicated that direct citizen involvement has probably decreased since 1979, but that the demand for, and actual (if indirect), involvement has probably increased. To some extent this has been a consequence of the general fragmentation of SNG that has been caused by, for example, removing services and functions from elected local government and establishing the 'Trust' system in the NHS.

While these changes represent a new departure for *citizenship* politics the overall politicisation of the SNG system that has been generated as a result means that the isolation and bypass strategies that lie behind fragmentation have actually served to make the organisations of SNG more obviously 'political' than they have been for many years. A consequence of this has been that *party* politics has increasingly become a dominant part of the SNG system. In practical terms this is hard to see: at Westminster, for example, the sizeable majorities that the Conservative governments have had since 1979 have meant that national party conflict has been almost irrelevant – the government can, more or less, pass any legislation it likes. In deeper terms, however, the impact of the Conservative changes to SNG has led to an increasing tendency to reappraise precisely what SNG is all about. Almost all the opposition parties have rethought their position on SNG, with the Liberal Democrat and Labour parties both proposing the establishment of some form of directly elected *regional* government.

The changes in the intensity of conflict within the SNG system, the demand for involvement within it, and the thinking of the opposition political parties have all served to increase the political awareness of SNG that exists. None of them, however, have essentially changed the day-to-day politics of the system in any significant way. Much deeper, and wide-ranging, changes to the entire system would be needed before these underlying political regularities could be seen to be affected.

The changes to the system of SNG that have taken place since 1979 have lacked any sort of consistency and coherence. The basically piecemeal approach that the centre has adopted has not really differed from that of previous governments, and the results of policy initiatives cast severe doubts on the extent to which a 'new' SNG could be seen to have been developed. In many ways the inability of the centre to control the internal workings of the organisations of SNG has acted against its desire to transform the entire system. Further, the difficulties of ensuring a trouble-free implementation of policy has created a succession of 'policy messes' (Marsh and Rhodes, 1992) over which the centre has effectively lost control.

This catalogue of difficulties might be taken to imply that SNG has hardly been touched at all by the actions of the centre. Such a conclusion, however, would be misleading. SNG is now a very different creature to what it was 20 years ago, and the working through of the changes that *have* been introduced implies that this process has yet to be concluded. The lack of control that the centre has been able to exert over SNG means that there will have to be a continuation of reform as parts of the system undermine central policy, or as central policy itself fails. The implications of this necessity to continue the process of reform forms the basis of the next section.

The Reform Tendency

The attempts by central government to reform and restructure SNG since 1979 have met with only limited success. However, clear lines of approach can be discerned that are characteristic of these attempts. Even while they have not been entirely successful in achieving the aims of the centre these paths to reform need to be identified to understand what the centre has been hoping to do, and to understand what the immediate future holds for SNG in the context of governing in the 1990s.

Essentially three themes can be identified as arising from the experiences of the past period of Conservative government. These involved a desire to:

- 'privatise' management in SNG;
- curb expenditure by SNG; and
- fragment the organisational structure of SNG.

The motivation for pursuing these three objectives can be found in many places and, importantly, a predisposition towards a distrust of SNG should not be overlooked. Whilst doubt can be cast on the extent to which recent Conservative governments have pursued a consistent ideological line with regard to SNG (Gray, 1994, ch. 3) a general sense of dissatisfaction with, and even outright hostility towards, SNG *has* been a common feature of both the rhetoric and the actions of these governments.

The mistrust that has been expressed towards SNG has certainly been a major factor in explaining the three policy themes that have been identified above. The desire to remodel SNG into more 'acceptable' forms ('acceptable' to central government at any rate!) has clearly affected the range of options that the centre has cared to pursue, and has meant that some alternative choices that *could* have been made have never been seriously looked at. The major consequence of this has been that SNG has felt itself to be under constant threat, if not outright attack, from a national government that appears not to care to listen to arguments that might undermine its own attitudes and approach towards SNG.

The reforms that have taken place have affected all of the organisational types that make up SNG, although in different ways for different organisational types. In financial terms, for example, the amount of income that local authorities directly control through taxation, fees and charges has been severely reduced with the introduction of the Uniform Business Rate, while the use of rate- and charge-capping has effectively limited the amount of money that local authorities are able to spend. With quangos, on the other hand, emphasis has been placed on searching for alternative sources of financing for the public sector, which has led to a rise in joint financing from the public and private sectors in fields as diverse as inner cities policy, with the UDCs and the City Challenge programme, and sponsorship of the arts, through the Arts Council and the Regional Arts Boards (Gray, 1994, ch. 7).

Such variation of approach should not really be too surprising given the range, number and variety of different organisations that are involved in SNG. However, the common themes of the reform experience do cut across these distinctions. In terms of the first theme, the 'privatisation' of public management, attempts have been made across the entire public sector, not just SNG, to introduce forms and styles of management that are believed to exist in the private sector, with the introduction of 'general managers' into the NHS being the clearest example. In terms of the desire to curb expediture new approaches to the allocation of grant aid to all of the organisations of SNG have been common, as has the attempt to introduce new concerns with 'value for money' and the three Es of efficiency, economy and effectiveness. Finally, in terms of the desire to fragment the organisational structure of SNG, this has been seen in the introduction of new quangos which have been allocated functions from local government, the increasing use of private suppliers of goods and services as a result of the process of compulsory competitive tendering, and the establishment of executive agencies from the old civil service and NHS Trusts.

These attempts at reform have followed an accelerating tendency in so far as increasing efforts have been made by the centre to ensure that the desired results are actually achieved. More recent events, such as the proposed reform of local government structure (Greenwood, 1991/92; Midwinter, 1992), and the increasing number of NHS Trusts in existence, indicate that the centre is not giving up the strategy of change for SNG and, indeed, the wish to push it on. The set-backs that have confronted the centre do not seem to have dampened this desire, and may even have encouraged greater efforts to be made. As a result of this the future of the other governments of Britain seems set to continue to be one of change.

The Shape of Things to Come?

The prospects for SNG in this context of reappraisal, restructuring and reform are not necessarily bleak. The extent to which the process of change will lead to a diminution of the role of SNG depends upon what, precisely, the centre intends for the coming years. It is safe to argue, however, that SNG will not vanish as an active centre for independent political decision-making and, indeed, it is possible that its role will be enhanced in the future as a result of broader currents of change that will influence the entire British political system.

The above paragraph contains two arguments that have relevance for any consideration of the future of SNG. First, that regardless of the wishes of the centre SNG will continue to be relatively free to make its own decisions and choices. Second, that the future of SNG in Britain cannot be understood simply by concentrating on events at home: the wider political context needs to be considered, and particularly the impact of developments within the European Union on British politics. (See Chapter 8, and Bongers, 1990, for a general review of this area.)

The full consequences of the reform process that has been under way since 1979 are by no means clear as yet. However, it is apparent that the status of SNG within the overall political and administrative system in Britain has been questioned and affected in a variety of both subtle and blatant ways. The accusation that central government is determined to effectively centralise the administrative system (see, for example, Jones and Stewart, 1983), and to change sub-national *government* to sub-national *administration*, has important implications for democracy, accountability and citizen involvement within this system.

The fact that the centre has attempted to change the understanding and practice of all of these areas should not be taken to mean that such attempts have actually led to *real* change. In many areas it could effectively be argued that the centre has largely failed to achieve *any* sort of change within the SNG system – at least to the present. The working through of some of the reform programmes that the centre has instigated may well lead to significant change in the future but, in very general terms, such change has not yet taken place.

This relative failure on behalf of the centre indicates that the idea that the centre *must* be able to get its own way in terms of SNG overstates, at the very least, the extent to which the centre can effectively manipulate the complex patterns of structure and behaviour that exist within the system. The relative independence that SNG has from the centre in so far as it is free to determine its own policies, management practices and relationships with other parts of the overall political–administrative system means that the prospect of a totally centrally-dominated system is unlikely to become a reality without a much grander redesign of the entire SNG system.

As long as some form of decentralised system of government and administration exists power must necessarily be dispersed between different organisations in different locations (Smith, 1985; Gray, 1994, ch. 1). In these circumstances it is unreasonable to assume that centralisation will lead to a complete homogeneity between the organisations of SNG and that the future for the system will be one of bland uniformity. Even when the centre is nominally in control of the organisations of SNG (such as the regional and local offices of central government departments) variation still exists in a significant fashion between them (Gray, 1994, chs 6 and 7).

Apart from anything else, the extent to which the centre would positively desire to manage and control SNG is open to doubt. The centre can find it convenient, both administratively and politically, to avoid direct control of the system (Bulpitt, 1989); this implies that central domination would have costs for the centre as well as benefits. While the benefits might include coherency of policy across the entire country and an organisationally more simple system, the costs would have to include an increased administrative burden for the centre and the potential for politically damaging results to occur as a result of the decisions that would have to be made, as the experience with the 'opting-out' of schools from local authority control makes abundantly clear.

While complete centralisation of the system is unlikely to occur it can be accepted that there has been a tendency towards a *greater* centralisation of the system than was the case before 1979. In practice the centre has used different strategies and tactics in its attempts to influence different parts of SNG so that the extent of this centralising tendency has varied between the types of organisation that are to be found. In the case of local government, for example, the desire to control expenditure has led to a major centralisation of the financing of the system, with local authorities being far more dependent for their financial resources upon the decisions of the centre than ever before. In the case of the NHS, on the other hand, the 'opting-out' of hospitals, in the form of hospital Trusts, would seem to be designed to actually *limit* the extent of central control and direction by allowing these Trusts to develop their own 'business plans' and financial strategies independently of both the health authorities *and* central government. One area where centralisation has been of increasing importance has been in the field of quangos, where the use of these has been accompanied by pressures from the centre for the introduction of styles and forms of management that are different from those that are normally found in the public sector. The indirect forms of control over the membership, finances, functions and the very existence of these organisations that the centre retains has meant that it has been able to dominate this area of SNG fairly effectively. A direct result of this has been that the presumed independence of these organisations from central government has been significantly reduced.

The variations that can, therefore, be found within SNG makes any assessment of the overall position problematic. Even if centralisation has been occurring the centre still finds great difficulty in *directly* controlling what happens within the organisations of SNG: even within the field of quangos central direction is not utilised in a direct form. As a consequence of this lack of directive capacity the centre has had to rely on the traditional weapons that are available to it to encourage the adoption of preferred stances towards policy and management. These weapons include both direct and indirect means, such as financial incentives and penalties and the provision of advice and other more subtle forms of encouragement.

It is probable that these forms of approach will continue to be dominant in the dealings that the centre has with SNG, as they are often concerned with areas of activity that the centre does not, and is unlikely to want to, directly control. If the commitment to change that the centre has displayed in the past is to continue then the tactics and strategy of the centre are largely restricted to past forms – unless, of course, the centre decides to grab the proverbial bull by the horns and move towards a much more directive approach to SNG than it has been willing to use in the past.

The prospect of the centre adopting anything other than the piecemeal approach to reform that it has used in the past is an unlikely one. Without such a total approach, however, the introduction of real change into SNG is destined to remain a possibility rather than a probability. As such, SNG is still in a relatively strong position compared with the centre as it is the organisations of SNG themselves that have to take responsibility for the implementation of preferred central government policies. Given that these policies are not necessarily popular with SNG the future is likely to see a continuation of the conflict that has marked relations between the two for their entire history.

In effect, central government is caught in a double bind: without direct intervention into SNG it is unlikely to find a complete and non-problematic acceptance of its ideas and policies; with such intervention, however, it will find itself being overwhelmed by a mass of specific and detailed work that it has neither the expertise nor, necessarily, the desire to manage. The fact that the centre will probably have to continue to operate through the same means as it has previously utilised means that at least some of the current features of SNG are likely to remain a constant fact whatever the result of future developments.

Central to this continuation is likely to be the political conflict between SNG and the centre. Attempts at reform have generated, not surprisingly, intense arguments between central government, health and local authorities and a wide range of quangos. Such conflict is generated both as a result of the effects that proposed changes have on the existing pattern of interdependence between the various parts of the governmental and administrative system; and also through the impact that such changes have on the internal power structures that exist within organisations. These structures have important political implications for what is likely to occur in any organisation, and those of SNG are no exception to this (see, for example, Stoker and Wilson, 1986, on local government).

In circumstances of change the consequent reappraisal of what is occurring in SNG will continue to generate perceptions that there are winners and losers. The interests that are affected are, as pluralist and neo-pluralist theories suggest (Gray, 1994, ch. 8), unlikely to simply accept changes in status, particularly if these interests are amongst the losers. As a result those interests whose position is seen to be under threat will seek to protect their position.

Professional groups have traditionally been adept at safeguarding (and, even, increasing) their status and position. Under the current 'managerialist' climate such groups are increasingly finding themselves being isolated and, often, ignored in favour of other groups which are not necessarily as knowledgeable on a given subject as the professionals themselves.

Examples to illustrate this are many in the case of SNG, with the declining status of the medical profession in the NHS being a prime case in point. The dominant position that the medical profession and its governing body (the British Medical Association) have had within the NHS since its inception has been increasingly eroded as 'general managers' have been introduced into the service. The inability of the profession to reverse the trend of steadily declining status and the intensely political campaigns that have been mounted around this issue indicate that in this area, at least, the centre has managed to achieve some success in controlling the actors within the system.

Attempts to control other public sector professions, however, have been relatively less successful than has been the case with the medical profession, although an increasing use of quasi-market solutions to what is perceived to be a problem of professional dominance may, yet again, lead to further changes. The use of compulsory competitive tendering (CCT) has been extended to cover professional services, such as legal and architectural services, alongside the already existing service delivery functions of, for example, refuse collection and leisure services. The extent to which such a 'privatisation' of professional services will actually lead to a diminution in professional power is, as yet, a wide-open question but is an area that will certainly deserve close scrutiny in coming years.

Of all of the areas discussed earlier in this chapter the one that will be returned to here is that of accountability. While the attempts of the centre to change SNG have had some implications for this area of concern it is only likely to be in the future that the full ramifications of these centrally-imposed reforms will be felt. The fragmentation of SNG and the preference for economic rather than political versions of democracy imply a very different future structure and meaning for SNG to those which are currently in force.

In essence the two features of fragmentation and an emphasis on economic interpretations of democracy are tied together through certain values and theories that are often lumped together under the heading 'the New Right'. The versions of public choice theory and bureaucratic theory that are associated with this school of thought have had some impact on the reforms that the centre has adopted, even if it would be misleading to see the Conservative governments of the post-1979 period as being straightforwardly 'New Right' in themselves (Gray, 1994, ch. 3).

Of particular importance here is that the theories of the New Right support a fragmentation of government into what are effectively *competing* organisations, and argue that an increasingly market-like public sector that operates on economic criteria of profit, efficiency and effectiveness is the only solution to the difficulties and problems that are seen to exist with the public sector as currently constituted. In this version of things accountability can only be guaranteed by the introduction of an economic basis to the work of the public sector. Democratic versions of accountability, usually through elected representatives, are seen as inefficient and ineffective and no protection against abuses by self-interested bureaucrats and politicians (Pirie, 1988).

The result of following through with the logic of this approach would be that SNG would have to be radically restructured in terms of how it operates, the organisations that are involved, the manner in which it is financed, and how it is controlled. Accountability would have to reside with the *consumer* and not with the *citizen*, implying a different form of relationship between the state and the citizen than is currently in force, and a very different manner of working for the public sector than currently pertains.

In other words, if the nature of accountability in SNG is changed then so must be all of the other features of the system. The democratic basis of SNG would have to be done away with in favour of an economic model of the relationship between the public and the state, implying that political choices and decisions would be made secondary to economic ones.

Such a development may seem to be relatively unimportant but, in practice, it has the greatest possible significance for SNG and for the entire political and administrative system of Britain. The acceptance of such an economic model as the basis for the work of all the public sector overturns accepted models concerning the nature of the public provision of goods and services by denying the essentially collective nature of much of what is undertaken within SNG. By doing so it denies that there is anything intrinsically different between the public and the private sectors of the economy and heralds the abandonment of values and beliefs that have been accepted since at least the eighteenth century.

In this context the future of SNG as a whole is important for more than the organisations and employees of SNG: it also has important implications for the entire public sector, not least for the meanings and understandings that are attached to the politics of the public sector and how it could, and should, be managed. These issues also raise further questions – such as who would benefit from such a changed system – that relate to the nature of democracy within Britain. Given that the government has indicated that it intends to make the political system more pluralistic in nature, the extent to which this is achievable in the context of a system that would be, at best, more *economically* pluralist and more *politically* elitist is open to question.

Conclusion

As can be seen from the above argument the future of the 'other governments' of Britain has an importance that extends far beyond the organisations of SNG, and raises questions about the future of democratic government in this country. At one level the future of SNG could simply be a case of 'more of the same': where the centre continues to attempt to exert increased control over the management and finances of this tier. Such an approach, however, also has implications for accountability and access to the system, both of which are intimately connected to these issues. As these then spill over into the general, and much broader, question of democratic government as a whole it would be misleading to simply look at these changes to the surface of SNG.

Certainly, the future of SNG promises to be an interesting one, with further changes to its organisation and structure being highly likely. As a consequence of this the political in-fighting over SNG that has been taking place almost constantly since the mid-1970s is likely to continue. Such politics, however, is unlikely to leave much scope for *citizen* politics to be increased, but is, instead, more likely to make *organisational* and *financial* politics the centre of attention for the rest of this decade and beyond. Given the piecemeal approach to SNG that the centre has adopted since 1979 these conflicts will continue to be isolated from each other so that the overall picture of change in all of the public sector is likely to remain a subtext to the debate.

References

Barker, A. (1992) 'Legitimacy in the United Kingdon: Scotland and the Poll Tax', *British Journal of Political Science*, 22, pp 521–33.

Bongers, P. (1990) *Local Government and 1992* (Harlow: Longman).

Bulpitt, J. (1989) 'Walking Back to Happiness?: Conservative Party Governments and Elected Local Authorities in the 1980s', in Crouch, C. and Marquand, D. (eds), *The New Centralism* (Oxford: Basil Blackwell).

Clarke, M. and Stewart, J. (1991) *The Choices for Local Government* (Harlow: Longman).

Gray, C. (1994) *Government Beyond the Centre* (Basingstoke: Macmillan).

Greenwood, J. (1991/92) 'Local Government in the 1990s', *Talking Politics*, 4, pp. 62–9.

Gyford, J. (1991) *Citizens, Consumers and Councils* (Basingstoke: Macmillan).

Holliday, I. (1991) 'The New Suburban Right in British Local Government', *Local Government Studies*, 17 (6), pp. 45–62.

Holliday, I. (1992) 'The Conditions of Local Change', *Public Administration*, 69, pp. 441–57.

Hood, C. (1978) 'Keeping the Centre Small', *Political Studies*, 26, pp. 30–46.

Jones, G. and Stewart, J. (1983) *The Case for Local Government* (London: Allen & Unwin).

Klein, R. (1989) *The Politics of the National Health Service*, 2nd edn (Harlow: Longman).

Marsh, D. and Rhodes, R. (1992) 'The Implementation Gap', in Marsh, D. and Rhodes, R. (eds), *Implementing Thatcherite Policies* (Buckingham: Open University Press).

Midwinter, A. (1992) 'The Review of Local Government in Scotland', *Local Government Studies*, 18 (2), pp. 44–54.

Midwinter, A., Keating, M. and Mitchell, J. (1991) *Politics and Public Policy in Scotland* (Basingstoke: Macmillan).

Pirie, M. (1988) *Micropolitics* (Aldershot: Wildwood House).

Ranson, S. and Stewart, J. (1989) 'Citizenship and Government', *Political Studies*, 38, pp. 5–24.

Rhodes, R. (1981) *Control and Power in Central–Local Government Relations* (Aldershot: Gower).

Rhodes, R. (1992) 'Local Government Finance', in Marsh, D. and Rhodes, R. (eds), *Implementing Thatcherite Policies* (Buckingham: Open University Press).

Smith, B. (1985) *Decentralization* (London: Allen & Unwin).

Stoker, G. (1989) 'Urban Development Corporations: A Review', *Regional Studies*, 23, pp. 159–73.

Stoker, G. and Wilson, D (1986) 'Intra-Organisational Politics in Local Authorities', *Public Administration*, 64, pp. 285–302.

Thody, A. and Wilson, D. (1988) 'School Governing Bodies and the Pressure Group Arena', *Local Government Policy-Making*, 15 (2), pp. 39–46.

Thornley, A. (1991) *Urban Planning Under Thatcherism* (London: Routledge).

Conclusion: Agendas for Reform

ROBERT PYPER and LYNTON ROBINS

As the chapters in this book show, the governing institutions in the United Kingdom are subject to a continuing process of reform. In some cases, academic analysts and politicians argue that this process is too slow and cumbersome to cope with the fundamental problems which need to be addressed, and they urge the adoption of radical measures which look beyond particular institutions to the wider system of government.

In recent years there would appear to have been a proliferation of reformist organisations producing an ever expanding volume of literature. Reform, broadly defined to encompass a variety of proposals for substantive political, institutional or constitutional change, is certainly in the air in the 1990s. We should note, however, that our period is not unique in this respect.

During the 1960s, as the country's relatively sluggish economic performance became increasingly apparent, confidence dwindled in the ability of government to deliver sustained growth, the size and shape of the government machine came under scrutiny, and academics and politicians began to raise fundamental questions about aspects of the UK policy. A vogue for broad-ranging institutional and constitutional soul-searching took hold.

The supporters of fundamental change were ultimately disappointed by a rather meagre harvest of reform. The advent of the Parliamentary Commissioner for Administration, some experimental Commons select committees, and abortive attempts to reform the House of Lords and alter arrangements for Commons sittings were the main outcomes of the wave of parliamentary reform. Local government reform and the devolution issue were placed on the agenda through referral to Royal Commissions, and the resulting reports provided the basis for legislation in the 1970s. However, by the end of that decade it was not difficult to detect growing disenchantment with the new system of local government, and popular interest in devolution had waned to the point where the 1979 referenda in Scotland and Wales failed to evince sufficient support for the proposed reform.

Beyond this, concern had been growing about the extent to which the system of government was suffering from 'overload': unrealistic expectations that government could and should attempt to solve problems of all kinds, and excessive demands emanating from increasingly assertive pressure and interest groups. A series of economic and political crises in the 1970s, epitomised by the events of the winter of 1973–74, which culminated in the fall of the Heath government, raised the question of 'ungovernability'. Had the problem of exercising power from Whitehall and Westminster simply become intractable (King, 1976)?

After 1979, the Thatcher government largely set its face against the type of constitutional tinkering which had preoccupied some of its predecessors. Reform, when it came, stemmed from a combination of managerial imperatives (chief amongst which was the unending attempt to secure 'value for money' in the public services) and ideological urges (get government 'off peoples's backs' and let the 'enterprise culture' do its work), rather than a penchant for re-ordering the constitution. Thus, for example, the establishment of the Next Steps executive agencies was presented not as the precursor of constitutional change but as part of the drive for greater efficiency and effectiveness, which involved grafting elements of the business culture on to the civil service. Even when fundamental questions arose concerning the impact of the new agencies on traditional concepts of responsibility and accountability, the government refused to rethink constitutional norms.

The managerial and ideological drives of the 1980s generated a substantial amount of change, but this was accomplished in the absence of anything which might be described as a new constitutional settlement. Constitutional change was almost occuring by default. By the early 1990s, it was being argued within the opposition parties, and beyond, that a breathing space was required in order to facilitate greater accountability, stem the burgeoning ranks of quangos, and generally allow the machinery of government to adjust to the realities of the enabling, contracting and regulatory state.

Major's Initiatives

There were some early indications that the Major government might adopt a more reflective attitude towards the constitution. This should not be taken to mean that substantive constitutional reform suddenly became feasible. The government's reform agenda was distinctly limited. Nonetheless, a series of initiatives was introduced in order to address, if only marginally, some systemic flaws.

Some reforms were, in fact, little more than gestures. For example, the 'taking stock' exercise which reviewed the government of Scotland in the wake of the 1992 general election only yielded the series of minor initiatives described by Roger Levy in Chapter 9.

The veil of official secrecy was lifted slightly when the government allowed publication of the membership of Cabinet committees for the first time, and the official rule book for ministerial conduct, *Questions of Procedure for Ministers*, was released. Of course, informed journalists had managed to publicise this type of information in the past, but now, at last, the government was releasing the information on its own initiative.

The next stage in this process came in the summer of 1993, when the government published a White Paper on *Open Government* (HMSO, 1993a) which proposed extending the statutory right of access to personal information held by the state, a less restrictive approach to the release of public records, and safeguards for the rights of 'whistle-blowers' who disclose information which is not highly confidential. Open government campaigners argued that the proposals fell far short of a freedom of information statute (Norton-Taylor, 1993).

More significant developments were to come in this field. In July 1993, the government published a brochure on the organisation of M15, *The Security Service* (HMSO, 1993b), in which the Director-General, Stella Rimington, was openly identified. Three months later similar information was released about the intelligence services (HMSO, 1993c). These were initiatives which certainly could not have been foreseen in the days of the Thatcher administration, although it will take some time before their full implications can be assessed. Have the first steps been taken on the path to a genuinely more open system of government, or do these measures simply represent an attempt to forestall the open government and freedom of information campaigners?

Those who subscribe to the negative interpretation of the government's motives tend to view the much-vaunted Citizen's Charter as a political manoeuvre, an underfunded sop to consumerism designed to circumvent the need for a more fundamental bill of rights. In a more positive light, this can be interpreted as a genuine attempt to give the consumers of public services the basic information they need about standards and quality targets, as well as the power to secure some kind of redress when these are not met.

The efforts of the Major government notwithstanding, there remains evidence of a sustained, and as yet unsatisfied, appetite for change. How are we to explain the revived interest in reform (broadly defined) in the 1990s, what are its manifestations, who are the proponents of change, and what impact would their prescriptions have on the government of the UK, if implemented?

Why Reform?

While it is not possible to establish the definitive causation of the type of wide-ranging proposals for reform we are discussing here, we can point to at least some possible contributory factors. These are not in any sense mutually exclusive; on the contrary, there is considerable overlap between some of the factors.

First, the duration, nature and style of the successive Conservative governments after 1979 played a considerable part in stimulating a desire for reform. Four straight election victories by a single party inevitably gave the main opposition parties considerable time to reflect upon the flaws in the existing system. Furthermore, the legitimacy of the Conservative governments was thought by some to be worthy of challenge due to the distortions of the plurality (first-past-the-post) electoral system. While this system had rarely been seriously questioned as long as it provided for a fairly regular alternation in power between the main parties, it was now failing to do this.

The Conservatives retained power over the four elections with between 42 per cent and 44 per cent of the vote: a majority of voters consistently supported the opposition parties. Moreover, the third party grouping (variously styled the Liberals, the Liberal/SDP Alliance and the Liberal Democrats) reaped only a handful of seats regardless of their share of the vote (the most glaring discrepancy came in 1987, when they won only 23 seats, with over 25 per cent of the vote). The apparent anomaly of the Conservative Party's minority status in Scotland, coupled with its secure grasp of the Scottish Office, was a further cause for concern. In these circumstances, even some previously committed supporters of the plurality system began to turn their attention to electoral reform.

However, it was not simply the fact and nature of the Conservative election victories which nurtured thoughts of reform. The style of the Thatcher administrations in particular contributed to these feelings. Under Margaret Thatcher the powers of the premiership were pushed to their limits. More generally,

These were not governments which sought consensus or practised consultation extensively. Far from adopting the mantle of 'one nation' Conservatism, Tory governments from 1979 to 1990 celebrated a tough-mindedness in implementing policies which departed from the consensual policies of their predecessors. Battle lines between the parties were more tightly drawn; demarcation lines between those included in and those excluded from government were more apparent. (Peele, 1993, p. 21)

A second contributory factor was the perceived encroachment upon what had previously been regarded as sacrosanct 'civil liberties'. Was there now perhaps the need for a new bill of rights, incorporating the European Convention on Human Rights? The banning of trade union membership at GCHQ in 1984, together with the general impact of the government's employment laws on the ability of unions to mobilise their members for strike action, provided grounds for concern in this sphere. The actions of the police when checking (and occasionally turning around) vehicles, and making blanket arrests during the miners' strike in 1984–85, added to this concern. Freedom of speech seemed to be under challenge too, as testified by the partial censorship imposed on spokesmen for Sinn Fein and other political groupings in Northern Ireland.

Third, the obvious malfunctioning of certain bodies or institutions undoubtedly created a desire for reform. This can be seen most clearly in relation to the police and the juridiary. A series of *causes célèbres* during the late 1980s and early 1990s, involving the Birmingham Six, the Guildford Four and Judith Ward, revealed fundamental flaws in the criminal justice system. These miscarriages of justice stemmed from failings at virtually every level of the system, from the conduct of police interrogations and the gathering of evidence to the functioning of the Court of Appeal.

In the case of the monarchy, the institution was not malfunctioning as such, but it certainly began to suffer a loss of credibility due to the publicity surrounding the disintegrating marriages of Prince Charles, Prince Andrew and the Princess Royal. Intensive press coverage of even the most minor peccadillos of members of the Royal Family did not help, and the protracted debate about whether the Queen should pay tax further lowered the esteem in which the institution was held.

Fourth, the calculated weakening of what Gillian Peele refers to as 'institutions which might act as a countervailing power to the government' (local government, the civil service, Parliament, the judiciary), and the more indirect undermining of 'mediating institutions' (finance, business, the universities and the trade unions – and, we might add, the churches), served to

> highlight the fragility of constraints on the power of the executive in the UK, and the extent to which the system relies on the executive itself exercising self-restraint. (Peele, 1993, pp. 23–4)

Economic circumstances partly explain a fifth possible impulse for reform. For example, the resurgence of nationalism in Scotland was caused by the complex interaction of a number of factors (not least of which was the collapse in Conservative support during the elections of the 1980s), but industrial decline and mass unemployment certainly gave the SNP an invaluable point of departure for questioning the validity of the United Kingdom.

A sixth factor was linked to membership of the European Community/Union. Closer connections with the states of Western Europe inevitably led to direct comparisons being made between the respective merits and demerits of the 'unwritten' constitution of the United Kingdom, and the written versions elsewhere. Beyond this, a particular concern developed regarding the propensity of Community/Union institutions to encroach upon elements of the UK constitution, and, correspondingly, some reformers argued the case for buttressing the constitution.

Finally, it can be argued that at least some proposals for reform have their roots in disappointment with the results of earlier initiatives. This is particularly true of the parliamentary reformers who had aimed to alter the balance of power between Parliament and the executive by means of 'internal' reforms.

A clear division opened up in the ranks of the parliamentary reformers due to the experience of the 1960s and 1970s. For some, epitomised by Philip Norton, the case in favour of continued procedural and structural change in Parliament remained strong. This could redress the imbalance of power between Parliament and the executive, particularly if it was accompanied by behavioural or attitudinal change on the part of MPs, without the need for root and branch constitutional reform (Norton, 1981, 1983). John Garrett, like Norton, stressed the need for practicable proposals to strengthen the hand of Parliament within the existing constitutional framework, and produced a cogent account of how this could be achieved (Garrett, 1992). Others simply lost faith in 'internal' reforms, and came to reject what they saw as mere tinkering with the powers and jurisdiction of committees and the Parliamentary Commissioner for Administration. These people turned their attention instead to the need for 'external' innovations: much wider constitutional change, centred on the introduction of electoral reform (Crick, 1989; Walkland, 1981, 1983).

The Reformers

Those who proposed reforming aspects of the UK polity can be categorised in different ways. However, a simple distinction can be drawn between the wholesale, root-and-branch, constitutional reformers and those who have a more narrow focus on specific institutions or parts of the system. There are also organisations such as the Rowntree Trust, which might be described as 'cheerleaders' for reform, in the sense that they provide some of the funding for the research and debates surrounding this issue.

The first broad category encompasses a range of bodies and individuals adopting wide perspectives and putting forward comprehensive agendas for reform.

More obviously, this would include the opposition parties themselves, whose proposals, as set out in their election manifestos, encompass electoral reform, parliamentary reform, curtailment of official secrecy and a move to a more open system of government, devolution/independence (the latter favoured only by the nationalist parties) for Scotland and Wales, a bill of rights, and local government reform.

Some prominent individuals also proffer their own schemes for constitutional reform. Tony Benn is a well-established campaigner in this sphere (Benn, 1982), and in May 1991 he went so far as to sponsor a Commonwealth of Britain Bill, which proposed, *inter alia*, an elected President, replacement of the House of Lords with a 'House of the People', national parliaments for England, Scotland and Wales, and an end to British jurisdiction over Northern Ireland (Benn and Hood, 1993). From the opposite political perspective, Ferdinand Mount, a former head of Margaret Thatcher's Policy Unit, tried to alert Conservatives to the dangers of ignoring constitutional reform (Mount, 1992). Some academics have a specialised interest in reform, producing theoretical and practical studies of the topic (Harden and Lewis, 1988; Lewis, Graham and Beyleveld, 1990).

A number of policy units and think-tanks operate in this sphere, organising seminars, conferences and debates, as well as publishing books and discussion papers. These include:

- Charter 88: a cross-party movement spanning academia and the world of politics, which claims 25 000 signatories for its charter of minimum constitutional reforms.
- The Constitutional Reform Centre: a non-partisan body which sponsors seminars and produces a range of publications.
- The Institute for Public Policy Research (IPPR): linked to the Labour Party, this think-tank has published numerous proposals for wide-ranging constitutional reform, including a draft for a written constitution.
- The Institute of Economic Affairs (IEA), the Adam Smith Institute, and the Centre for Policy Studies: these 'New Right' think-tanks have a fairly comprehensive remit, covering the

full spectrum of public policy issues. While they all address constitutional issues from time to time, the IEA in particular (especially its former Deputy Director, Frank Vibert) has argued for the incorporation of market principles into the constitution (Vibert, 1990, 1991, 1993).

The second broad category covers bodies which adopt a more specific focus, and have ostensibly limited agendas for reform.

Thus, for example, the Electoral Reform Society, as its name implies, concentrates on proposals for changing the plurality system (the Society currently favours adopting the single transferable vote). Electoral reform also formed the focus of activity for the Plant Commission, an internal Labour Party body designed to provide options for the leadership on this issue.

Leaving aside the arguments about the pros and cons of electoral reform, it seems clear that if this was introduced, it would probably act as a catalyst for broader change. Any move away from the plurality system would increase the chances of coalition government, and this would, in its turn, lead to a reordering of the relationships between Prime Minister and Cabinet, executive and Parliament. Cabinets containing representatives from more than one party would probably be obliged to adopt new working habits in order to keep members 'on board' since the price of having even a single ministerial malcontent could be catastrophic for a government. The adversarial nature of the House of Commons would certainly be affected to some extent by the advent of coalition government: one or more of the minority parties would have representatives in the government, and this would feed into the operation of the chamber and the committees.

Another example of a body proposing reform in a particular sphere would be the Scottish Constitutional Convention. In the period leading up to the 1992 general election, the Convention (a forum within which the churches, local authorities, trade unions, the Labour Party and the Liberal Democrats were represented) produced plans for the future government of Scotland within the United Kingdom. The centrepiece of these was a Scottish Parliament, which would have had significantly greater power than the Assembly proposed by the 1978 Scotland Act. In the wake of the 1992 election, the Constitutional Convention faded into relative obscurity.

Once again, however, the introduction of devolved power in Scotland (whether based on the Constitutional Convention's blueprint, or any other plan) would probably have a catalytic effect. New elected bodies in Wales and the English regions could emerge within a UK bearing the hallmarks of a federal rather than a unitary state.

The Freedom of Information Campaign directs its efforts towards challenging the prevailing culture of official secrecy in UK government. The Campaign publishes a newspaper, *Secrets*.

Individuals figure in this category too. In February 1993, Labour's Mark Fisher became the latest in a line of MPs to introduce a measure designed to challenge official secrecy and achieve greater freedom of information. His Right to Know Bill would have severely limited the government's discretion over the release of official documents. Of course, it lacked government support (unacceptable cost was cited as one reason for this), and was consequently rejected by the Commons. Fisher's party colleague, John Garrett, has already been mentioned as a proponent of procedural and structural reform in Parliament.

Prospects

David Judge has asserted that,

> What forces reform on to the political agenda is not support for 'bright ideas' but the weight of politico-economic events. (Judge, 1989, p. 411)

This is a convincing argument. Traditional notions of parliamentary sovereignty in the UK did not come under threat from academic theorists, but from the impact of participation in the European Community/Union, which was itself impelled by broad economic and political factors. Consideration is given to reordering the relationship between Britain and Northern Ireland because of the perceived need to end 'the troubles', rather than the attractions of abstract notions of devolution or federalism. Conversely, substantive reform of the government of Scotland, which would probably have been necessary had the Conservatives retained power in 1992 with only three or four seats and less than 20 per cent of the vote north of the border, could be avoided because the Scottish Conservatives marginally improved their position as a result of the election.

The process of reform is, therefore, primarily driven by political and economic factors. This is not to belittle the efforts of campaigners and theorists: when the time comes for the consideration and implementation of reform, their contributions can be highly influential. However, the publication of pamphlets and the collection of signatures in favour of electoral reform, open government, devolution or a bill of rights do not, in themselves, force reform on to the most important agenda of all: that of the government.

References

Benn, T. (1982) *Arguments for Democracy* (Harmondsworth: Penguin).

Benn, T. and Hood, A. (1993) 'Constitutional Reform and Radical Change', in Barnett, A., Ellis, C. and Hirst, P. (eds), *Debating the Constitution* (Oxford: Polity Press) pp. 24–9.

Crick, B. (1989) 'Beyond Parliamentary Reform', *The Political Quarterly*, 60 (4) (October–December), pp. 396–9.

Garrett, J. (1992) *Westminster: Does Parliament Work?* (London: Victor Gollancz).

Harden, I. and Lewis, N. (eds) (1988) *The Noble Lie: The British Constitution and the Rule of Law* (London: Hutchinson).

HMSO (1993a) *Open Government* (London: HMSO).

HMSO (1993b) *The Security Service* (London: HMSO).

HMSO (1993c) *Central Intelligence Machinery* (London: HMSO).

Judge, D. (1989) 'Parliament in the 1980s', *The Political Quarterly*, 60 (4) (October–December), pp. 400–12.

King, A. (1976) 'The Problem of Overload', in King, A. (ed.), *Why is Britain Becoming Harder to Govern?* (London: BBC).

Lewis, N., Graham, C. and Beyleveld, D. (1990) *Happy and Glorious: The Constitution in Transition* (Milton Keynes: Open University Press).

Mount, F. (1992) *The British Constitution Now: Recovery or Decline?* (London: Heinemann).

Norton, P. (1981) *The Commons in Perspective* (Oxford: Martin Robertson).

Norton, P. (1983) 'The Norton View', in Judge, D. (ed.), *The Politics of Parliamentary Reform* (London: Heinemann).

Norton-Taylor, R. (1993) 'Minister "Maintains Culture of Secrecy"', *Guardian*, 24 August.

Peele, G. (1993) 'The Constitution', in Dunleavy, P., Gamble, A., Holliday, I. and Peele, G. (eds), *Developments in British Politics 4* (London: Macmillan).

Vibert, F. (ed.) (1991) *Britain's Constitutional Future* (London; IEA).

Vibert, F. (1990) *Constitutional Reform in the United Kingdom: An Incremental Agenda* (London: IEA).

Vibert, F. (1993) 'A Free Market Approach To Constitutional Reform', in Barnett, A., Ellis, C. and Hirst, P. (eds), *Debating the Constitution* (Oxford: Polity Press) pp. 30–5.

Walkland, S. A. (1981) 'Whither the Commons?', in Walkland S. A. and Ryle, M. (eds), *The Commons Today* (Glasgow: Fontana).

Walkland, S. A. (1983) 'Parliamentary Reform, Party Realignment and Electoral Reform', in Judge, D. (ed.), *The Politics of Parliamentary Reform* (London: Heinemann).

Index